Written in Water, Written in Stone

Written in Water,

Written in Stone

Twenty Years of *Poets on Poetry*

Edited by Martin Lammon

Foreword by David Lehman

Ann Arbor

THE UNIVERSITY OF MICHIGAN PRESS

Copyright © by the University of Michigan 1996
All rights reserved
Published in the United States of America by
The University of Michigan Press
Manufactured in the United States of America
⊗ Printed on acid-free paper
1999   1998   4   3   2

*A CIP catalog record for this book is available
from the British Library.*

Library of Congress Cataloging-in-Publication Data

Written in water, written in stone : twenty years of Poets on poetry /
    edited by Martin Lammon.
        p.   cm.
    ISBN 0-472-09634-6. — ISBN 0-472-06634-X (pbk.)
    1. American poetry—20th century—History and criticism—Theory,
etc.   2. Poetry—Authorship.   3. Poetics.   I. Lammon, Martin, 1958–.
II. Poets on poetry.
PS323.5.W75   1996
811'.5409—dc20   96–43380
                                                                CIP

Contents

DAVID LEHMAN

Foreword

When a magazine editor commissions a piece about the publishing industry, it's never about what's going on in the book business. It's always about the "crisis in publishing," it being generally assumed that a state of crisis is a perennial, if not permanent, feature of the literary-industrial complex.

Something similar is true of the way poetry is covered in the print and broadcast media. Poetry is the eccentric aunt or outlandish nephew patronized at family gatherings and otherwise ignored. The very word is an honorific usually applied to campaign oratory or rock music or even, when used with the words "in motion," a skillful 6-4-3 double play. The message is that poetry is okay when it is not really poetry.

People are intimidated by poetry, modern poetry in particular. In some readers it wakens the anxiety that they are inadequate, in others the suspicion that they are being had. Part of the problem is that readers try too hard. They are constantly wondering what the poem in front of them means. When you go to the movies you don't worry about the meaning of what you're watching; you just let it happen. The same should be true of reading poems. Later, there will be time for speculation and reflection. For now sit back and enjoy it.

What can we do to lessen or remove the intimidation factor? We can do our best to make the discourse about poetry as compelling and as vivid and as real as we think our poetry deserves. We can work to create the taste by which our writing will be understood. It is not that we have had too little criticism. It is that so much of it has been irrelevant, wrongheaded, or deadly. If that were true of the 1940s and 1950s, when the New Criticism was new, how much truer is it now that literary theory rules the academic roost. As poets we cannot rectify this problem entirely by ourselves, since it goes to the root of a larger academic malaise. But we can and should remember that the best critics of poetry have historically come from our own ranks and that we have an obligation and a mandate to continue this rich tradition. "I said at one point that there can't be a good poetry without a good criticism," James Wright remarked in an interview reprinted in the present volume. "I did not mean that there has to be a great body of formal criticism in print. I meant that a person who is writing and reading is going to be able to write better and more truly if he tries to think about language, if he tries to imagine what his own writing is going to look like and smell like and sound like to an intelligent person of good will. These are critical efforts. Or if he tries to determine what relation he has or can have to the authors whom he, himself, genuinely considers to be great and enduring. What do I have to do with Horace? It is a question that I have to ask myself if I am a serious man."

Wright was propounding one of the rationales for the Poets on Poetry Series, now on the verge of its third decade at the University of Michigan Press. The series is dedicated to the proposition that the prose of poets—critical, expository, technical, autobiographical— offers satisfactions to be found in no other field of writing. In one sense Poets on Poetry was launched by Donald Hall in the mid-1970s, just as he was making the transition from being a tenured professor in Ann Arbor to being a freelance man of wits in New Hampshire. But in another sense Poets on Poetry began when Horace wrote his *Ars Poetica* (stating that the aim of poetry is to delight and instruct) and was extended when first Sidney and later Shelley wrote their defenses of poetry. Poetry has had, in fact, to defend itself from an accusatory charge ever since Socrates banished the poets from his Republic and dared anyone to persuade him to change his mind. The decisive essays in literary history—Wordsworth's Preface to the *Lyrical Ballads,* Arnold's "Study of Poetry," Eliot's "Tradition and the Individual Talent"—are implicitly attempts to come to terms with the Platonic veto.

In our own century, the ideal of the poet who was also a critic, an essayist, and an editor was embodied in their differing ways by both T. S. Eliot and W. H. Auden. One could teach a course—I would like to—on the prose works in which poets have discussed their vocation. We might begin with Keats's letters and Emerson's essays and go on to Gertrude Stein's lectures, Rilke's *Letters to a Young Poet,* Auden's *The Dyer's Hand,* Wallace Stevens's *The Necessary Angel,* and Randall Jarrell's *Poetry and the Age.*

This is the tradition in which Poets on Poetry participates. Donald Hall in his original prospectus foresaw a series that would "constitute an informal poetics" and answer the need for intelligent, passionate, informed talk about poetry. As an editor he was intent on being as generous and ecumenical as possible, publishing not only such longtime friends and associates as Robert Bly and Galway Kinnell but poets with whom he had far less in common. "Conflict makes energy, and I'm all for it," Hall said. "I started the series because I wanted to read the books."

Critical unanimity is as rare as it should be. But the opinion of Robert McDowell in *The Hudson Review*—that Poets on Poetry "is a triumph of small press production and courageous editing"—is one that the writers themselves seem to share. There are book-stores—the Grolier in Cambridge, Massachusetts, for one—in which an entire bookcase is devoted to Poets on Poetry and its companion series, Under Discussion. When the books are encountered together this way they make a powerful impression.

The eclecticism of the series virtually ensures that any group review will render a mixed verdict, since reviewers are partisans and it would require a rare postmodern genius to subscribe to all of the views presented in the series. Donald Hall's "role as sponsor borders on anomaly," John Malcolm Brinnin commented in the *Washington Post Book World* in 1984. "This most urbane of mentors has opened his umbrella over talents so at variance with his own as to suggest he has conspired to promote what by temperament he deplores and in practice avoids."

Brinnin felt that one danger of the series was its "invitation to self-advertisement at the expense of self-portraiture." The danger may be considered acute at a time when the interview is gaining acceptance as a form of critical exposition. Yet Brinnin exempts from his stricture Philip Levine's wittily titled *Don't Ask*—a book consisting exclusively of interviews. Other surveyors of Poets on Poetry, such as Reginald Gibbons, have wondered whether contemporary poets are really applying themselves to the "great tasks of criticism" or shirking them, failing to take a stand. Gibbons particularly disliked William Stafford's *Writing the Australian Crawl*— "probably the most puzzlingly destructive and unwittingly dismissive book about poetry by a poet that has ever been written"— which, as it happens, is far and away the most popular title in the series, with 15,000 copies in print. Is Gibbons right about Stafford? And just how legitimate a form is the interview? Readers of *Written in Water, Written in Stone*—which includes Stafford's "The End of a Golden String" plus interviews or excerpts from interviews with Levine, Kinnell, Bly, Wright, and Robert Creeley—may decide for themselves.

Like the player/manager of a baseball team, Donald Hall has so far come to bat four times in the series, and his contributions have been among the most widely admired and hotly disputed. The reader of this book will find the famous essay in which Hall advocated the abolition of MFA programs and decried the "McPoem" that was mass produced in the workshops of "Hamburger College."

Several poets represented in these pages put into practice Matthew Arnold's idea of poetic "touchstones," as Amy Clampitt does when she quotes lines from Robert Frost that engraved themselves in her memory and furnished the criterion for judging poetic greatness. Others—Donald Justice and Thom Gunn, for example—set out to account for the genesis and development of specific poems they had written. Marge Piercy gives out sensible advice to struggling young writers: "Never thank anybody sexually, and never use your body as payment or prepayment for help." Robert Hayden, imagining being interrogated by Chekhov's Black Monk, rises to the occasion with eloquence: "Let there be poets and more poets—just as long as they are poets."

The various styles of exposition on display here add a dimension to our understanding of the poets. How apt that Charles Wright favors an aphoristic style ("Each line should be a station of the cross") and Robert Creeley a conversational idiom ("Franz Kline was being questioned—not with hostility but with intensity, by another friend—and finally he said, 'Well, look, if I paint what *you* know, then that will simply bore you, the repetition from me to you. If I paint what I know, it will be boring to myself. Therefore I paint what I *don't* know.' And I write what I don't know, in that sense"). Apt, too, that Anne Sexton writes with urgent intimacy ("Some day I may go forth on some jet and look for that one person again and read my goddamned heart out"), while a story told by Charles Simic resembles a parable ("Marcel Duchamp suspended a book of Euclidean geometry by a string outside his window for several months and in all kinds of weather, and then presented the result to his sister as a birthday present, and of course as an art object. A lovely idea").

William Matthews humorously demystifies poetic practice. Here is his complete subject index of poetry:

1. I went out into the woods today and it made me feel, you know, sort of religious.
2. We're not getting any younger.
3. It sure is cold and lonely (a) without you, honey, or (b) with you, honey.
4. Sadness seems but the other side of the coin of happiness, and vice versa, and in any case the coin is too soon spent and on we know not what.

In the same spirit, I might propose the following as a comprehensive list of the great critical questions that will not go away:

1. Is anything central?
2. Does joy come from within or without?
3. How can you justify your aimless afternoons—Hitler is going to come again, and what are you going to do, write a poem?
4. Is it good enough to read on your deathbed?

5. What did T. S. Eliot know and when did he know it?
6. What are the poets in Ghana doing these days?
7. What are days for?
8. What do you think of: (a) the New Formalism, (b) Surrealism, (c) the Language School, (d) writing workshops, (e) poetry readings, or (f) the Internet. (Choose one.)
9. Was it a vision or a waking dream?
10. Lord, what would they say, did their Catullus walk that way?

Poems make something out of little more than nothing, and this is true of criticism as well. Luckily, the imaginative possibilities are limitless for critics who take after Henry James in habitually chewing more than they bite off.

MARTIN LAMMON

Introduction

The Second Language of Poetry

The University of Michigan Press's Poets on Poetry series began under Donald Hall's general editorship nearly 20 years ago—a long time for any publishing venture, but remarkable for a project devoted to poets and poetry. As I write these words, more than fifty books have been published. For those who follow contemporary poetry closely, the Michigan series is a model of endurance, much like the poets gathered together here, whose works in this anthology are among the best of Poets on Poetry. And the series goes on—now with David Lehman at the editorial helm.

In his own Poets on Poetry book *Goatfoot Milktongue Twinbird: Interviews, Essays, and Notes on Poetry, 1970–76,* Hall includes a short preface, as much to introduce readers to the new series as to his own volume. In it, he summarizes the historical context and literary rationale that helped to shape the Michigan series:

> After the thirties and forties, when American poets lost themselves in their own New Criticism, younger poets reacted by putting literary criticism on the poetic index. Or so it seemed. In fact, poets kept on talking about poetry, and criticizing each others' work, but they used forms more tentative than full-dress essays published in literary quarterlies. The interview printed as dialog, initiated by the *Paris Review,* became the dominant form by which poets made public their poetics. For more practical purposes, like defining or urging taste, there was still the book review; some even tried their hands at an essay from time to time, while looking the other way. But for many years, poets did not collect criticism into books.

Hall then describes his aspirations for the book and for the series as a whole: "I would hope this book might be useful to young poets trying out their ideas. Most likely to sharpen their claws on."

By the thirties and forties, T. S. Eliot, John Crowe Ransom, Allen Tate, Randall Jarrell—poet-critics who, among others, one might say "lost themselves in their own New Criticism"—had become the teachers, both formally and informally, of the poets who would begin to mature after World War II. New poets of that time grew up very much in the New Critical tradition, and that upbringing is discernible in the early work of many of the older poets (and many younger ones) represented in this anthology, with notable exceptions, such as Robert Creeley. One way or another, however, radically or subtly, these younger poets began to rebel against their elders, a rebellion that often led to personal claims for poetry that the New Criticism's emphasis on aesthetic distance would have restrained. Thus, James Wright would finish a dissertation on Charles Dickens; would publish in 1957, to much acclaim from the literary establishment, *The Green Wall*, his formal collection of poems; and would despair of ever writing poems again after his second book, *Saint Judas* (1959). Later came the intuitive, surrealistic poems of *The Branch Will Not Break* (1963), which disappointed Wright's earlier admirers. In these more personal poems, however, Wright would pursue a poetics of intimacy that rejected his early training in the New Criticism.

What James Wright and other poets of his generation found, I think, was a sense of the world in which he, an individual man, lived. Unlike the New Critical emphasis on the necessity of emotional distance, the New Poetry (to borrow a phrase Robert Bly was fond of using in his magazine *The Fifties,* and later *The Sixties*) was about getting closer to trees, deer, city streets, stray dogs, lovers, husbands and wives, mothers, children, fathers, farmland covered in snow, midwestern prairies, Indian ponies, long bridges across the Monongahela or Hudson Rivers. For example, in his essay collected here, "The Necessity of the Personal," David Ignatow borrows an idea from William Carlos Williams's 1936 article "How to Write"—a point of view that is diametrically opposed to the ideas expressed in T. S. Eliot's "Tradition and the Individual Talent." Where Eliot would locate the poet's genius in the world's historical artistic tradition, Williams looks "backward through the night of our unconscious past" and "down to the ritualistic, amoral past of the race, to fetish, to dream, to wherever the 'genius' of the particular writer finds itself able to go." Williams and Ignatow claim a more organic, personal, even messier tradition than Eliot's well-crafted metaphysics. Ignatow insists that poets must obey their own instincts, must listen to their own authentic voice. Likewise, James Wright explains in his 1979 interview with Dave Smith that "the writer's real enemy is his own glibness, his own facility"; instead, Wright continues, the poet must go where personal genius leads, "to discover something in his own mind, or in the language which is imaginative."

One might also apply "the necessity of the personal" to Alicia Ostriker's essay "A Wild Surmise: Motherhood and Poetry."

Ostriker describes being a graduate student in 1960 and trying to write poems "as nearly resembling those of Keats, Hopkins, and W. H. Auden as I could" and then meeting a "distinguished gentleman poet" from whom she coveted praise but from whom instead she received a dismissal: "You women poets are very graphic, aren't you." It was a personal poem—Ostriker had written about being in bed with her husband, "probably nude"—that disturbed this older, "distinguished" poet. Ostriker recalls that experience as the moment she began to see herself in a new way ("All right, then, I'll *be* a woman poet") and decided to "write about the body." In the new poetics, the body was alive and essential—and not just the human body, but also animal bodies. It was also the world's body of the prairie, the pasture, the forest (see Maxine Kumin's essay "Estivating—1973").

In Northrop Frye's *Anatomy of Criticism* (1957), he dismisses poets writing criticism, arguing that they could only promote their own notions of what poetry should be, not what poetry is. He would have had in mind a poet exactly like Robert Bly, who in 1958 *did* publish critical prose in his magazine *The Fifties*, except that the criticism included statements such as this one: "We need poets now who can carry on a sustained raid into modern life, and in work after work, carry on the green and vigorous waters of this profound life" ("Five Decades of Modern American Poetry," *The Fifties*, no. 1, 1958). Robert Bly was no doubt one of the poets Hall had in mind who had rebelled against the older generation that had "lost themselves in their own New Criticism"—one among many poets who in the fifties and sixties had begun to discover a body of poetry and poetics more lively, and more alive, than what their New Critical predecessors had impressed on them.

Many of the essays, interviews, book reviews, memoirs, and other kinds of articles included in the Poets on Poetry series are not what most people would call criticism—certainly not Northrop Frye, or many other intelligent scholars and literary critics. However, among the many ways of talking intelligently about poetry, I would make one admittedly simple but important distinction: A thoughtful reader relies on an intellect that either includes intuitive, emotional, and irrational approaches to poetry or that excludes these approaches as too subjective and uncritical. Thus Northrop Frye, or a bibliographical scholar, or a well-heeled "New Formalist" poet might diminish, or even dismiss intuitive, emotional responses to literature as too personal, too messy. There is something less ambitious, however, about a critical approach that forgoes mystery and seeks instead what is quantifiable and objectively redeemable. In the *Anatomy of Criticism*, Frye acknowledges that mystery cannot be the object of criticism, but he does not regret the loss. Like the clinical scientist, he insists that objectivity is a fundamental premise of critical inquiry and thus, de facto, he validates objective criticism to the exclusion of other possible approaches. Northrop Frye, of course, is only one critic. But his *Anatomy* expresses the essential intellectual drift of that era.

The intuitive poet's typically broader approach is inclusive rather than exclusive, and that openness is more ambitious, I believe, if less subject to scrutiny and proof. Lacking proof, an open approach creates rather than proscribes critical possibilities for addressing poetry. Thus we have Charles Wright's fragments and notes as "Improvisations on Form and Measure"; Jane Miller's poetics as travelogue; Louis Simpson's intelligent and more traditional essay on narrative poetry; Robert Francis's satirical "Pot Shots" at poetry; interviews with Robert Creeley, James Wright, Robert Bly, Philip Levine, and Galway Kinnell; Maxine Kumin's journalistic summer memoir; and Thom Gunn's poignant essay on revision that connects one's craft to one's life.

We also have William Stafford suggesting a distinction between personal and objective approaches to poetry in his essay "The End of a Golden String." In discussing the question of literary influence, Stafford challenges the "system that has served so long and been used, explicitly and implicitly, by our whole culture, in the schools." He laments the "relay-race assumption in the arts" that "lends itself to sustained scholarship . . . a life preserver for teachers on the long float through the afternoon." The fact of such literary influence would seem obvious, a valid product of cause-and-effect reasoning, but Stafford offers a different point of view:

> Somewhere, each life has its validation, not in a sequence of ciphers influencing each other down through time, but in immediate encounters that have their own individual worths, no matter how small.

In *The Weather for Poetry,* Donald Hall writes the following about William Stafford's idea of a "second language of poetry":

> Stafford has referred to an unspoken tongue that lives underneath the words of poetry. This second language is beyond the poet's control, but we can define a poet as someone who speaks it. English teachers afflicted with students who lack control over their own language—ignorant, illiterate, wordless—often assume that the best language is the most controlled and the most conscious. Not so, or not always so: poets are literate, poets control, poets command syntax and lexicon—but the best poets *also* write without knowing every-

thing that they are up to, trusting in the second language's continual present hum of implication.

Often, the poet writing critical prose will also work through the mystery of poetry's second language, which is about having *faith,* and therein lies the higher ambition I perceive when I read poets on poetry. If poems are the object of a poet's hope and ambition, what poets write about poetry can encourage high ambition—not only for writing poems, but for reading them—encouragement that is palpable for me when I read the poets collected here. Their ideas dig deep, like sharpened claws.

When I read traditional criticism and scholarship, I miss the camaraderie, the community, and even the caterwauling that poets on poetry can express—something more passionate than the scholar-critic's typical wryness, sarcasm, or irony. In the fifties and sixties, poets and poetry were being divided into camps ("Beats" vs. "Academics"; "raw" vs. "cooked" poetry—in fact, Diane Wakoski recalls in her essay collected here the discouraging labels "Dionysian" and "Apollonian"). Battles were being fought, alliances made, allegiances pledged. Granted, so-called "schools" were more the invention of journalists and anthologists. But poets were arguing with each other, claiming new ground for poetry not only from their elders but also among each other. It was a lively time indeed, and very different, at least in character, from the kind of public debate T. S. Eliot, John Crowe Ransom, or Allen Tate engaged in. Ezra Pound's passion unfortunately degenerated into incoherence.

Young poets today may not need so much to "sharpen their claws" against their elders, or on each other. Their immediate past is populated neither by Eliot, declaring himself Anglican and Loyalist; nor Ransom, offering a clinical analysis of the "world's body"; nor Pound, broadcasting his overwhelming madness. This was the past that, variously, Robert Creeley, David Ignatow, Robert Bly, and, a little later, Alicia Ostriker confronted and perhaps *had* to fight against because it was their artistic and personal freedom that was being threatened. But sustaining that "raid into modern life," as Bly described it, could be dangerous. Often, belligerence leads to using the tactics of one's adversary. Certainly an original thinker, Robert Bly (in one of his infamous "Crunk" essays) in the early sixties had examined the work of Denise Levertov, but (much like the influence-seekers that William Stafford had observed) he claimed that Levertov had learned her style and form from Robert Creeley and others. In a letter to the editor, Creeley responded, firmly but gracefully, that none of the poets exerted undue influence over each other, that "all of us were looking for water to drink."

In the essays that follow, a reader will find that stones are often not weapons, but are the flat stones near rivers good for walking on, and that the poets are all looking for good water to drink—an image that comes to mind in what James Wright calls "the pure, clear word."

Even if the immediate past is not so threatening, younger poets and readers of poetry must pay attention to the past, to encounter and challenge old and not-so-old ideas if new ground might still have the chance to be explored. More recently, the threat that compromises the younger poet's freedom may be the MFA workshop. Teachers are restrained by academic calendars and thus focus on students' own writings, leaving little time to develop in the classroom a sense of history, even recent history. This is a phenomenon that concerns many of the poets in this anthology. I am concerned that the young poet today is often not aware of Galway Kinnell's Avenue C, let alone Pound's ABCs. Unlettered, how can the young poet even guess at Dante's *De vulgari eloquentia?*

But I agree with William Stafford. The young poet should not be looking to find influences. The goal might instead be to become an individual within a community of poetry, past and present. Therefore, one has to know the past. I would hope, then, that this anthology challenges a reader not only to address contemporary ideas about poetry but also to look more deeply into the origins of these ideas. In these essays and interviews, a reader will find many references to poets and critical ideas that range from the present to the distant past. In her essay "Robert Frost and the Better Half of Poetry," Amy Clampitt ranges far indeed, from contemporaries Jonathan Holden and A. R. Ammons back to Frost, Milton, and Spenser. Her essay challenges a reader to think about poetry's language, about the sounds that words make. One cannot help but hear Frost's old complaint about there being no pleasure in writing free verse, which to him was like playing tennis without a net. Pay close attention, and you may be compelled to reread Milton and rediscover his claim that only blank verse satisfies the requirements of the serious epic poem in English; or if you're persistent, you may even go looking to find out why Dante wrote in vulgar Italian. Such a sense of history, both recent and old—not to mention both Western and non-Western; after Dante, then Basho—also promotes a higher ambition for one's work, and for one's life.

Clampitt's essay opens the first part of this anthology. There are five parts, each devoted to issues important to anyone interested in looking more closely at poetry: "Poets on Form and Content," "Poets on the Modern Tradition and New Directions," "Poets on the Academy and Literary Industry," "Poets on Politics and Poetry," and "Poets on Influence and Identity." These divisions are conveniences established to help a reader, especially a teacher, organize ideas and issues. The essays and interviews, however, explore ideas and issues that are hardly convenient, neither intellectually nor emotionally. I would hope that readers of Clampitt's essay will on their own look more closely into Milton and Spenser (not to mention Holden and Ammons) whom she cites, and perhaps seek out Basho, Dante, or Sappho, whom she does not. This book will challenge readers, I hope, to go in search of connections to the larger community of poets and poetry that no anthology can fully represent.

An excerpt from an interview with James Wright opens the second part. Anyone interested in contemporary American poetry needs to be familiar with Wright's poetic renaissance in the early sixties, culminating in his 1963 collection *The Branch Will Not Break*. The excerpt focuses mostly on this period, but Wright also directs us to Dickens and Katherine Anne Porter, to Samuel Johnson, to Robert Creeley. In the third part, Donald Hall directs us to Horace and to whomever or whatever leads us away from the triviality of the MFA workshop, the "McPoem," and "Hamburger University." In much the same way, Robert Bly directs us away from the workshop in the fourth part; he also opens up a world that is not primarily Anglo-American.

In the final part, William Stafford directs us back to ourselves, even insisting that there is no tradition influencing poets today. That is an idea hard for us to accept. Such a poet would require much integrity, discipline, and conviction. Stafford was a conscientious objector during World War II and a man who wrote a poem every day. But he was also a reader aware of the traditions that did not influence him. The language and idea for his essay "The End of a Golden String," he explains disingenuously, come from William Blake's *Jerusalem*.

A sense of shared history enriches the affection, the inevitable bickering, the common and uncommon goals that arise among a community of readers and poets. I hope this anthology offers the kind of reports, insights, arguments, declarations, claims, tributes, and criticisms that may help new readers think about the past— logically and intuitively, disinterestedly and passionately—so that they might move on to their own new ground.

My goal in selecting these pieces was to choose works that made demands on readers, whether they be poets younger or older, teachers of literature or creative writing, or merely women and men in pursuit of the modest question Donald Hall poses at the end of "Poetry and Ambition": How shall we lead our lives? In the books of the Poets on Poetry series, one may find such inspiration, and while I hope that this anthology represents the best the series has to offer, I would hope, too, that readers of this anthology will also seek out the individual poets' books in the series. In making selections for this anthology, I was keenly aware of what I could not include. It was a little like those occasions at parties and in airports when a stranger asks, Who's your favorite poet? or What's your favorite poem? Restrained, you cannot spend an hour naming dozens of poets and explaining the various ways you favor work by all of them. In this endeavor, I could not make a nine hundred–page book. For balance, I could not choose an essay or interview that was thirty or forty pages long (in a few cases, I excerpted from longer works). I chose not to include tributes, attacks, and reviews that focused on a single poet, preferring instead to have, as much as possible, poets on a broader range of topics, ideas, and issues. I preferred to have essays but selected five interviews. In some cases a book was devoted only to a poet's interviews, which did not leave me much choice, while in other cases it was an interview that offered a poet's best ideas.

Obviously, I chose works that I thought challenged, engaged, inspired, riled, informed—works that touched me and taught me. As is always the case, an editor must consider what an audience needs but finally be represented by one's own taste and instinct. Whatever criticism, then, a reader may levy against this book, the toll is mine to pay and no one else's. I am, however, thankful for the help and support of many people. Always, of course, I am thankful for the camaraderie of colleagues, friends, and family—at this time in my life, especially for those people I live among in West Virginia. But I thank especially for their help on this project John Burke of the Fairmont State College library and Jenny Smith. I thank my former teacher David Heaton of Ohio University for the model of endurance and integrity that he provided his students. And for her insight and help, her patience and guidance, I offer special thanks to Libby Davis.

I. The Better Half of Poetry ✑
Poets on Form and Content

AMY CLAMPITT

Robert Frost and the
Better Half of Poetry

Some years ago I came upon one of those single passages that can be so arresting as to call for an immediate rearrangement of one's ideas. The context was a *Georgia Review* essay by Jonathan Holden (later reprinted in *The Rhetoric of the Contemporary Lyric,* Indiana University Press, 1980):

> by and large the emphasis on metaphor . . . in American poetry of the 1970s is a natural outgrowth of the recession of music in favor of closure as the dominant convention that seems at times virtually to define "poetry."

The recession of music in favor of closure: that was the phrase that leaped at me from the page, and made me wonder all at once where I was, where I had been, and what was going to happen next. At the time I had not so much as heard of Barbara Herrnstein Smith's *Poetic Closure: A Study of How Poems End* (Chicago, 1968). If I had, no doubt I would have taken note of her statement that "analogues between music and poetry are always suggestive, particularly so in connection with closure," and of her reference to the "conventionalized" situation in, for example, Petrarchan love poetry; as well as, a little further on, her observation that "the concluding lines of many sixteenth-century poems . . . would be as alien to a modern poem as a pavan in a modern dance." If what Jonathan Holden proposed is correct, the conventions of lyric poetry have so far departed from those of the sixteenth century as to have produced "the poem that is all metaphor and that is *without* music" (my italics). He was writing of things in the seventies. Now that not only the seventies have come to an end, but the eighties as well, what new thing sits waiting to leap off the page?

For this reader, one such thing is a concept encountered for the first time in an essay on A. R. Ammons, in Willard Spiegelman's *The Didactic Muse* (Princeton, 1990):

> Current literary wisdom holds that all literature gives prominence to the *lisible,* because language is inscriptive. No priority is granted

to voice, transcendent reality, or "world" because language itself creates, commands, and precedes the meanings that it inscribes, submerging its "referents" more and more deeply into a scribal palimpsest. I do not wish to tackle, let alone refute, Derridean orthodoxies. . . . Still, it seems legitimate to credit Ammons with having created a poetry, like that of William Carlos Williams, that is genuinely unhearable.

The prominence of the lisible, as opposed to the merely audible: if this is indeed the way things are going, one can only conclude that the recession from music continues—toward what end I myself quail at the very thought of. It's not that aural poetry is dead: pop music on the airwaves and rap all over the place prove otherwise, not to mention the food-hawkers who are still at it, half a century after Gershwin put the strawberry woman and the deviled-crab man of Charleston onto the operatic stage—or, indeed, the caller at Penn Station whose chanted Allll-a-bo-*oht!* surely qualifies as an aria. None of this is exactly literature, at any rate literature as Mary Renault in *The Praise Singer* conceived of Simonides conceiving it at the beginning of the fifth century B.C.:

> So what can I do, unless I'm to be remembered only by what's carved in marble? *Tell them in Lakedaimon, passerby, that here, obedient to their word, we lie.* They'll remember *that.* . . . Men forget how to write upon the mind. To hear, and to keep: that is our heritage from the Sons of Homer. Sometimes I think I shall die their only heir. . . . I shall leave my scrolls, like the potter's cup and the sculptor's marble, for what they're worth. Marble can break; the cup is a crock thrown in the well; paper burns warm on a winter night. I have seen too much pass away. . . . The true songs are still in the minds of men.

What happens when the true songs are no longer in the minds of men? We are seeing what happens. Memory is elsewhere—on library shelves, squirreled into microfilm, cramming the reductive labyrinth of a microchip. The only exceptions to its seemingly irreversible atrophy are among the illiterate. We are drowning in print, and yet (with a few rare and glorious exceptions) nobody remembers anything. In my darker moments I wonder sometimes whether anybody *reads* anything, aside from those who do so because they earn their keep that way—the literary theoreticians and (can it truly be?) those whose function is now to give them employment. In moments less glum, I still wonder whether, so far as the printed page is concerned, the aural, the hearable, the ear itself, are on their way to being regarded as passé. From a review of my own work I learned that it owed "everything to the eye and rather less to the ear." Well, that shook me. For as long as I can remember, however interesting the look of things (my earliest ambition having been to be a painter), in poetry the sound came first. The better half of poetry, Robert Frost called it.

> The ear [he wrote] is the only true writer and the only true reader. I have known people who could read without hearing the sentence sounds and they were the fastest readers. Eye readers we call them. They can get the meaning by glances. But they are bad readers because they miss the best part of what a good writer puts into his work.

He was referring to the kind of blank-verse dialogue you find all through *North of Boston*—blank verse like this, from "A Hundred Collars":

> I like to find folks getting out in spring,
> Raking a dooryard, working near the house.
> Later they get out further in the fields.
> Everything's shut sometimes except the barn;
> The family's all away in some back meadow.

That's a Yankee voice, and what makes it lively has been neatly spelled out by Frost himself:

> I am never more pleased than when I can get the very regular preestablished accent of blank verse, and the irregular accent and measure of speaking intonation, into strained relation. I like to drag and break the intonation across the metre as waves first comb and then break stumbling along the shingle.

He also knew how to slow down the pace, for an effect that is not a bit colloquial—as in this monologue by a census-taker who comes upon a house with nobody in it:

> This house in one year fallen into decay
> Filled me with no less sorrow than the houses
> Where Asia wedges Africa from Europe.
> Nothing was left to do that I could see. . . .

That deprecatory drop is pure Frost, and he fell into it often— letting you know that though some rather grand ruminations occasionally slip past, he's still the same pawky rural character. Nobody was ever going to catch him opening all the stops, the way Spenser had:

> The trembling ghosts with sad amazed mood,
> Chattring their yron teeth, and staring wide
> With stony eyes, and all the hellish brood
> Of feends infernall flockt on every side,
> To gaze on earthly wight that with the Night durst ride.

You're not going to catch him being grandly polemical either, the way Milton was:

> Avenge O Lord Thy slaughtered saints, whose bones
> Lie scattered on the Alpine mountains cold. . . .

Nobody writes like that these days, and it's not hard to imagine why. Humankind has simply been put in its place too unmistakably, has been taken in by its own overweenings, and then shown up for a dolt, a few times too often to leave room for all-out sublimity any more. Just why this should make poets wary of open vowel sounds ("Ay me! whilst thee the shores, and sounding Seas / Wash far away, where ere thy bones are hurled"), I'm not so sure, but it must be the same reason opera is so often thought of as not grand but ridiculous—and how we all do fear and dread to be that! What interests me about Frost, though, is how in his own way, with his own resolutely middling intentions, he does arrive at a kind of grandeur. He was not going to think of writing another "Lycidas." All the same, in "Once by the Pacific," he used simple couplets and still did justice to an ancient theme:

> It looked as though a night of dark intent
> Was coming, and not only a night, an age.
> Someone had better be prepared for rage.
> There would be more than ocean-water broken
> Before God's last *Put out the light* was spoken.

Milton's grand open O is made into a smaller sound: broken, spoken in those falling final syllables—a sort of cutting of sublimity down to size. But it's there all the same: the echo is there in the language for us to hear, when it's given a chance to be heard.

Nobody would accuse Robert Frost of being lush, either—in fact, as Howard Moss memorably put it, his Yankee wariness showed itself by refusing to be either naked or gorgeous. But there are poems of his that, though chilly by comparison with, say, "The murmurous haunt of flies on summer eves," do contain an almost Keatsian synesthesia:

> Let them think twice before they use their powers
> To blot out and drink up and sweep away
> These flowery waters and these watery flowers

in "Spring Pools," or

> And with these sky-flakes down in flurry on flurry
> There is more unmixed color on the wing
> Than flowers will show for days unless they hurry

in "Blue-Butterfly Day"; or, in a poem more famous for the sense, the almost sixteenth-century closure of its "what to make of a diminished thing," than for the internal melody of

> He says the early petal-fall is past
> When pear and cherry bloom went down in showers
> On sunny days a moment overcast;
> And comes the other fall we name the fall.
> He says the highway dust is over all.

I'm not trying to separate the melody from the meaning of "The Oven Bird"—only to say that the melody is there: the sound of the English language being turned into music.

It was a dryer, sparer sound, by the time Frost took it up; and when you consider Wallace Stevens, it would seem that the drying-up process had gone a bit further:

> The lacquered loges huddled there
> Mumbled zay-zay and a-zay, a-zay.

But even that jazzy little buzz would seem to be on its way out. Consider, for a last example, the unmistakable tone (lisible or whatever) of A. R. Ammons:

> probably this is why nature says nothing—
> it has nothing to say

is an extreme example—as is

> we were talking about our MFA program
> (pogrom) in Creative Writing when I said
> should we, can we, professionalize
> delight

Irresistible though I find this, the music is a vibration in the brain rather than the ear. Can it be that what's in store for us is indeed the poverty of living elsewhere than in a physical world?* People, including poets, living more and more inside their own heads: is this what's happening? Is it why people turn out in such droves for poetry readings, the merely lisible and inscriptive notwithstanding? In a time when there is so little agreement about what the conventions are—if there even are any—anything is possible.

---

*Perhaps some sort of analogy may be drawn from the remarks of Arthur G. Danto in the *Nation* for July 9, 1990: "The history of Modernism is an erratic progress of self-purification. Thus the figure was discarded as contingent in pictorial representation by Abstractionists. Pictorial or illusionistic space was discarded as being inappropriate to abstraction, even if not filled with recognizable scenes and figures. Geometrical forms were discovered to be not altogether mandated by abstraction, which could be achieved by swipes of pigment across a flat surface. The brush stroke was demonstrably unrequired, as the drip-stick showed." And so on.

WILLIAM MATTHEWS

Dull Subjects

"And what are your poems about?" a poet might be asked by, let's say, an affable seatmate on an airplane. And what would our poet say?

The question makes immediate sense about other sorts of books, and answers are not hard to imagine.

> "*Unsafe at Any Speed* is about the wanton and cynical triumph of style over safety in American-built automobiles," said Mr. Nader.

> "It's an odd book," said Mr. Melville, ringing the stewardess's bell with, among the other objects in his teeming mind, a second Bloody Mary in view. "A one-legged whaling captain monomaniacally pursues a white whale. It's a novel about whaling, male bonding, obsession, and it's about the mute and lulling allure that ideas of good and evil bear for Americans. It's hard to talk about; that's why I wrote the book." Mr. Melville heaved an ambiguous noise, a sort of stifled, ecstatic sigh, and for that instant it was hard to know if he was satisfied by his *précis* or only beginning to describe.

> "*New Hope for the Dead* is the ultimate self-help book," its author explained.

Robert Creeley has used as an essay title a puzzled question once asked him: "Are those real poems or did you make them up yourself?"

Among the other confusions behind the question posed to Creeley is a predisposition to the idea that all real poems were written by people now dead, and since Creeley is alive he must be an imposter. Also important here is the notion that poetry should not be merely personal, that someone inspired, as a poet in the popular imagination must be, has breathed in the spirit of poetry and is temporarily the vessel and conduit of some larger force, as indeed we all are until we cease to inhale.

But, paradoxically, poetry in the popular imagination is assumed to be among the most personal of the arts, if not the most personal of them, and indeed, doesn't the durable injunction against the merely personal suggest how prevalent the merely personal might be?

Perhaps we could begin thinking about the use of subject matter to poetry by considering the poet's needs. Here is a brief excerpt from an interview with James Merrill.

> You hardly ever need to *state* your feelings. The point is to feel and keep the eyes open. Then what you feel is expressed, is mimed back at you by the scene. A room, a landscape. I'd go a step further. *We* don't *know* what we feel until we see it distanced by this kind of translation.

Merrill is close here to drawing the body of Eliot's elusive Cheshire Cat, the "objective correlative." It isn't that you know what you feel and devise alchemically a scrap of language that transmits accurately such complex information to a reader. The implicit model for such a process, were it possible, is the genetic code. With that thought in mind we can see how much hubris has been attached by others to Eliot's modest catch phrase.

The poet is struggling to make something, and then, secondarily if it comes to that, to make something clear. Something subjective, of which one was the helpless owner, is ex-pressed, pushed out, made objective. Both poet and reader can now gaze on it with some curiosity, for it is in this world a new thing. It is, so far as words can create such effects, palpable, malleable, mysterious, in all three of these ways like matter itself. That the poet and reader, or any two observers, might describe it quite differently goes, almost, without saying.

A poet beginning to make something needs raw material, something to transform. An ambition or a hope to transform suggests a process, and so a good analogy for subject matter in poetry might be a chunk of matter with process already alive in it, like mother of vinegar or sourdough starter. Or like decay.

If subject matter is chosen in order that it be transformed, then a Subject Index to Poetry would be an especially unneeded and impossible reference work.

Indeed it must seem to those as casually curious about poetry as Creeley's interlocutor that poetry has all too few subjects, and I suspect the earnest compilers of a Subject Index to Poetry would find their major headings both borderless and few. To forestall such fruitless labors, I hereby offer a short but comprehensive summary of subjects for lyric poetry.

1. I went out into the woods today and it made me feel, you know, sort of religious.

2. We're not getting any younger.

3. It sure is cold and lonely (a) without you, honey, or (b) with you, honey.

4. Sadness seems but the other side of the coin of happiness, and vice versa, and in any case the coin is too soon spent and on we know not what.

One could, I suppose, if one were possessed of a mania for condensation and categorization, offer a single ur-plot for lyric poetry and indeed for all imaginative literature, and if so, one could do worse than the following four-word sentence, a plot summary of the Bob Hope, Bing Crosby and Dorothy Lamour film, *The Road to Bali:* "Amorous gorilla pursues Hope."

Hope is the most difficult of industries, for it manufactures nothing from something. But poems make something out of only a little more than nothing. It is perhaps in fear of the generative power of the best poetry that so much bad discussion of poetry reduces the fully exfoliated poem to a seed, the poem's theme or topic, which of course is not what the poem grew from but a poor, bare paraphrase of what the poem grew to be if every leaf and bud and detail be ignored and an idea be made to stand for the poem the way in children's drawings a stick figure is made to stand for a person.

Our Subject Index to Poetry, then, would turn out to be a Theme Index to Poetry—even less useful than we first supposed.

Let's consider the way so many passages by Wallace Stevens turn on a quick shift of perspective.

> In my room, the world is beyond my understanding;
> But when I walk I see that it consists of three or four hills and a
>   cloud.

So begins "Of the Surface of Things," and here is the third of "Six Significant Landscapes."

> I measure myself
> Against a tall tree.
> I find that I am much taller,
> For I reach right up to the sun,
> With my eye;
> And I reach to the shore of the sea
> With my ear.
> Nevertheless, I dislike
> The way the ants crawl
> In and out of my shadow.

And here is the eleventh of "Thirteen Ways of Looking at a Blackbird."

> He rode over Connecticut
> In a glass coach.
> Once, a fear pierced him,
> In that he mistook
> The shadow of his equipage
> For blackbirds.

There is always in poetry a kind of plot. After all, grammar has a plot: sentences open and then, according to the rules and habits of grammar and syntax, they close. And in a poem line 1 precedes line 2. So the two primary units of a poem, the grammatical unit and the line, both have built into them considerations of time and rhythm, which is to say narrative and suspense.

In poems where large and readily recognizable events are the controlling elements of plot and narrative—let's take obvious examples like "Casey at the Bat" or "Gunga Din" or "The Highwayman"—subject matter may well be the single controlling factor in a reader's response. There are plenty of baseball fans who know "Casey at the Bat" who don't know Marianne Moore's various passages of encomium to the Brooklyn Dodgers. The difference in appeal to such a reader between Ernest Thayer's ballad and Marianne Moore's lines is likely to be that for Moore, subject matter is not in itself important, except that it gives her the opportunity to speak about something that engages her passions. What is important instead is what she can discover to say.

In passages like those I've quoted from Stevens, where the ordinary elements of drama, conflict and narrative suspense are almost wholly suppressed, we have a clear opportunity to see how provisional ostensible subject matter is.

In a poem where subject matter is the finish line for discovery, rather than the start, a first line like

In my room, the world is beyond my understanding.

would lead, probably, to a quest: the speaker would go into the larger world, undergo significant experiences, and, likely as not, return symmetrically to his room, older but wiser.

But the speaker in Stevens's poem goes out and finds, without insisting that the event increases his understanding, that when he is outside the world consists of what he can see of it.

In the passage from "Six Significant Landscapes" we could almost be hearing the preternaturally intelligent babble of an immense, precocious baby. The discovery that the senses are an extension of the body, in lines 3–7, recapitulates a recognizable stage in infant development, and there is in the switch between this discovery and the imperious dislike of the ants (what are *they* doing to *my* world, which is my body) a very small child's promiscuous attention to the world as a waterfall of sensations.

About the passage from "Thirteen Ways of Looking at a Blackbird" we should note how thoroughly unanswered are questions the passage might provoke in a reader for whom subject matter is a resting place.

Where do you get a glass coach outside of fairy tales? Why Connecticut? Were blackbirds in themselves fearful? or the mistake of the shadow of one thing, a glass coach, for many blackbirds? Or what?

Stevens has a short poem in *Harmonium* called "Theory" that seems apposite.

> I am what is around me.
>
> Women understand this.
> One is not duchess
> A hundred yards from a carriage.
>
> These, then, are portraits:
> A black vestibule;
> A high bed sheltered by curtains.
>
> These are merely instances.

The first sentence is a tautology, we could say, the way all sentences using the verb *to be* tend toward being tautologies. I don't mean to suggest by the word "tautology" that the sentence is self-evident. For one thing, Stevens's proposition about the nature of the self is not an ordinarily creditable one. And for another, the whole notion of self-evidence is a problem, for what we call "self-evident" is only so after we have noticed it; before that moment it was invisible. What I mean to emphasize is the way the verb *to be* resembles, in mathematical notation, an equals sign. It's like a fulcrum, and it balances the two halves of the sentence by the variable poise of a teeter-totter.

So if a person can be what is around that person, a temporary portrait or an instance of that person can be made by sketching a scene or situation. As if to underscore how one can serve for the other, Stevens gives us two instances where the person would in fact be hard to see, hidden by the scene that is, anyway, that person. So what does it matter that this person's face is hard or impossible to see in a black vestibule? It probably doesn't matter, even, if the person in question is inside the sheltering curtains of a high bed when we look at the bed or is out, somewhere else, touring Connecticut in a glass equipage, let's say, and merely might as well be behind those sheltering curtains.

But these portraits aren't emblems, they're instances: they're in rather than out of time, and that's why, I take it, fastidious Stevens adds the word "merely."

Subject matter, then, is often in poetry a place to begin, and it need not, we can see from an admiring glance at these few passages from Stevens, refer to an event or to a drama larger or more melodramatic than the shifting play of perception.

Sometimes poems refer for their beginnings to exactly those topics conventional wisdom considers so dull that even knaves know it: weather, how time flies, how grass grows, etc. William Carlos Williams's celebrated "Spring and All" touches on all these dull subjects and more.

> By the road to the contagious hospital
> under the surge of the blue
> mottled clouds driven from the
> northeast—a cold wind. Beyond, the
> waste of broad, muddy fields
> brown with dried weeds, standing and fallen
>
> patches of standing water
> the scattering of tall trees
>
> All along the road the reddish
> purplish, forked, upstanding, twiggy
> stuff of bushes and small trees
> with dead, brown leaves under them
> leafless vines—
>
> Lifeless in appearance, sluggish
> dazed spring approaches—
>
> They enter the new world naked,
> cold, uncertain of all
> save that they enter. All about them
> the cold, familiar wind—

Now the grass, tomorrow
the stiff curl of wildcarrot leaf
One by one objects are defined—
It quickens: clarity, outline of leaf

But now the stark dignity of
entrance—Still, the profound change
has come upon them: rooted, they
grip down and begin to awaken.

Reading this poem again during a summer of Bread and
Circuses—two political conventions, the grandiloquent tedium of
the endless presidential campaign, ABC's jingoistic Gee Whiz cover-
age of the Olympics—is a great, grounding pleasure.

Often in poems incomplete sentences mean incomplete thoughts
and emotions, but in this poem, where we don't have a technically
complete sentence until the fourth stanza, what seems missing at
first is exactly what a verb is for—process, change. They go on
overhead, in weather, but the ground on which Williams's eye is
fixed is strewn with stuff: matter seen at a stage almost before
growth has given it form. It barely has color (not red, but reddish;
not purple, but purplish). It's in waste, without apparent pattern or
meaning. It's sluggish and dazed and uncertain.

I can't think just now of a poem that celebrates better the usual
work of the vegetable world, nor of a poem that makes more grace-
fully the analogy of such work to the endless and ordinary labor of
human consciousness. After a summer of tatty glory and hypno-
tized praise of a selective American past, it's good to dowse one's
dusty face in the stream of Williams's poem, made, like life itself,
from scruff and blur and effort, into, at life's best, clarity and
outline and shadowing.

"What is there here but weather?" Stevens asks in "Waving Adieu,
Adieu, Adieu," a poem aching from the speed by which one percep-
tion is replaced by the next.

That would be waving and that would be crying,
Crying and shouting and meaning farewell,
Farewell in the eyes and farewell at the centre,
Just to stand still without moving a hand.

In a world without heaven to follow, the stops
Would be endings, more poignant than partings, profounder,
And that would be saying farewell, repeating farewell,
Just to be there and just to behold.

To be one's singular self, to despise
The being that yielded so little, acquired
So little, too little to care, to turn
To the ever-jubilant weather, to sip

One's cup and never to say a word,
Or to sleep or just to lie there still,
Just to be there, just to be beheld,
That would be bidding farewell, be bidding farewell.

One likes to practice the thing. They practice,
Enough, for heaven. Ever-jubilant,
What is there here but weather, what spirit
Have I except it comes from the sun?

It's not only that dull—or modest, or unassuming—subjects provide a useful place to begin, or that they can be in themselves a constraint against melodrama and easy grandeur. Inherently dramatic and shapely subject matter lends itself to a certain neatness—conflict, resolution, and calm—that may appeal to a poet's craft and perfectionism, on the one hand, but may well, on the other hand, incite a poet's suspicion of the perfected certainties of art in the face of a life—not the poet's, necessarily, but anyone's—that is unruly, unfinished, and unstoppable.

Here is Howard Moss's "The Summer Thunder."

Now the equivocal lightning flashes
Come too close for comfort and the thunder
Sends the trembling dog under the table,
I long for the voice that is never shaken.

Above the sideboard, representation
Takes its last stand: a small rectangle
Of oak trees dripping with a painted greenness,
And in the foreground, a girl asleep

In a field who speaks for a different summer
From the one the thunder is mulling over—
How calm the sensuous is! How saintly!
Undersea light from a lit-up glen

Lends perspective to an arranged enchantment,
As peaceful as a Renaissance courtyard
Opened for tourists centuries after
Knights have bloodied themselves with doctrine.

The first stanza bristles with a nearly subliminal syntactical discontent like that caused by shifting barometric pressure before rain. At the end of each of the first two lines, the grammar of the unfolding sentence is in doubt: (1) Is *flashes* a verb or a noun? (2) Is *thunder* part of a dual noun—*comfort and the thunder*—or is it the beginning of a new clause beginning with "and"?

And consider the understanding that makes possible the link between "perspective" and "arranged enchantment" and "doctrine"; this short lyric poem contains not a theory but an understanding of the relationship between technique in painting and technique in religion. No wonder "sensuous" and "saintly," at first glance an odd pair of adjectives, snuggle comfortably together in line 11, bonded by an idea of containment, contentment even, that we are lured to by its promise of respite from thunder at the poem's beginning—and eager to escape from, as from blood, by the poem's end.

The ability to hold such opposites in balance without resort to mere paradox is a signature of our best writing. A related passage is in Vladimir Nabokov's *Speak Memory.*

Nabokov's beloved father is, after memory itself, the hero of his memoir. His father is being tossed from a blanket by villagers who are ceremonially celebrating his father's role in settling a local dispute. The custom is like the one in which the coxswain of a winning crew is thrown into the water after a race. I mention this only to point out that it has nothing to do with the intellectually lazy and politically sentimental view of Nabokov's family as White Russians, those stuffed reactionaries coddling Fabergé eggs in the Wax Museum of Political Stereotypes. Nabokov's father was in fact a leader of the Kadets (a liberal opposition party before the Revolution), was jailed for issuing a revolutionary manifesto, and died in 1922 in Berlin, at an emigré political meeting, when he stepped in front of a speaker who was the target of two monarchist assassins.

From my place at table I would suddenly see through one of the west windows a marvelous case of levitation. There, for an instant, the figure of my father in his wind-rippled white summer suit would be displayed, gloriously sprawling in midair, his limbs in a curiously casual attitude, his handsome, imperturbable features turned to the sky. Thrice, to the mighty heave-ho of his invisible tossers, he would fly up in this fashion, and the second time he would go higher than the first and then there he would be, on his last and loftiest flight, reclining, as if for good, against the cobalt blue of the summer noon, like one of those paradisiac personages who comfortably soar, with such a wealth of folds in their garments, on the vaulted ceiling of a church while below, one by one, the wax tapers in mortal hands light up to make a swarm of minute flames in the mist of incense, and the priest chants of eternal repose, and funeral lilies conceal the face of whoever lies there, among the swimming lights, in the open coffin.

Nabokov's famous phrase-making abilities are on full display in this virtuoso passage, but it is perhaps the stark and off-hand "as if for good" that is the most haunting in this hallucinatory performance. The more lovingly remembered and painstakingly rendered a loss is, the more on the one hand it is ours, and the more on the other hand it is already given over to memory and to art, which have, each of them, their own uses for loss. The clear light of Nabokov's prose shines on everything here, lingeringly (the tapers light up "one by one"), though it can't, or perhaps won't, penetrate the funeral lilies to illuminate the handsome and now wholly imperturbable features of Nabokov's father.

How easy it would have been for a lesser artist than Nabokov to make this scene conventionally picturesque and sentimental; indeed, it may well have given him considerable private pleasure to have picked an incident with such inducements to gauzy writing and to have persisted, with the apparently perverse courage that marks the true artist, to find in the *trompe l'oeil* of his father ascending into heaven the gravity of his real interest in the scene.

Oddly enough it is the incident that seems, at the start, already artistically shaped and full of feeling that is most likely to finish dull, perhaps because it conceals by its first appeal how much work can be done with it.

It is not, of course, the subject that is or isn't dull, but the quality of attention we do or do not pay to it, and the strength of our will to transform. Dull subjects are those we have failed.

(1985)

CHARLES WRIGHT

Improvisations on Form and Measure

The line is a unit of Measure: measure is music: the line is a verbal music. Which is to say, until we start talking about poems again, and not Poetry, we are still lost. Poems are put together with words, not Language. Word by word. Theory comes after the fact, it is not the fact. The line is a fact, it is not a theory.

In poems, all considerations are considerations of form.

A well-known poet once said to me, "I don't worry about the ends of my lines. I feel if the beginnings are good, the ends will take care of themselves." Wrong. They will not. Things have ends as well as beginnings. The line must be strong all the way through and not finish in a dying fall. This sort of sloppy thinking and practice is what leads people to dwell on, and work toward, line breaks in free verse instead of imagining the line as a whole, a unit. It leads to the anemic and careless practices we see executed in most free verse poems today, where the accent is on the *free* and not on the *verse,* as it should be.

Form is nothing more than a transubstantiation of content.

The asyntactical endings William Carlos Williams used so brilliantly for syncopation and measure—and which Robert Creeley used so well in the poems collected in *For Love*—in his short-line poems have crept along gradually to the ends of longer-lined free verse poems in our time. Any thought of a jazzy syncopation is gone because of the lengthened line, and the surprises to the ear and eye that Williams created, pleasurably, are now muted or totally over-whelmed by a sense of incompletion, as though the last part of the poem, horizontally, had been torn off, right down the page, the lines ending where the moving hand had left them.

What you have to say—though ultimately all-important—in most cases will not be news. How you say it just might be.

I myself am interested in a kind of structural investigation of the line, an attempt at some kind of harmonics involving new patterns and new designs using a long image-freighted line (the odd marriage of Emily and Walt) that can carry information (and "sincerity") and a lyric intensity at the same time. Not only will it sing, but it will tell time too. Or as Fats Domino once observed, "I don't want to bury the lyrics, man; I want 'em to understand what I'm saying."

The poetic line gets harder to blow each year. Keep your chops.

When a poem is constructed imagistically, line by line, it is built up. When it is constructed discursively, when the ideas in the sentences become the basic building blocks rather than the images, it is broken down. In the former, the writer thinks in lines, in the latter he thinks in line breaks. Both ways are workable, I suppose, but the music of one will be very different from that of the other. As I've said already, I believe it is preferable to think in lines rather than line breaks. In one, you construct, in the other you deconstruct. In fixed meters you have a built-in check against the excesses of the latter. In free verse, such checks exist only in the integrity of the writer's ear; hence, I suppose, the prolixity of so much slack free verse nowadays.

All great art has line—painting, poetry, music, dance. Without line there is no direction. Without direction there is no substance. Without substance there is nothing.

There is an organization to the universe, but it's not personal.

One has to learn to leave things alone. It's best to keep unwritten as much as possible. Poetry is just the shadow of the dog. It helps us know the dog is around, but it's not the dog. The dog is elsewhere, and constantly on the move.

The poem that is spatially tight and formally loose is what we have had too much of lately—what has come to be known as "the workshop poem," the merely well-made poem or the poem that is only a shaped and ordered prose trying to pass as a poem with a sense of, and integrity of, line. What we could use a bit more of is the poem that is spatially loose and formally tight, where the line is rib and bone and object, where the line is a thing, tactile and unrepentant. The spider's web, not the empty bee's body.

Each line should be a station of the cross.

If the true purpose and result of poetry is a contemplation of the divine and its attendant mysteries, as I believe it is, then content is a constant and a given: only the proper subject matter, and the innovative presentation of that subject matter, becomes, then, a concern.

Form is finite, structure is infinite.

All the great masters of free verse in this country—Whitman, Williams, Pound, Stevens, Eliot—came to that form from traditional meters. This meant they already had an idea of what a line was, and its integrity. They therefore tended to think of lines as lines, and not as a series of breaks. They had a sense of the measure, the music, of the linguistic energy that a true line can generate. You just can't not know the traditions of English verse if you expect to write in English. You have to know why you don't write—if you don't—in traditional meter. As Philip Johnson has said about architecture, you cannot not know history. If you write in a free verse line, you'd better know *why* you do so. Merely because it's in vogue is not enough. Your line has to be as good as the traditional one, and you'd better have a reason for using it.

What's more tactile, sin or a tree?

Only technique can tell us what we don't know. The content's a given we've heard before, the essence of the subject matter, its *virtù*. The poem should be a mixture of revelation and arrangement: measure and matter, matter and measure.

GREGORY ORR

The Interrupted Scheme

*Some Thoughts on Disorder and Order in the Lives
of Poets and the Lives of Poems*

> *[Imagination] reveals itself in the balance or reconciliation of
> opposite or discordant qualities: . . . a more than usual state of
> emotion with more than usual order.*
>
> —Coleridge, *Biographia Literaria*

Coleridge, who was one of the first to introduce the word "psycho-
logical" into English, gives us formulations that go to the heart of
poetry's human importance. Faced with disorder, the human mind
needs to respond with an ordering principle that will sustain it and
console it. Nowhere is that more graphically evident than when
individual victims of violent crimes like rapes or muggings struggle
to cope with the event. Again and again, they construct poignant
and pathetic retrospective stories ("If only I hadn't . . .") that *prove*
the world is not random disorder. Rather than accept that they
were simply in the wrong place at the wrong time, they will "blame
themselves," as so many of these stories do, if that is the only way
they can assert that some ordering principle does indeed determine
what happens in the world.

We all know the overwhelming power of chance, accident, ran-
domness, disorder. How lives, our lives, can be altered or ended
abruptly, catastrophically. It's a truth we can't live without and can't
live with. It's a truth that calls up a countertruth: the human need
to believe in ordering principles, even if we have to invent them
ourselves. And that is what the human imagination does—the vic-
tim going over the event again and again is trying to create or
discover the ordering principle, the story, that will make it bearable.

And don't poems do the same thing? Don't they present us with a
disorder that represents the randomness we feel threatened by in
our lives and then respond with an ordering that seems to answer
that disorder? Isn't that what makes poems vital—a genuinely threat-
ening sense of disorder and an equally convincing order? The two
forces together seek some balance, reconciliation, or resolution.

In poems, disorder tends to be thematic. Love and Death, the great
lyric themes, are essentially disordering as they impinge on the

individual life. Think of Dickinson's poem "I cannot live with You," where love is so deeply disruptive as to cause her to offend even divine order. Yet not all disorder is destructive. In the West, love's disorder may be pleasurable and vitalizing, as in Herrick's "Delight in Disorder" ("A sweet disorder in the dress / Kindles in clothes a wantonness"), though here the theme of arousing disarray unfolds in the context of the ordering of costume just as his plea for disorder is expressed in the context of highly ordered rhymed couplets.

Disorder can be present formally as well as thematically. French Surrealism utilized an intentional formal disorder of syntax and imagery as a means of social and political revolt in pursuit of that higher ordering promised by the term itself, defined by Breton in the First Manifesto as a resolution of the two states of dream and reality into a higher or sur-reality. The surrealist poem, a late Romantic development, uses a formal disorder in the services of a higher order, just as Rimbaud's "long, intentional disordering of all the senses" was the necessary disorder of the life that led to the creation of the higher order of "voyant," or visionary poet.

Order, the ordering principle, can also be either thematic or formal. In terms of thematic ordering, we may no longer be as convinced of the cosmic governing principles of divine love and harmony as Sir John Davies was when he constructed his hundreds of lines of "Orchestra," in which all nature from insects to galaxies did its formal dance, but we are still easily convinced that love orders our lives. And meter, rhyme, and traditional forms, the primary historical ordering principles of poetry, again and again assert their power. Not to mention the fact that each poem in the tradition becomes a model for subsequent poems and endorses their orderings when it is imitated, evoked, or alluded to.

Poems that continue to engage us enact this contest, this Aristotelean agon of disorder and order. The poem unfolds or initiates its particular version of disorder only to have it answered by a final sense that (to use a phrase from Robert Duncan's poem) "certain bounds hold against chaos."

Individuals vary enormously in their sense of what is genuinely threatening and what is adequately ordering, and much disagreement over the "greatness" of this or that poet or poem really hinges on the subjective response of the reader to these issues. This response, in turn, has been created by the circumstances of the reader's life and his or her innate temperament. In this deep sense "de gustibus non est disputandum" holds—there's no arguing taste. It's like the first time you move in with another person and discover that the way they arrange their furniture and physical space can be nonnegotiable, your two distinct senses of order and disorder creating a series of tensions and collisions curious in their intensity.

I think it's fair to say that poetry exerts a powerful attraction on people who have an intense consciousness of disorder. The art has an enormous reservoir of ordering principles and historical models which it offers the individual as he or she enacts the "difficult balance" of making sense of the world. However, the very ordering powers of poetry can represent a possible danger. What if, in the complex interaction between the poet and the poem, the poem comes to represent *only* an ordering—what if its order suffocates all wildness in the process of offsetting the psychic imbalance of the poet?

Gerard Manley Hopkins is a wonderful example of someone impelled by a need for strong ordering principles, both in his life and in his art. I wish to sketch his ordering efforts, not belabor them, because my goal is to focus some thoughts and perceptions on a particular poem of his.

Perhaps the clearest hint about Hopkins's personality is contained in a letter of 1882 to Robert Bridges. After denying Whitman's influence on his own work, Hopkins says the following:

> But first I may as well say what I should not otherwise have said, that I always knew in my heart Walt Whitman's mind to be more like my own than any other man's living. As he is a great scoundrel this is not a pleasant confession. And this also makes me the more desirous to read him and the more determined that I will not.

How that last sentence reverses itself perfectly in midsentence— desire leading not to the acts that fulfill it, but to a moral determination to resist, to turn against that with which he identifies. He slams the door in Whitman's face, Whitman who would have all doors removed from their hinges. Why? Both Whitman and Hopkins were exquisite sensibilities—intense and emotional in their response to nature and to sensation:

> Is this then a touch? quivering me to a new identity,
> Flames and ether making a rush for my veins,
> Treacherous tip of me reaching and crowding to help them,
> My flesh and blood playing out lightning to strike what is hardly
>   different from myself
>
> (*Song of Myself,* sec. 28)

Where they differed is in their response to this intense sensibility that they possessed, that possessed them. Whitman felt confident that he could give his sensibility celebratory expression and that this expression would discover or create an adequate new form for it, that the "original energy without check" he "permitted to speak" would create or discover an original ordering principle. That he was right in his risk is the glad judgment of history.

But Hopkins had no such confidence, either for his person or for its expression in language. And so he took this wild spirit, this chaotic sensibility he recognized in himself, and submitted it to numerous successive and progressively more stringent orderings to make it either bearable or acceptable. He converted to Catholicism and became a priest (celibacy—a rejection of the disturbing erotic component of his personality), and then past that to joining the Jesuits, the soldiers of Christ, severe, ascetic, disciplined. (Imagine Whitman as a Jesuit!)

As part of his religious renunciations, he gave up poetry entirely, only returning to it seven years later, when, at the request of his rector, he composed "The Wreck of the *Deutschland*"—in part to memorialize the five Franciscan nuns who perished in the shipwreck. The poems he subsequently wrote had to be theologically acceptable, to confirm and conform to his religious compass and that of his order.

Another entire essay could be written about how, "safe" in the double ordering of life and art form, Hopkins felt finally free to let his disorder loose. Nor is that disorder simply the thematic anguish of his so-called "dark sonnets." It manifests itself constantly in rhythms, sounds, and syntax:

> As kingfishers catch fire, dragonflies draw flame;
> As tumbled over rim in roundy wells
> Stones ring; like each tucked string tells each hung bell's
> Bow swung finds tongue to fling out broad its name.

Even his sonnet forms disorder into "curtal sonnets" and other invented variants. This upheaval within the double ordering of life and art is like an orgy taking place inside a locked room inside a locked house. That we still read Hopkins with interest and pleasure attests that he was right to impose such restraints.

But I want to focus here on one small phenomenon of disorder in a poem of profound order and beauty.

> *Spring and Fall*
> to a young child

> Margaret, are you grieving
> Over Goldengrove unleaving?

Leaves, like the things of man, you
With your fresh thoughts care for, can you?
Ah! as the heart grows older
It will come to such sights colder
By and by, nor spare a sigh
Though worlds of wanwood leafmeal lie;
And yet you will weep and know why.
Now no matter, child, the name:
Sorrow's springs are the same.
Nor mouth had, no nor mind, expressed
What heart heard of, ghost guessed:
It is the blight man was born for,
It is Margaret you mourn for.

"Spring and Fall" even in its title proposes a balancing of birth and decay. According to the poem's symbolic structure, the theme of disorder written in human terms is mortality, written in vegetative nature's terms is decay; further, that the two are parallel and even interfused in a deeply felt, primal way.

But it is the subtitle that interests me: "to a young child." The subtitle announces another person to whom the poem is presumably addressed. The *reference* to another person is itself unusual in Hopkins's poetry, but this child is not a reference, she is a *presence* in the poem. The poem's opening word is her name, "Margaret," and the same name will return to give the last line its power and poignancy. Alerted to her existence in the poem, we could alter Yeats's title and say: in names begin responsibilities. This girl is not simply a symbol, the "spring" end of the symbolic seesaw, but a dramatic presence in the poem. In the highly ordered world of Christian Hopkins, it is rare to find another person. Typically, nature, God, and the poet's emotions come together to confirm a cosmic order. But such an order has, in Hopkins, a tendency to exclude other humans, to exclude human otherness. It is the disorder of Margaret's human otherness that challenges Hopkins's ordering impulse to deepen and enlarge its embrace.

The poem's opening lines present a dramatic situation: the speaker and the girl are confronting each other. The girl is upset (perhaps they are in the woods called Goldengrove, or near it):

Margaret, are you grieving
Over Goldengrove unleaving?

Disorder is present in two forms: in the child's weeping and in the fall and decay of the autumn leaves. No sooner does disorder appear than Hopkins's ordering impulses rush forward to cope with it:

Ah! as the heart grows older
It will come to such sights colder
By and by, nor spare a sigh
Though worlds of wanwood leafmeal lie;

(lines 5–8)

These lines are an ordering response that attempts to control the disordering otherness of the child's grief. Paraphrased roughly, they say: you'll get used to it as you get older. The tone here verges on smugness; the speaker is telling her, instructing her, but he is also condescending to her. Smugness is the tonal giveaway of any poem where the ordering outweighs the disordering.

And here Hopkins's genius asserts itself: the child interrupts Father Hopkins's little disquisition with her urgency. Her dramatic otherness bursts his formal bubble:

And yet you will weep and know why.

(line 9)

His extra stress on "will" is just right—the child's feelings cannot be bought off or silenced by glib intimidation. The highly organized fifteen-line "sonnet" pivots here at its triple-rhymed center, pivots on its syntax ("And yet"), and pauses heavily as line and meaning unit are coincident for the first time in the poem. In addition, the key thematic word "why" culminates a cluster of end rhymes and internal rhymes. "Why." This single line, and the dramatic opposition it presents to the poem's initial ordering principles, hurts the speaker to a deeper level of engagement with the themes at the same time that it asserts the imperative of authentic feeling. The poem's preliminary ordering, a false ordering, a human controlling ordering (like that of a dismissive parent) gives way before the child's insistent, instructive grief.

The poem, through this single line, dramatizes another dimension of the poem's greatness: the disparity between secular orderings and sacred orderings. The worldly and worldly wise "understanding" of human nature and experience the speaker exemplifies in lines 5 through 8 only satisfy *his* needs. But the child's needs, the needs of deep grief, can only be understood in relation to a sacred ordering that brings human innerness into play—what the heart has heard of, ghost has guessed.

Only a sacred order can explain her sorrow, can place her tears in an ordering context. The sacred ordering Hopkins proposes is the Christian myth of the Fall of Man through original sin, which brought death into the world. Since this myth presupposes God's complete and total ordering of the world since its beginning, it can subsume Margaret's individual grief at a deep enough level—scoop it up, roots and all, not just blossom, carry if off toward that future in which she will be transplanted in heaven's garden, beyond all ill. Yet it seems to me that the same language also expresses a pagan ordering which is equally convincing (and thus consoling): you, Margaret, are a part of this timebound, natural world; you intuit your own death in the falling of leaves because of the mystical unity of all life. This pagan ordering is tragic at the personal level, but its consoling power is equally profound or a poem like Whitman's "Crossing Brooklyn Ferry" could not move us as it does.

The two endings call for a slight difference in tone. The Christian version has Father Hopkins back in the saddle—it's a homily, a deep homily directed at the child. The other, the pagan version, has more feeling for the rightness of her grief, and the repetition of her name in the final line makes her individual identity a part of the universal order. To me, there's enough of Whitman still unexpurgated in Hopkins's imagination to make this second reading equally believable.

But, to return to my earlier assertion, in either poem (the pagan or the Christian), it is the child's presence that turns the poem away from the self-enclosed certainties, it is the disorder of her interruption ("And yet you will weep and know why") that lets a deeper order in.

The nature of the disorder in a poem tells us what the poet's human concerns are. The orders he discovers, creates, or imposes to respond to that disorder are his gift to the human community— a representative manifestation of the human encounter with disorder and a possible response to it. What makes Hopkins's poem important is that he is able to take on two disorderings: the universal disorder of death/decay and the immediate dramatic disorder of personal emotional demand on the self. Both challenge his ordering impulse, the child's grief especially, pushing his poem past its easy answers to a vision of a deeper order more adequate to the deep disorder the child has glimpsed.

MARVIN BELL

What Does Art "Imitate," and How?

What does art "imitate," and how?

Aristotle told us that art imitates life, and thereby created The University of Chicago Department of English. Sergeant Joyce Kilmer said he's never seen a poem lovely in the way that a tree is lovely, and of course in his silly way he was right. Frank Lloyd Wright, and Ernest Fenollosa before him, said that form follows function, and Robert Creeley gets credit for saying that form is never more than an extension of content. In 1915, the second rule of Imagism mentioned that in poetry, "a new cadence means a new idea." Charles Olson is credited with saying that the poetic line is a function of one's metabolism, and Allen Ginsberg swears that each line of "Howl" takes one human breath.

What does art imitate, and how? Specifically, what does poetry imitate, and how?

Of course, I have some possible answers to the tentative question I have asked, but first I must make a petty distinction between verse that is metered and verse we call "free." In the case of metered poems, we might say that meter imitates our heartbeat—indeed, by extension, the heartbeat of the mother in the perfect world of the amniotic fluids—and at the same time "imitates" in some sense the mathematical ideal, which becomes also the musical ideal, of interval.

But I want to make the question harder by concentrating our investigation on so-called "free verse." Frost, as everyone knows, said that writing free verse is like playing tennis without a net. My friendly tongue-in-cheek variation of this has always been that writing free verse is really like playing jai alai without a net. Free verse can differ so much and so significantly from rhymed and metered verse that the difference may become one of kind rather than of degree.

What does form imitate, and how?

Let me say more about so-called "free verse." No verse is "free," said Eliot, for the man who would do a good job. And we know that expectations established by patterns of rhyme and rhythm—that is, meter—are powerful advantages. In verse which has no regular rhyme and rhythm, there must be other "formal" concerns.

We can name some possibilities: the phrase, the line, diction and syntax, the image, metaphor, the stanza, etc. But these are aspects, after all, of all poetry—"free" or not. In discussing such matters, it is a question of emphasis and frequency. In free verse, pattern and repetition are surprises, and continuing variation is the norm. The formal ideal is something called "organic form," and the presupposition in calling such form "organic" is that it grows naturally, as does a living organism. Form follows function. Form is never more than an extension of content, etc.

But that sort of talk pales in the face of examples. For we all know that singular line division is not sufficient to engage us for very long, nor is peculiar imagery, quirky diction or seemingly unique metaphor-making. And we all know of many poems written to no discernible pattern which seem to us engaging, convincing, consequential and inexhaustible. Often, these poems are written so simply, so straight-forwardly, if you will, so—modestly—that they put into proper perspective our technical obsessions by nothing more complicated than their sheer, sometimes overwhelming, humanity.

Now I admit to a tendency to wince when the talk turns to the "humanity" of poets, and I want to draw a thick line right away between my notion of humanity and the fraudulent critical notion of sincerity which has turned the minds of many reviewers and writers to mush.

The critical notion of sincerity surfaces every few years, and has more than one meaning for those who employ it. Sometimes, it means writing without ornamentation. Sometimes, it means writing colloquially. Sometimes, it means writing in the first person. Sometimes, it means writing only about what the author has physically experienced in his or her space- and time-bounded life. And there are always false gurus around to tell us that we can only have meaningful lives if we take this or that job, enlist in or avoid this or that school. More than one poet blinded by intensity has said that he or she didn't care for poems in which the poet's entire life had not been brought to bear on the writing of the poem. Surely, that is self-delusion at best and dangerous advice at worst. It is based on the false notion that art replaces and becomes life. It invites, and attempts to justify, the causing of pain to others and, ultimately, suicide. (For contrast, I would mention Denise Levertov's fine essay about Anne Sexton's death and the artist in society in the December–January, 1975 issue of *Ramparts*.)

What's more, few of us will live lives of extreme danger or unusual consequence, in the general view of many others. Few of us will live the life of a Nadezhda Mandelstam. Indeed, like the Chinese poet who foresaw the dilemma in describing what he hoped for his granddaughter, we should probably not wish to live in what will later be known as an "interesting" time.

In any event, I would like to deflate the language with which we speak of our poems. I would like to think of poems we might read together as poems not of urgency but of immediacy. I would like us to think of them as poems not of vision but merely of intelligence. Of course, I don't mean "merely." I confess I no longer know what the word "vision," applied to poets, means, if ever I did. I think I understand what a personal mythology is, and what imagination is, and what lucky prophecy is. The word "vision," however, seems to have become for many poets a self-congratulatory term meant to help us pretend that we are more unequal than we really are. One dictionary definition of "vision" is "the work of the imagination." In that case, vision is something we all have, or none of us have, and in either case it is not a useful term. I would prefer, also, not to use the word "inspired" in speaking about poems.

I have always believed, as I have said, that the critical notion of "sincerity" is, in any of its recurrent forms, invalid and beside the point. I would prefer to speak of the "modesty" of poems. The poems which survive for me are essentially modest . . . in attitude. They may not be modest, may even be outrageous, in diction, in syntax, in range or subject matter, in ability and willingness to teach, or in other ways, but they are modest with regard to: (1) the necessity for evidence; (2) the necessity for form.

The first necessity means that content must be based in reality—probable, possible or actual—no matter how made up the meta-phorical landscape. Coleridge's distinction between the "fancy," which is essentially frivolous because merely associational, and the "imagination," is relevant again here. The second necessity means that works of art do not exist except as *art* first, no matter how far into "life" they may take us.

It occurs to me that the notions of "sincerity" and "modesty" in poems are too close not to be related. I insist, however, on their difference. Sincerity may be present without modesty, but modesty may never be present without sincerity. Sincerity may derive from passion, whereas modesty always derives from wisdom.

Going perhaps uncomfortably further, it is modesty which allows a writer to hold in mind opposites, apparent contradictions, at the same time, and to resolve them within a poem.

Such poems—poems of wise humility, if you will—often make uncommon good sense by paying attention to the ordinary. When they do, they seem uncommonly genuine expressions. They are in special touch with life and accept it. They are not self-con-gratulatory, they are clever at times but not self-consciously or pridefully so, and they do not distort reality for the sake of the poem—either by investing it with a drama it does not contain, or by pretending it is "cooler" than it really is: they do not pretend that the amount and kind of life portrayed in the poem means either everything or nothing.

At this point, I would like to point to a poem by William Stafford—not one that's likely to be anthologized often. It appears in the collection *Allegiances,* available from Harper and Row.

With Kit, Age 7, at the Beach

We would climb the highest dune,
from there to gaze and come down:
the ocean was performing;
we contributed our climb.

Waves leapfrogged and came
straight out of the storm.
What should our gaze mean?
Kit waited for me to decide.

Standing on such a hill,
what would you tell your child?
That was an absolute vista.
Those waves raced far, and cold.

"How far could you swim, Daddy,
in such a storm?"
"As far as was needed," I said,
and as I talked, I swam.

Writing about another of his poems ("The Farm on the Great Plains") for a 1962 anthology, *Poet's Choice,* Stafford said that he could "confront and accept something of my portion in writing: an appearance of moral commitment mixed with a deliberate—even a flaunted—nonsophistication; an organized form cavalierly treated; a trace of narrative for company amid too many feelings. There are emergences of consciousness in the poem, and some outlandish lunges for communication; but I can stand quite a bit of this sort of thing if a total poem gives evidence of locating itself."

Here is a small clue to what art imitates: "an appearance of moral commitment." We mustn't leave out the word "appearance." Does it mean that it just seems that way? Or does it mean that the moral commitment appears, shows up, makes itself known? Might I hazard that the choice was cagey, perhaps honestly modest, but that it means the latter—that moral commitment makes itself known in the poem.

But Baptist preachers aren't often poets. When I say "moral," I mean "of, relating to, or acting on the mind, character, or will." Do you like that definition? It's the most tentative one I could find— the last offered, in my Webster's Seventh. You see, I didn't want to go to any heavier dictionary for this discussion of the uncommonly ordinary. By "moral commitment," I *don't* mean didacticism. Consciousness and a sense that there can be right and wrong in human behavior will do it. Indeed, a true-seeming view of human nature seems to me sufficient evidence with which to impeach the poet on the grounds of uncommon virtue.

Stafford makes other gestures in this poem which keep us on the ground and at ease. Lines one and two of stanza three are, I feel, disarmingly straightforward. And they put us on the spot, which is what morality always does. Now it is true that these lines are each trimeter lines with reversed first feet and that the poem as a whole is mostly trimeter—sprung trimeter. It is likewise true that the language is casual, off-handed, colloquial; and not caught up in complaint or congratulation.

Certainly, it's a minor accomplishment just to be able to get into a poem such an apparently "unpoetic" line as, "How far could you swim, Daddy, / in such a storm?" Of course, the history of poetry is to a large extent the history of the accommodation of manner and substance hitherto thought to be unpoetic or even antipoetic. Wordsworth's language, after all, was thought to be too "common" in its time; and it wasn't long ago that Whitman's was thought vulgar. The vulgar and the controversial are large parts of poetry— the writing of which, in its insistence on clarity and individual perceptions and, ultimately, individual decisions, is always a subversive activity. Even Miss Dickinson was probably wisely advised not to print many of her poems during her lifetime because of what could be anticipated: an angry reaction to her seeming informality. (The lunge for prose-poetry in America at this moment seems to be a desperate attempt to incorporate the seemingly unpoetic, but it has so far taken the form mostly of clutter and comedy.)

Apart, however, from the petty thrill I get at just seeing in a poem such a common question, commonly phrased, it's that last stanza which makes this poem one of uncommonly good sense for me. "How far could you swim, Daddy, / in such a storm?" asks the daughter. And the speaker's answer is both cagey and seemingly straightforward. Surely, it is the sort of reassuring answer the speaker in this poem senses the situation demands. Yet it pretends nothing. "As far as was needed, I said, / and as I talked, I swam." How far is "needed"? The implication of this poem is that nature will decide what is needed. In the realm of *human* nature, *we* can decide what is to be *said*. There is a great deal of difference, and the poem refuses to blur the difference.

What does art imitate, and how? An appearance of moral commitment? The distance between speech and action, between nature and thought? What our gaze should mean? Standing on such a hill, what would you tell your child?

Good poems refuse to blur essential differences, even as they seek what is common in the seemingly disparate. A general impression of "sincerity" or passion is a poor substitute for this ability. It is just such a defiance born of intelligence which reveals what we might call "authentic" character. Authenticity goes far beyond an appearance of sincerity.

Given unlimited space, I would reproduce a variety of poems to illustrate further. One would surely be John Ashbery's brilliant poem, "Illustration," which appeared in his first book, *Some Trees* (Yale, reissued by Corinth). Indeed, Stafford and Ashbery seem to me two poets who consistently risk uncommon mental gestures in poems. In the work of both, what was formerly thought unpoetic or antipoetic is absorbed into poetry time and again. Next to their best poems, the flash of neo-surrealism is little more than poetic vaudeville: clams playing accordions, etc.

"Illustration" is about a suicide, but it is neither an expression or hysteria nor an attempt at total (and false) identification with the tragic heroine. Rather, the poem is about one's distance from the event. We might, says the speaker (after a girl has jumped to her death from a tall building), have felt and acted differently. We might have cared more. But she was only an "effigy of indifference." Solely of *our* indifference? It would be easy to say so. But no. The indifference which the poem speaks of is the indifference in nature. The final illustration in the poem is of a tree losing its leaves at the approach of winter.

> But she, of course, was only an effigy
> Of indifference, a miracle
>
> Not meant for us, as the leaves are not
> Winter's because it is the end.

The young girl who plunged to her death, that is, is no more ours than are the leaves which fall to winter the property of winter. To believe otherwise would be to deceive ourselves quite as much as those well-intentioned bystanders who thought they knew what she wanted, offered it to her, and in so doing became merely part of the ceremony she desired. "I want to move figuratively," she had said, "as waves caress the thoughtless shore." But it is not the thoughtlessness of human nature which those lines speak of anymore than winter is a blunder of physical nature.

What does art imitate, and how? "Illustration" imitates, in its diction and syntax, in its plot, in its weaving philosophic discourse, in the necessity it finds for illustrations, the distance from that event to the mind which survives it, and the process by which apprehension of the physical becomes the mental.

Here are some other examples of poems of ease, attentiveness, and unusual awareness and "modesty." One is "¿*Habla Usted Español?*," from James Reiss's book, *The Breathers* (Ecco), which spots the distance between the language of a child's reassuring imagination and the more practical and allegedly "useful" definitions which accompany the child's loss of innocence and security. Another is "Willy Lyons," by James Wright, available in his *Collected Poems* (Wesleyan), because the poem makes a crucial distinction between the speaker and the lives and arts of his uncles (now dead), and between himself and his weeping mother. Although by resorting to mythology the speaker allows for the possibility of "the other world," he recognizes also that, if the other world is unknown to the grieving mother, it is equally unknown to him. A lesser poet would have claimed to know.

Wright's powerful poem, "To the Muse," is another example. In this poem, the speaker brings back to life a childhood friend who drowned. But he does not allow her to go on living in the poem, as many poets would have. Rather, he pulls back. He is not, he realizes, the agent of creation. He is more like the frightened garter snake that he and the drowned girl caught long ago—writing his poems and listening, just as the snake moved its tongue in and out. He can be the agent only of his own death. That is why he says, at the end of the poem, "Come up to me, love, / Out of the river, or I will / Come down to you." As he wouldn't, he has said at the outset, lie about the pain he would cause the dead girl in bringing her back to life, so he does not lie finally about his own powers.

To recognize one's limits in this regard may be an important basis for moral commitment. What does art imitate? Neither the agency of life, nor the agency of death, but the coming into consciousness of the presence of the moral agency.

(At this point, I simply want to note, for anyone who might be interested, that at another time and in another place I used the following poems to further illustrate that level of poetic awareness which manifests itself in a refusal to compromise essential differences or the human condition, a willingness to apprehend one's judgments and reconsider, and a refusal to take credit or to freely condemn others: Randall Jarrell's "Washing," "Next Day," and "The Truth," Alan Dugan's "Elegy" ("I know but will not tell . . . "), "Portrait from the Infantry," and "To a Red-Headed Do-Good Waitress," and Gary Snyder's "Hay for the Horses." Other poems by these poets could have been used, of course, or poems by many other poets. A look at these, however, will not misdirect the attention of anyone who wishes to continue the analysis, or the praise.)

Of course, I have been trying to do two things at once in this essay. First, I have been asking, What does art imitate, and how?—the implication being that the usual answer, that art imitates life, is insufficient and misleading because it is not life in its physical immediacy that art imitates, and because art is itself a part of life. Does life imitate art sometimes? Is the difference between art and life that you can't do anything about life?

"How" art does whatever it does we can answer. Every poem is another answer. But it is more difficult to say just "what" art imitates. Art, like life, needs no purpose to come into being. Its destiny, like man's, is its character. And it is a part of life we can have nowhere else in life. The title of a new book I saw advertised notwithstanding, life is not the ultimate poem any more than a poem replaces life. The green of a pine is all we will know of green. All we will know of the dark is sleep's forgetfulness. Time is all we will know of the end of time.

Second, I have tried to draw a thick line between fashionable notions of sincerity and that authenticity of speech and writing which derives from attention, wisdom and conscience.

In asking what art imitates and at the same time discussing the sensible and the genuine, I have tried to merge two long-opposed doctrines.

Aristotelian notions of imitation are part of classical poetics. Plato had condemned art because, in its imitation of characters, it gave the young themselves the opportunity to imitate the low and the base. But Aristotle defended poetry against Platonic condemnation by saying that poetic imitation is of plot, rather than of characters; that it is a valid representation of the actions of men according to the laws of probability and necessity. By plot, Aristotle meant not a sequence but a structure of events, firmly welded to form an organic whole.

Whereas the notion of imitation is central to classical poetics, it was of little interest to the Romantics, for whom imitation was felt to be out of keeping with the new spirit of spontaneity and self-expression. For them, sincerity was a genuine correspondence with, or expression of, the poet's state of mind and feelings, from which the poem derived its vitality. The Victorians, however, gave sincerity a moral twist. To Matthew Arnold, the touchstone of great poetry was "the high seriousness which comes from absolute sincerity."

So what does art imitate? Specifically, what does poetry imitate? One tentative, general answer is that it imitates a quality of authenticity of thought and perception; that is, sincerity. Put another way, sincerity might be thought of as—to use Stafford's phrase—"an appearance of moral commitment."

The poetic notions of imitation and sincerity cross where we recognize the distance between physical reality and mentality or speech. To pretend that that distance does not exist is to be a vagabond among poets. You can cross the country, but you won't get anywhere. Nor will fancy, the ability to associate, travel that distance. Only the imagination can get from one to the other, and about that our knowledge is limited to examples.

The line is that, in a poem, anything is believable. But that is not true. In a poem, anything is *provable*. There is a difference.

Finally, here are three Yiddish proverbs which bear on the questions of truth, reality and sincerity: (1) Dumplings in a dream are not dumplings, but a dream; (2) For example is no proof; and (3) If a horse had anything to say, he would speak up.

1975

DAVID LEHMAN

Notes on Poetic Form

I.

A distrust of received forms seems endemic to American poets. It is predicated on the conviction that depth or complexity of vision, force of passion, profundity of insight, or whatever it is that distinguishes art from mere craft will invariably precede rather than follow from a formal maneuver. This view found its first great exemplar in Whitman's "Song of Myself"—and its first great sponsor in Emerson:

> For it is not metres, but a metre-making argument, that makes a poem,—a thought so passionate and alive, that, like the spirit of a plant or an animal, it has an architecture of its own, and adorns nature with a new thing. The thought and the form are equal in the order of time, but in the order of genesis the thought is prior to the form.

That Emerson's edict continues to have its adherents is clear. Alice Fulton has restated the case: "During the act of writing, technique and meaning are inextricably linked, and it is only for the convenience of critical discussion that one could wish to separate them. The realization that craft depends on content leads to the concept of organic form and the idea that whatever elements help us experience a poem as a whole can be called its form."

Perhaps it betokens the rise of a new formalism that a rival notion—that "in the order of genesis" form may precede thought—seems on the ascendant. (By "a new formalism" I mean to designate the tendency as such rather than the specific group or movement of poets who have banded together under one or another label, issuing proclamations.) Certainly there has been a resurgence of interest in forms traditional or exotic—forms that can themselves create the occasion for poetry. Some regard this development as yet another manifestation of the back-to-basics spirit evident in other areas of cultural activity. Or is it that the emerging generation of poets is acting in filial rebellion against predecessors who valued nothing so much as what Whitman called the "barbaric yawp"? In any event, it is possible that the preoccupation with poetic form is precisely what distinguishes this generation from the last. A number of celebrated younger poets are clothing their poems in the traditional raiments of rhyme and meter. Others have embraced a principle of poetic form that follows from two key premises: that imaginative freedom can flourish amid self-imposed restrictions and that originality starts from a mastery of tradition, not an ignorance thereof. There are also those who remain solidly committed to free verse—they might write prose poems, but never a villanelle (never one that rhymes anyway)—but who are nevertheless engaged to the point of obsession with the form and appearance and design of their work. In this category one thinks of Jorie Graham, whose meanings are inextricable from the effects she obtains through her experimentation with form: for example, her substitution of blanks for words in several poems, or her unusual lining and punctuation—she may end a poem in the middle of a sentence with a dash instead of a period. These are formal choices, as crucial to the outcome in Graham's case as another poet's decision to write a double sestina using the same end-words that Swinburne used in *his* double sestina a hundred years ago.

II.

Subscribing to the traditional paradox that liberty most flourishes when most held in check, John Ashbery offers a shrewdly pragmatic explanation for his interest in the exotic pantoum. "I was attracted to the form," he writes, "because of its stricture, even greater than in other hobbling forms such as the sestina or canzone. These restraints seem to have a paradoxically liberating effect, for me at least." Ashbery concludes with sly deadpan: "The form has the additional advantage of providing you with twice as much poem for your effort, since every line has to be repeated twice."

To an important extent, such formal scheming casts the poet in the guise of problem-solver. In the course of working out the puzzle he has set for himself, a poem will get written—not as an afterthought, but as an inevitable by-product of the process. By this logic, the tougher the formal problem, the better—the more likely it is to act as a sort of broker between language, chance, and the poet's instincts. "And this may indeed be one way that 'form' helps the poet," Anthony Hecht observes. "So preoccupied is he bound to be with the fulfillment of technical requirements that in the beginning of his poem he cannot look very far ahead, and even a short glance forward will show him that he must improvise, reconsider and alter what had first seemed to him his intended direction, if he is to accommodate the demands of his form." This is desirable, notes Hecht, if the aim is—as Robert Frost said it was—an outcome that is both "unforeseen" and "predestined."

No doubt it's the prevalence of this aim that accounts for the sestina's unprecedented popularity among modern poets. The votaries in the sestina chapel may begin with Sir Philip Sidney ("Ye Goatherd Gods"), but there then follows a gap of three centuries before the procession is renewed by Rossetti and Pound, Auden and Elizabeth Bishop, and innumerable poets since. Allowing for maximum maneuverability within a tightly controlled space, the sestina has a special attraction for the poet in search of a formal device with which to scan his unconscious. Writing a sestina, Ashbery once remarked, is like riding downhill on a bicycle while the pedals push your feet. The analogy makes the whole procedure sound exhilarating, risky, and somewhat foolhardy, making it irresistible. Paradoxically, the very ubiquity of the sestina—it's a favorite in creative writing workshops—has recently begun to argue against it. The logic is Yogi Berra's: "Nobody eats at that restaurant anymore—it's too crowded."

III.

The question of measure and meter has been undergoing reexamination of late—inevitably, as poets discuss and dispute their ideas about form. Brad Leithauser, in a controversial essay entitled "Metrical Literacy," has argued that "poetry is a craft which, like carpentry, requires a long apprenticeship merely to assimilate its tools" and that meter is a true and perhaps indispensable implement in the trade. "Metrical illiteracy is, for the poet, functional illiteracy," Leithauser concludes. Nor is he alone in taking arms against plain speech: more than one poet has noted, with pleasure or alarm, that their contemporaries have brought back meter as a vital concern. The debate on the question is far from being one- or even two-sided. Douglas Crase, for example, doesn't place any the less value on finding a true measure even if he is little concerned with anapests and dactyls. What Crase wants is a meter suitable to an American vernacular and an American reality. He proposes "the 'civil meter' of American English, the meter we hear in the propositions offered by businessmen, politicians, engineers, and all our other real or alleged professionals. If you write in this civil meter, it's true you have to give up the Newtonian certainties of the iamb. But you gain a stronger metaphor for conviction by deploying the recognizable, if variable patterns of the language of American power."

Perhaps it would help to clarify the question of prosody, without simplifying it too much, if we rephrased it as an issue involving the desired amount of resistance that the poet wishes his medium to exert. Let two English poets argue the question for us. Here is Craig Raine defending his preference for unrhymed couplets in his book *A Martian Sends a Postcard Home:* "Technique is something you learn in order to reach a point where you're writing what you want with the minimum of interference. The unrhymed couplet interested me as something in which I could write fluently. Any verse, however, with a fair amount of freedom in it is actually much harder to write than strict verse." By contrast, Geoffrey Hill endorses "the proposal that form is not only a technical containment but is possibly also an emotional and ethical containment. In the act of refining technique one is not only refining emotion, one is also constantly defining and redefining one's ethical and moral sensibility." What Hill wants is more resistance, not less; he distrusts the very fluency that Raine prizes, and opts for a "harder" severity than "freedom" allows for. Hill endorses C. H. Sisson's remark: "There is in Hill a touch of the fastidiousness of Crashaw, which is that of a mind in search of artifices to protect itself against its own passions." Form as artifice or form as the path of least resistance, a maze or a straight line, a way of reining in the imagination or a method for letting it roam free, a container or a ceaseless stream: the permutations are endless.

JANE MILLER

Sea Level

Sun and rain—the words in English are strong and feel as if they belong coupled. The moon somehow is not far away, in sound, in power, in connotation. One thinks of Hardy in English, or of Lorca in Spanish. A friend was telling me the other day the story of Daedalus, and of the many tasks he was asked to accomplish in the service of King Minos. I especially liked the tale of the King's daughter who went to Daedalus to have him help her track the man she had fallen for on first sight, a man intended to serve as a slave to her father and be sent into a maze so he wouldn't escape. She is given a simple golden thread for her lover to take with him, that he might find his way out—that single thread by which we are all tethered to earth. Some of us feel we are tethered to earth by words. Each day here I feel that I am pulled down from the mountain, Tourrette to Vence, through Cagnes-sur-Mer to Nice, until finally I see the great calm waters of the Mediterranean.

They're azure, and gold where the sun plays on the small crests. It isn't difficult to find the words for the sun on the sea, for the light on the waves, for the gold on the water. But it is another thing to have them serve as a thread from poet to populace. It has always been standard to give them a tune and to repeat it if need be. Free verse has made the tune more subtle, burying the tune, contorting it, repeating rhetorical devices and syntax rather than relying on the marching count of feet. For those who continue to use or who have reverted to the use of traditional measure, or who occasionally use it, the power of poetry must appear to have a lot to do with sound. Those who write free verse still handle a lot of sounds, though they aren't so busy weighing them on scales with their arms outstretched. But are the words we have chosen really expressive, these words that sound so good, or sound pretty good, or have, anyway, a mesmerizing whisper because of an arrangement of vowels and consonants?

The drive from Tourrette-sur-Loup, a fortified city, into Vence is down a fine road of views that runs no more than four miles. Along it lies the perfume museum (Le Château Notre Dame des Fleurs) and testing boutique (Château des Aromes), and there you can see what became of the early mimosas last year, and the lavender and violets and roses that followed, and the carnations and jasmine and geraniums. If you head west you'll run into the Fragonard factory on the way to Grasse, the center of the perfume world. The buses en route south to Nice are full of women with terrific French haircuts, bouffant, assymetrical, and they smell for all the world as if they are wearing fruit, and the rose scents are the worst because they can't be reproduced. But there are less sweet scents and on the right person there is a gentle lilt of the first almond blossoms in February and that's fine. And who knows, someone might think it's possible to become the right person simply by choosing the right scent.

The flower industry pervades the Côte d'Azur, but in the mountain towns, where the flowers grow, there is their raw, wild beauty before they are gathered in spring and then sold. They are watched over as delicately and obsessively as the French care for their wines. (Although wine production is more central to the Spanish economy, the French are still fussier with the vines.) The lavender and violet festival in Tourrette is a rare rehearsal of the hoopla that will follow later in advertising. This will invade the culture at subliminal and corporeal levels, for there is a universe of pictures and poses and fast cars and models that goes with the territory. The more well-known manufacturers use blow-up glossies of exotic pubescent women, with scarves and sashes around their hips, and then cover the pineapple plants or palm leaves in the background with their logos: *Opium* (Yves St. Laurent); *Eau Savage* (Christian Dior); *Charlie* (Revlon); *Joy* (Jean Patou); *Fidji* (Guy Larouche); *Arpège* (Lanvin)—names we recognize that turn us on to a hyped world of pseudo-pleasure.

The glee of the children in the parade of flowers starts it. One year I saw the parade in the rain, and the smear of purple, violet, magenta, prussian, and lavender blossoms has soaked that end of the color spectrum into me forever. One can only imagine the serious chemical business of combining and defining and inventing and reconstituting the mixtures after they have been boiled. The process has fascinated me for years and is easily culled from the *Michelin Red Guide*—the process of *enfleurage*. First the essence is extracted from the flowers and plants by the process of distillation.

This is done with water vapors, or by vacuum to get to the more rarified core. The essences become soft; they're steeped in fluid to separate them into their constituent elements. In dissolution, they completely break down and disperse. Then the scent is literally pressed out, or "expressed." But like anything else, the making of a truly fine scent, like the making of a fine day, is magical.

For a poet, the mistakes that are made in processing can be fascinating and often produce a perfect and fleeting moment for the senses and state of being, like perfume. Many of the samples in the museum, *Our Lady of Flowers* (one wonders what she wore), are ruinous, and smell as if safflower oil, gone bad, has been cut with banana left in the sun. The more subtle chemical exchanges produce whimsical and sugary effects, but the winners to my taste are the honeylike ambers that smell like, well, one flower that doesn't really have a scent, the tulip—a white one in a sunny room, and near it is an open sack of berries, and someone comes in who has just bathed with a bar of olive soap, and her cousin is whistling on the porch.

By the time it sifts down into additives for products that are a "melange vif de sauge des Alpes, d'essence de sarriette, d'essence de pins et menthe sauvage"—a lively blend of sage from the Alps, essence of pine, savory, and raw mint—the thing stinks, it's too much, and it ends as scent for toilet paper.

I don't have many books of poetry with me, but I have been thinking about language, about the essence and power of language, and it is not so different from learning about perfumes, or about wine, where in essence one is dealing with rain and sun. It hasn't rained here for four months (now it has, for five straight nights), but this year's wine crop has been in since October. Not so with the flowers. The same fields of violet and lavender hilariously overrun in 1981 today are meager bursts of color in otherwise quiet soil that the residents say ought to have bloomed simply from overnight dew.

Lavender generally sticks out in a straight cropped look like teenage hair combed up with mousse. Most mousses are artificially scented, and the chemical derivatives are nearly always "burned." They smell as though electricity has gone through the flavor, or as if there's been a thunderstorm from inside the head, followed by a dry wind.

A poet catches the bus down from the flower-growing mountains through the subtle lowlands of vineyards to the sea. It takes most of a morning to get started because the sun rises late in February. The dew is thick in the morning in the mountains, it's cold and it's been too dangerous to leave *le bomb*—the gas heater—on all night, so the stone house is freezing. But even with the heater on, the place is like a tomb. The bus takes forever stopping at every last fortified town that now sells herbs and seeds and soaps, the latter perfumed with extracts. At high noon the bus plows through Nice and dusts the local air of the wide Promenade des Anglais. The grandstands are still set up from *Le Carnaval*. They face the facades of the 1940s and 1950s hotels, Le Casino Ruhl of the Meridien Hotel, a square-jawed building, and further west, Le Negresco, with its pink breastlike dome. The adornment of pink and white balustrades and capped roofs of the buildings flashback to a more leisurely time, if one happened to have been rich. Now they house retirees. The old port in the old part of town is rich in turquoises and oranges and reds; the Italian and Greek influences mock the fey pinks and flesh tones of the main drag.

Further along lies St. Jean Cap Ferrat, where the old money and the new rich have estates and the Arabs paint the fences and water the fruit trees. The notorious French hegemony is like a rot and stench in the soil, so the culture thrives but not without tremendous abuse to outsiders. It feels somewhat like the old South, but without the Faulknerian inbreeding and bent communion. Around the peninsula lies a pedestrian path no more at any time than thirty yards from the sea, but between it and the sea are honeycombed white stones and spectacular rock-sponge outcroppings. Every now and then you can see where the wealthy have cut a pool into the rocky hill above. Hydraulic lifts bandy them from the house to the pool so, without much of a trek, they can go for a swim in the sunshine. "Swim" and "sunshine"—already we are a far cry from rain and sun. Imagine "a dip to catch some rays" and you have a range of action and power.

The walk around the peninsula takes hours, especially if you keep doubling back or if you lie down on a rare flat rock. I have a friend who is working on a project of "safe space" sculptures, whimsical and colorful but sturdy open spaces that house people and fresh air and feel "safe," that is, protected and encouraging. In the maquettes they are made of twig and tubing and telephone wire and pipe cleaners and feathers, they're maybe five inches high, but they stand for— because she doesn't have the funds to "create" them—monumental pieces. It's impossible not to think of the shore ring as a safe space, open to pedestrians and monitored by the open sky and the fact that you can see for miles as it gently curves. It is easy to get from the stone path to the rough outcroppings by simply leaving it and acting like a goat. Sydney Hamburger—we have joked about her French name too, in Berlitz phonetics, "Sydnay Hamberjhay"—says her sculpture is meant to be rough and undefined and to set general parameters only; one can be in and out of a safe space easily, and hardly know it. The whole metaphoric quality appeals to me. The naming of things in Sydney's case is significant because she was adopted as a child and is struggling to find her birth parents. Given a particular number from the adoption agency, she has been able to trace, not her parents, but the name they originally gave her. She thought about taking it as her new name but "it" didn't resonate in her. She is Sydney Hamburger, spritely with its gender confusion. My calling this sea walk a safe space doesn't necessarily mean nothing dangerous can happen, but that it would be a danger of my own making, whose meaning I am open to apprehend on personal, metaphoric, and universal levels.

We all have oracles that we go to for definition. The Temple of Fortuna, mother of all the gods, takes up the entire area now occupied by Palestrina in Italy. We trust its dark strata and antechambers. It is another matter to ask to trust oneself. That one listen to oneself is perhaps adulthood, completely giving over to intuition. There has crept into the process of making these feelings known in words a certain healthy doubt. As if the feelings for things and the words for things have grown distant. And to make them touch again unfortunately has the air of being a presumptuous and an immodest act. In America you can sense a poet by the modesty he or she feels. Words, it is often said, are merely passing through the vessel of the poet. Of course, there are many others who feel no such thing, who feel completely in control. Both are false and represent posturing.

We fill something completely and then leave it in much the same way Picasso was given the Château d'Antibes to work in for five months, July to November of 1946, and then in gratitude gave the city the work he fabricated there. The place is now a museum of two dozen paintings, nearly eighty pieces of ceramics, forty-four drawings, thirty-two lithographs, eleven oils on paper, two sculptures, and five tapestries. The numbers hardly tell the story. But the names of the pieces begin to: *Dish of Grapes, Guitar and Two Apples on a Plate* (1946); *Basket, Three Sea Urchins and Lamp* (October 19, 1946); *Three Lemons, Dish of Grapes and Bottle* (October 15, 1946); *Three Fish, Moray Eel and Green Lime* (September 28, 1946); *Owl and Three Sea Urchins* (November 6, 1946). He seems to have been happy there, working quickly and apparently effortlessly; at any rate the work that came out, in the ceramic plates with spunky fauns' faces and smiling sea creatures, in vases of women's torsos and in the large paintings that are homages to living, bathing, planting, there is this, the happiness of the artist. For it can be said of an artist that he or she has chosen to be attentive, and this may be what happiness is.

At the simplest level of function, the poet imagines. Yet these images in a very real sense have always existed. Of what use is description, of what use is it to name what already exists? Words have connotative value that is fulfilled by a poet, like a wind-god, unseen and serendipitous, who reveals by transfusion, transmission, transformation. Though it may indeed be the very same sun and moon, the very same rain across them, these are touched and gilded by passion, by compassion, and, ultimately, by comprehension.

For many decades the attention in American poetry has been on the verb—the drama, the motility of the verb has been difficult to equal in power. Meanwhile the nouns we use have fallen into disrepair. One thinks of the abuse *stone* and *blackness* and *time* have taken over the last two decades; though their appeal is universal, they are only useful if they reassert themselves from the depths of a writer. Naturally a noun doesn't stand alone. But for an instant to take it out of context with a golden thread, and pull it into isolated view: a noun may have power because we associate it with a story, a myth, but we remember only the word and not the thing it represented. In this case we have forgotten that a word is an embodiment of something rather than a symbol for it. Sometimes a noun has power because it is seized quickly before any adjudication—how about the word *morning*? Here the noun is personal and apprehendable before it is synthetic. Somewhere in between, shy of someone else's mythology yet hinting of new intentions, lies a noun to serve as a building block for a vital poem, like an old engine block oiled. And it is not like having a pet, unless the pet is big enough to eat you.

Monumental sculpture—from "miniature" monuments like Rodin's *Burghers of Calais* to David Smith's ironworks to Christo's wrapping of a bridge or a coastline in polyurethane—has the appeal of the noun: it is expansive and expressive and solid, square, present with a high center of gravity; it isn't going anywhere easily. The verb, by contrast, is light, flexible, capricious, with a low center of gravity. Its soul is therefore erotic, erogenous. But the noun has a soul too, and its soul is intellectual and symbological. It's clear that I believe parts of speech can be associated with zones in us, and nouns must retain the vitality of blood being pumped to the head. Most of what happens to us as writers happens through the body—we experience feelings because we feel experience (a useful tautology, I hope)—and then a third thing, the power of the subterranean world below the self impinges on the words we need to work. We cue in to the life of words themselves, their independent authority meets our reckless hold. If I say I had a dream last night about a robin's egg, the word "egg" has its connotations about birth, beginnings, protection, resiliency, delicacy, terror, separation. Then there is its visual representation, the blue shell, the sky, world, sea reflections. And then the social and spiritual overlay—blue as in sad, blue as in boy, blue as in transparent. It happens that this particular blue color shows up in a lot of the second and third rate pottery on display in Vallauris, where Picasso went to work after discovering Madame Ramie there. She and her husband owned a ceramic studio, and she made virtuoso hand-painted plates and bowls. Nobody there now seems to have the knack. The ceramic paints look milky and sickly and the pots are cumbersome and clumsy, merely decorative. As sculpture they are dead weight. Three-dimensional objects ought to aspire to airiness in space, since interest in an object lies in how it enters into association with its opposite. At the outdoor sculpture garden of the Maeght Foundation, in St. Paul de Vence, huge animated pieces by Miró and the anguish of the slender Giacomettis are planted near a pool Braque tiled in fish and a Calder red and yellow mobile. Out of the mouths of fountains by Miró spouts an endless talk of water. The whole outdoors is lively like cubism, disorienting, multi-faced, unexpected, a surrealism.

> Surrealism touched me, I think, from this side. A protest of our slavery that, rather than become a lament as it had until now, juxtaposes exaltation and the imagination in order to propose intellectual solutions in accord with eternal human desires. Here was something not in disharmony with the white open shirts the more bold of us had begun to wear in those years.

Greek poet Odysseus Elytis goes on to say that landscape "is not simply the sum of some trees and mountains, but a complex signifier, an ethical power mobilized by the human mind." Nouns have this great capacity for inclusion; suddenly we find something or are somewhere unexpected. A problem with contemporary writers drawn to surrealism is that the oneiric can become merely dreamy, fuzzy. Yet a real surrealistic image, or supra-realistic one, doesn't represent something larger than life but that life itself is large. One enters surrealism at the hub of experience, as if entering an ancient tomb at Tarquinia and finding the walls painted with swimmers and flying fish, and a flautist in sandals and tunic playing a double pipe. There in the dampness underground, someone's inventiveness called forth to assuage the dead. These messages are available to the poet who travels underground and who raises the objects to sea level and beyond. A process of distillation that requires refinement, experience—in the sense of experimentation—trust, and a return to the deep watery antechamber of the human psyche to fire up the relics of language, which all along have been preceded by instinctual activities, sweating, breathing, eating, killing, sharing, distilling.

According to a papyrus dating from 2000 B.C., Egyptians were the first perfumers, taking the scent of myrrh, cinnamon, galbanum, and other spices down to their essences. The myrrh and frankincense came stolen from Arabia. The earliest perfume was Kiphi (*kap* in Old Egyptian, meaning incense or perfume), found in the tomb of Tutankhamen. Plutarch named thirteen ingredients that make it up: honey, wine, cyprus, grapes, myrrh, genista, sesel, stoenanthe, safran, patience, juniper berry, cardamom, and sweet calamus. For centuries the Arabs supplied the world with jasmine and rose too, and taught the Greeks the process of distillation. A Greek, Dr. Aricemma, perfected the method of extracting volatile oils from flowers by means of a still and was the first to make rose water. Musk was used as a fixing agent, and with the widespread practice of Buddhism, incense hung in the air. In the fourteenth century, perfume was made from a paste of sweet-smelling substances and combustibles carved into the shape of small birds. Finally, the discovery of alcohol by the Spanish Moor Rhases offered the newest method of going after the essence of beauty.

There is no end to an audience's need to have a name for the mysteries and correspondences evoked by sensory impressions and objects, no end of this "clay," the noun. Like freedom to a poet, the noun offers gravity and elasticity. One may recognize some of the names of perfumes that have come to embody the needs of a culture as determined by the commercialism of the word, advertising *Timeless* (Avon, 1974); *Explosive* (Aigner, 1986); *White Shoulders* (Evyan, 1945); *Intimate* (Revlon, 1955); *Shalimar* (Guerlain, 1925); these are variously described—how suggestive and vague the adjectives in a world of scents and essences!—as green, fruity, fresh, floral, oriental, sweet, and spicy. The names of the scents for men are equally dreamy, as if in the underworld all is permitted, nothing is circumscribed: *Fantasy* (Armani pour Homme, 1984); *Old Spice* (Shulton, 1937). For men (one wonders how the divisions are made—is a geranium more or less female, is an iris root more or less masculine?) the adjectives alter. The perfumes are described as lavender, or woody, or leathery, coniferous, fresh, or citrusy. Adjectives have adolescent energy, the appeal of the evanescent. Everyone responds to the scents themselves, finding them enchanting, compelling, nauseating, biting, demanding, alluring. The names for them, for things, aspire to authority, often inspired by poetry, music, and legend. In general, essences made vibrant by the recombinant process go by the name of poetry. As for the notion that only other poets read poetry—that number has become large. I'm not saying great poets, I'm saying poets, but where there is poetry there can be great poetry. The essences of poetry are always available. Someone is always imagining the sun, the moon, and the rain.

If not for that dark cloud in the heavens today, it might be the first of spring in late February. The truth is the almond blossoms are already out, and the mimosa festival was three weeks ago. But there are levels of demarcation and it is clearly not yet spring—it is winter because, well, it is cold in the morning and the day is spent on the move, keeping warm, and the nights are raw. These sensations are received while the mind is timelessly recording, that is, remembering, in the lower recesses. Re-membering. For the instant someone hesitates at the image of the bird on the typewriter, he or she is capable of going down, out of time, as easily as one might drive down the mountain to the coast.

Special among these birds is the nightingale, who sings night and day, a fact its name omits—mere naming is never enough—and whose arrival is looked upon as a message and a joy. There is no end to the objects of desire. How shall we describe them again? For there is nothing like the duplicitous scent, odorless in the mind, that leads intentionally away from essences. The function of the poet is ample in our culture. It is not a matter of practicing to write every day, as some would say, nor a matter of abstinence out of respect for matter. It is important to say that one thing is like another and that this world exists in others. Correlatives must be made out of vigorous and elastic material, so that the value of any world is demystified by comparison. There is the dubious value of an odor, for example, as soon as it is co-opted and bottled merely for profit, as suspect as a dirty hand in the preparation. The poet's milieu has a secret and telling air about it, ambivalent but not ambiguous, fresh and suggestive, a countryside accessible to others.

ROBERT CREELEY

From an Interview with Linda Wagner

Wagner: You have said that poetry is "the basic act of speech, of utterance." Are you implying that self-expression is the poet's motivation, or is there more to be said about his desire to communicate, his interest in possible readers?

Creeley: I don't think that "possible readers" are really the context in which poetry is written. For myself it's never been the case. I'm looking for something I can say—I'm not looking for a job or an easy solution to problems—but I'm given to write as I can and in that act I use whatever I can to gain the articulation that seems to me called for. And I certainly will pay no attention to possible readers insofar as they may not respond to what I've offered in this way. I have found, for example, that the poems I wrote in the fifties, which at that time had only the sympathetic reading of friends, that those poems have gained the audience here implied, not because I intended it but simply because I have gained them—but I could never have anticipated that. If one in that way plays to the gallery, I think it's extraordinarily distracting. The whole performance of writing then becomes some sort of odd entertainment of persons one never meets and probably would be embarrassed to meet in any case. So I'm only interested in what I can articulate with the things given me as confrontation. I can't worry about what it costs me. I don't think any man writing can worry about what the act of writing costs him, even though at times he is very aware of it. Again, when Stendhal dedicated his work in effect to readers who would be alive—in say 1930, 1935, a hundred years later—he recognized the political and social circumstances that would make him politically suspect; so that he obviously wrote for the sheer pleasure and relief of the articulation so to be gained. And I would say, I do too.

Wagner: Communication per se, then, isn't a primary motive for the poet?

Creeley: It is for some; for others, it isn't. It depends on what is meant by communication, of course. I, for example, would be very much cheered to realize that someone had felt what I had been feeling in writing—I would be very much reassured that someone had felt with me in that writing. Yet this can't be the context of my own writing. When I come to write, I frankly cannot be distracted by what people are going to think of what I'm writing. Later I may have horrible doubts indeed as to what it is and whether or not it will ever be read with this kind of response by other persons, but it can never enter importantly into my writing.

So I cannot say that communication in the sense of telling someone is what I'm engaged with. In writing I'm telling something to myself, curiously, that I didn't have the knowing of previously. One time, again some years ago, Franz Kline was being questioned—not with hostility but with intensity, by another friend—and finally he said, "Well, look, if I paint what *you* know, then that will simply bore you, the repetition from me to you. If I paint what I know, it will be boring to myself. Therefore I paint what I *don't* know." And I write what I don't know, in that sense.

Communication, then, is a word one would have to spend much time defining. One question I have—doesn't all speech imply that one is speaking with what is known, is possible of discovery? "Can you tell someone something he doesn't know?" has always been a question in my own mind. And if it is true that you cannot tell someone something "new," then the act of reading is that one is reading *with* someone. And I feel that when people read my poems most sympathetically, they are reading with me as I am writing with them. So communication this way is mutual feeling with someone, not a didactic process of information.

Wagner: I have increasingly felt that to some poets—Allen Ginsberg, William Carlos Williams, yourself—this being read with, *sympathetically, was very important.*

Creeley: There are many, many ways of feeling in the world, and many qualifications of that feeling. At times in my own life I've been embarrassed to feel I had a significant relationship with other people—that is, I felt that my world was extraordinarily narrow and egocentric and possible only to some self-defined importance. So that reading in that sense I've just spoken of—that sympathetic being with—has always been an important possibility for me. What Robert Duncan calls the ideal reader has always been someone I've thought of—but not *in* writing, *after* it.

Wagner: One question that's fairly relevant here might be this issue of using so-called prose rhythms in poetry, of taking the language of poetry from natural speech. How does the poet himself decide what is poetry and what is conversation? And are they as close as the theory seems to indicate?

Creeley: If we think of Louis Zukofsky's poetics as being "a function with upper limit music and lower limit, speech," perhaps that will help to clarify what the distinctions are. Really, the organization of poetry has moved to a further articulation in which the rhythmic and sound structure now becomes not only evident but a primary coherence in the total organization of what's being experienced. In conversation, you see, this is not necessarily the case. It largely isn't, although people speaking (at least in American speech) do exhibit clusters or this isochronous pattern of phrase groups with one primary stress; so there is a continuing rhythmic insistence in conversation. But this possibility has been increased in poetry so that now the rhythmic and sound organization have been given a very marked emphasis in the whole content. Prose rhythms in poetry are simply one further possibility of articulating pace; these so-called prose rhythms tend to be slower so that therefore they give perhaps a useful drag.

I would like to make the point that it isn't that poets are using "common" words or a common vocabulary. This kind of commonness is deceptive. For example, if one reads Williams carefully, he finds that the words are *not* largely common. What is common is the *mode* of address, the way of speaking that's commonly met with in conversations. But when that occurs in poetry, already there's a shift that is significant: that fact in a poem is very distinct from that fact in conversation. And I think what really was gained from that sense of source in common speech was the recognition that the intimate knowing of a way of speaking—such as is gained as Olson says with mother's milk—what's gained in that way offers the kind of intensity that poetry peculiarly admits.

These words known from one's childhood have the most intense possibility for the person writing. Whatever language is removed from that source goes into an ambivalence that is at times most awkward. Now a very accomplished man—say Duncan—can both attempt and succeed in a rhetorical mode that's apart from this context, although it may well *not* be; yet Duncan's virtue is that he can move from one to the other with such skill and ease. As in "Two Presentations," he moves to the immediate context of speech (literally, to quotation) yet gathers it into a mode of rhetoric that is the basic speech pattern of the whole poem. In other words, it isn't simply an imitation of common ways of speaking, it's rather a recognition that the intimate senses of rhythm and sound will be gained from what one knows in this way.

Wagner: You have written recently that it is not the single word choices so much as it is the sound and rhythm of entire passages that determines the immediacy of the language. Is that concept relevant to this discussion?

Creeley: In conversation with Basil Bunting last fall, he said that his own grasp of what poetry might be for him was first gained when he recognized that the sounds occurring in a poem could carry the emotional content of the poem as ably as anything "said." That is, the modifications of sounds—and the modulations—could carry this emotional content. He said further, that whereas the lyric gives such an incisive and intense singularity, usually, to each word that is used in a longer poem such as his own "The Spoils," there's an accumulation that can occur much more gradually so that sounds are built up in sustaining passages and are not, say, given an individual presence but accumulate that presence as a totality. So that one is not aware, let us say, that the word *the* is carrying its particular content, but as that *e* sound or *th* sound accumulates, it begins to exert an emotional effect that is gained not by any insistence on itself as singular word but as accumulation. To quote Pound again, "Prosody consists of the total articulation of the sound in a poem"—and that's what I'm really talking about.

Wagner: Is line and stanza arrangement still used to indicate what the poet intends, rhythmically? Are poets today more concerned with the sound or with the visual appearance per se *of their work?*

Creeley: For myself, lines and stanzas indicate my rhythmic intention. I don't feel that any poet of my acquaintance whose work I respect is working primarily with the visual appearances except for Ian Finlay, and in Finlay's case he is working in a very definite context of language which has to do with the fact that there have been *printed* words for now, say, 400 years. The experience of words as printed has provided a whole possibility of that order as visual as opposed to oral or audible. Ian's working in the context of language as what one sees on signboards, stop signs, titles of books— where the words *are* in that sense; and there is an increasing school of poets who are involved with concrete poetry in that way. But for myself the typographical context of poetry is still simply the issue of how to score—in the musical sense—to indicate how I want the poem to be read.

Wagner: I have noticed in your own readings that you pause after each line, even though many of the lines are very short. You're not just creating quatrains of fairly even shape, then?

Creeley: No, I tend to pause after each line, a slight pause. Those terminal endings give me a way of both syncopating and indicating a rhythmic measure. I think of those lines as something akin to the bar in music—they state the rhythmic modality. They indicate what the base rhythm of the poem is, hopefully, to be.

The quatrain to me is operating somewhat like the paragraph in prose. It is both a semantic measure and a rhythmic measure. It's the full unit of the latter. I remember Pound in a letter one time saying, "Verse consists of a constant and a variant." The quatrain for me is the constant. The variant then can occur in the line, but the base rhythm also has a constant which the quatrain in its totality indicates. I wanted something stable, and the quatrain offered it to me; as earlier the couplet form had. This, then, allows all the variability of what could be both said and indicated as rhythmic measure.

Wagner: Where in this whole discussion does your often-quoted statement, "Form is never more than an extension of content," fall?

Creeley: Olson had lifted that statement from a letter I had written him, and I'm very sure it was my restatement of something that he had made clear to me. It's not at all a new idea. I find it in many people, prose writers as well as poets—Flaubert, for example. I would now almost amend the statement to say, "Form is what happens." It's the fact of things in the world, however they are. So that form in that way is simply the presence of any thing.

What I was trying then to make clear was that I felt that form—if removed from that kind of intimacy—became something static and assumptional. I felt that the way a thing was said would intimately declare *what* was being said, and so therefore, form was never more than an extension of what it was saying. The what of what was being said gained the how of what was being said, and the how (the mode) then became what I called "form." I would again refer the whole question to Olson's "Projective Verse." It's the attempt to find the intimate form of what's being stated as it is being stated. A few weeks ago I was moved to hear Hans Morgenthau in the teach-in which was televised saying, "Facts have their own dynamic." Which is to say something in one way akin—content has its own form.

Wagner: Some people use the term "organic" poem to refer to one in which this principle of form applies. How does the organic poem differ from what is usually called the "traditional" poem?

Creeley: The traditional poem is after all the historical memory of a way of writing that's regarded as being significant. And I'm sure again that all those poems were once otherwise—as Stendhal feels, Racine *was* modern at the time Racine was writing those plays. But then for his work to be respected in the nineteenth century as being *the* way of writing—this, of course, was something else again. This is a respect merely for the thing that has happened not because it is still happening but because it did happen. That I find suspect. If one is respecting something that continues to happen, as with Shakespeare, then I agree. But if one respects a thing that isn't happening anymore, that is now so removed by its diffusion into historical perspective, then of course "traditional" becomes a drag indeed. But the traditional is, after all, the cumulative process of response. It has its uses without question. But it can only be admitted as the contemporary can respond to it.

Wagner: What of the modern poets who write in sonnets, quatrains, blank verse? Can they still be using the organic rationale?

Creeley: Certainly, if these forms can occur. If they offer

possibility of articulation, then of course they can be used. Valéry, for example, in *The Art of Poetry* makes some very astute comments about his own methods of working, and he found these forms in this "formal" sense to be very useful to him insofar as they provoked him to extraordinary excitement and to extraordinary ability. He loved the problem of them. Now you see, each according to his nature again, to quote from Pound's quote of the Confucian text. There's no rule. Only when sonnets become descriptive of values that are questionable, do I find them offensive. But I don't think they are *per se* to be written off, except that they are highly difficult now to use because society does not offer them a context with which they are intimate, anymore than society offers a context for dancing the gavotte.

Wagner: A side issue here, perhaps. Does an artist's "sincerity" have any influence on the quality of his work? Can a poet write good poems about a subject if he has no feeling about it?

Creeley: I don't see how. If one respects Pound's measure of "Only emotion endures" and "Nothing counts save the quality of the affection," then having no feelings about something seems to prohibit the possibility of that kind of quality entering. At the same time, there are many ways of feeling about things; and it may be that—as in the case of poems by Ted Berrigan—one is feeling about the fact that there is no attachment of subjective feeling to the words. It's a very subtle question.

I remember one time Irving Layton wrote a very moving poem, "Elegy for Fred Smith." Later, Gael Turnbull, very impressed by the poem, said to him, "You must feel very badly that your friend has died, and your poem concerning this fact is very, very moving." And Irving then explained that there was no man named Smith; he simply wanted to write this kind of poem. But you see, he wanted the feeling too; he wanted to gain the way one might feel in confronting such a possibility. There wasn't, as it happened, a real fact that provoked this poem, but there was certainly a feeling involved. And it was certainly a "subject" that Irving had "feeling" about.

This issue of sincerity in itself, however, can be a kind of refuge of fools. I am sure that Goldwater was sincere in certain ways, and I don't think that that necessarily protects him from a judgment that's hostile to his intent. But it will gain him a hearing, as it obviously did. The zealot is often sincere. In other words, sincerity as a quality is one thing—well, I'd simply point to Louis Zukofsky's discussion of sincerity in his notes for the Objectivist issue of *Poetry* in 1931. But I'm going to take sincerity in my own reference which again goes back to Pound, that ideogram that he notes: man standing by his word. *That* kind of sincerity has always been important to me and is another measure of my own commitment to what I'm doing.

*   *   *   *   *

Wagner: You are one of the few modern poets, Bob, to escape the charge of "all means and no matter." Did you—do you—consciously choose your subjects?

Creeley: Never that I've been aware of. I may make too much emphasis upon that, but I can't remember ever setting out to write a poem literally about something that I was conscious of before I began to write. Again I fall back on Williams' sense which I may misquote. It's in the *Autobiography*, where he says in answer to the very usual charge of his lack of profundity that dogged him all during the forties and into the fifties (that was when he was being attacked for being involved with "nonpoetic" subjects and for things which were "trivial," etc., etc.,—again, you see, that's what "meaning" in the secondary sense can land on someone. It seems to qualify them as being specious or insignificant. In other words, if the meaning in this secondary manner is not addressed to something that seems very ponderous indeed, then the man writing is charged with being "unprofound." It's a very, very silly way to think of poems, and I suppose that what has come to correct that "meaning" is something partly akin to haiku where it's very evident that a few words indeed about extraordinarily common things or sights or feelings can provoke an endless wave of emotion, as long as it's held in mind). But in any case, Williams says, "The poet thinks with his poem. In that lies his thought, and that in itself is the profundity."

For myself, writing has always been the way of finding what I was feeling about what so engaged me as "subject." That is, I didn't necessarily begin writing a poem about something to discover what I felt about it, but rather I could find the articulation of emotions in the actual writing. I came to realize that which I was feeling in the actual discovery possible to me in the poem. So I don't choose my subjects with any consciousness whatsoever. I think once things have begun—that is, once there are three or four lines, then there begins to be a continuity of possibility that they engender which I probably do follow. And I can recognize, say, looking back at what I have written, that some concerns have been persistent, e.g., the terms of marriage, relations of men and women, senses of isolation, senses of place in the intimate measure. But I have never to my own knowledge begun with any sense of "subject."

In fact, I fall back on that sense of Olson's where—I think it's "Letter 15" in the *Maximus Poems* where it goes: "He said, 'You go all

around the subject.' And I said, 'I didn't know it was a subject.' "
You see, I don't know that poetry has "subjects" except as some sort
of categorical reference which persons well distinct from the actual
activity put upon poems for, I suppose, listing in library catalogs.
Poetry has *themes,* which I feel are somewhat different; that is,
persistent contents which occur in poetry willy-nilly with or without
the recognition of the writer. These themes are such as I've spoken
of, war and the others. But I don't feel that these "subjects" are
really the primary evidence of the poem's merit or utility in the
society in which it occurs.

*Wagner: You don't, then, have any "point" to make, to use a
common term of reference?*

Creeley: I have a point to make when I begin writing inso-
far as I can write; that is, the point I wish to make is that I am
writing. Writing to me is the primary articulation that's possible to
me. So when I write, that's what I'm at work with, or that's what I'm
trying to gain, an articulation of what confronts me, which I can't
really realize or anticipate prior to the writing. I think I said—to
egocentrically quote myself—in the introduction to *The Gold Dig-
gers,* well over ten years ago, that if you say one thing it always will
lead to more than you had thought to say. This has always been my
experience.

*   *   *   *   *

*Wagner: Could we return to associations for a moment? You've
mentioned Olson and Duncan and Ginsberg frequently. I know you are
friends, but what influence has the writing of, say, Olson, had on your own
poetry? Have any poets really been important in the development of your
art?*

Creeley: It's almost impossible to qualify that sufficiently.
Olson was the first reader I had, the first man both sympathetic
and articulate enough to give me a very clear sense of what the
effect of my writing was, in a way that I could make use of it. His
early reading of my stories particularly was very, very helpful to
me. I found him the ideal reader, and have always found him so. At
the same time, his early senses of how I might make the line inti-
mate to my own habits of speaking—that is, the groupings and
whatnot that I was obviously involved with—was of great release to
me. I had been trying to write in the mode of Wallace Stevens and it
just hadn't worked. The period, the rhythmic period that he was
using, just wasn't intimate to my own ways of feeling and speaking.
And so, much as I respected him, I couldn't use him at all. Williams
came in too and he had large influence, but it was Olson curiously
enough in the "Projective Verse" piece (I think I'm right in saying
that the first section of that is taken in part at least from letters that

Olson wrote me, the part about from the heart to the line, where he's explaining his sense of the line and the relation to breath). So he really made clear to me what the context of writing could be in a way that no other man had somehow ever quite managed.

Denise Levertov certainly in those early years was very important to me. We talked so much and exchanged so much sense of mutual concern while living in France. She's very important to me; we both share the respect for Williams and the interest in problems of writing. Paul Blackburn in the same period also. Robert Duncan is one of the most warm and sympathetic friends I've ever had, which is very important to me, and again is one of the most astute and involved readers I've ever had. And Allen equally, because Allen reassured me as Williams had that my emotions were not insignificant, that their articulation was really what I was given to be involved with. Ed Dorn—many, many men. It's impossible to list them all.

Wagner: Would you say that the influence of a poet's contemporaries is as strong as his "ancestors," so to speak?

Creeley: Very, very much so. I think as in the case of a university, very often students teach each other more actively than they are taught by their professors. Except that there will usually be one or two people of the so-called, "ancestor" type that are very important; Pound is very important in this way. Williams, although I felt him in a questionable way contemporary always; Whitman finally comes to have for me this possibility, although I must confess I'm beginning to know Whitman in a way that I hadn't known him previously. Hart Crane had this effect for me. Then the very precise beauty in Stendhal; for example, the way the thought was so free to find its own statement—and to only move as it was feeling some response. Then the peculiar beauty of, say, Wyatt or Campion. Shakespeare in this particular period was very, very moving to me. Coleridge, I used to love to read Coleridge in the diversity and the multiplicity of his statement, as I loved James for very like reasons. Or Jane Austen. In other words, I don't think one can make an absolute statement apropos which of these two possibilities is the more important. It depends. It depends simply on who one is and what one's particular nature leads him to.

Wagner: Do you credit any one writer with a strong influence on your poetry?

Creeley: I think Williams gave me the largest example. But equally I can't at all ignore, as I've said, Olson's very insistent influence upon me at that early time and continuingly. Nor can I ignore the fact that the first person who introduced me to writing as a craft, who even spoke of it as a craft, was Ezra Pound. I think it was my twentieth birthday that my brother-in-law took me down to

Gordon Cairnie's bookstore in Cambridge and said, "What would you like? Would you like to get some books?" "Gosh, yes," and I bought *Make It New*, the Yale edition. That book was a revelation to me insofar as Pound there spoke of writing from the point of view of what writing itself was engaged with, not what it was "about." Not what symbolism or structure had led to, but how one might address oneself to the *act* of writing. And that was the most moving and deepest understanding I think I've ever gained. So that Pound was very important to my craft, no matter how much I may have subsequently embarrassed him by my own work. So many, many people.

I could equally say Charlie Parker—in his uses of silence, in his rhythmic structure. His music was influential at one point. So that I can't make a hierarchy of persons.

Wagner: There exists at the moment a large group of young poets writing what have been called by some, "Creeley poems," short, terse, poignant. Will these young writers stay imitative?

Creeley: No, they won't. Imitation is a way of gaining articulation. It is the way one learns, by having the intimate possibility of some master like Williams or Pound. Writing poems in those modes was a great instruction to me insofar as I began to "feel" what Williams was doing as well as "understand" it. And so I found possibility for my own acts.

I think therefore that this imitative phase is a natural thing in artists; and I would feel it should be encouraged. I think that if so-called writing classes would use this possibility, possibly they would produce a more interesting group of craftsmen than is now evident. This is one way to learn, and it's the way I would respect, coming as I do from a rural background where learning how to plow is both watching someone else do it and then taking the handle of the plow and seeing if you can imitate, literally, his way of doing it; therefore, gaining the use of it for yourself. But what you then plow—whether you plow or not—is your own business. And there are many ways to do it.

*II. The Pure Clear Word ✒ Poets on the Modern
Tradition and New Directions*

JAMES WRIGHT

From the Pure Clear Word

An Interview with Dave Smith

(On September 30, 1979 Gibbons Ruark and I met James Wright in his New York apartment and conducted the following interview. Wright, nearing his fifty-second birthday, appeared trim and healthy. He is a solidly built man who moves with an obvious dignity that creates the impression of forceful grace. Like the music which is so much a part of his life and his imagination, his voice and gestures reveal oscillations of exuberance, enthusiasm, sobriety, and joy which these printed words cannot well convey. During the interview, which lasted more than four hours, Wright sat before a large wall-to-wall-to-ceiling array of books. I remember clearly the sense that these books were virtually husks because Wright held all that was alive in them within his own mind. And I remember the intense, bright vitality of his eyes that flared or lulled as he spoke or was silent.—Dave Smith, November 1979)

*   *   *   *   *

D.S.: During the writing of your first collection of poems, The Green Wall, *you said in a letter to Roethke that "I work like hell clipping away perhaps one tiny pebble per day from the ten-mile-thick wall of formal and facile 'technique' which I myself erected, and which stands ominously between me and whatever poetry may be in me." Can you comment on your meaning?*

Wright: I think that quotation is confused. I would enlarge on it by saying that I was starting to feel then, and I still feel, that the writer's real enemy is his own glibness, his own facility; the writer constantly should try to discover what difficulties there truly are inherent in a subject or in his own language and come to terms with these difficulties. If he does that, then he might be able to discover something in his own mind, or in the language which is imaginative. I did not say very clearly what I was trying to think my way toward. What I was trying to suggest, trying to think, trying to realize is just that it is fatally easy to write in an almost automatic way. After you master certain gimmicks, whether in formal verse or in rhyme or in so-called free verse, then it is pretty easy to repeat them. I wrote a piece in my notebook about the purity and the force, really the great strength, of Richard Wilbur. He has always written regular verse and with wonderful purity and a beautiful music and great accuracy and clarity, and with great emotional depth. For a while during the fifties most writers were tending to write in too facile, too glib a way in regular meters and rhyme. Some of us turned away to free verse. Since then I think that whenever one opens a magazine nearly all the poems one sees will be in free verse. More and more they strike me as being just as facile and automatic in their way as the earlier poems had been in other ways. That is, it isn't a solution to one's artistic problems just to stop rhyming.

Here is one of my favorite themes. This is what I call "trite surrealism." The French surrealists, and there are some very good ones, understood that Dadaism and Surrealism were comic reactions to certain preestablished conventions of rationality in writing. They started to be deliberately irrational. They were able to write good poems when in one way or another they were comic. Americans who have tried to follow the Surrealistic way don't get the joke. There are many bad surrealistic poems and there are horrible examples of the most automatic, unimaginable kind of thing. They are straining toward imagination and something new. They are like the Puritans in Dr. Seuss' old pocket book of boners. Some student wrote that the Puritans came to America to worship God as they saw fit and to see that everybody else did the same thing.

*   *   *   *   *

D.S.: How do you feel about your early poems?

Wright: I haven't read them for a while. About three years ago I sat down and read my whole *Collected Poems*. Some of them I couldn't remember having written and some of them I didn't understand. It is true that I wrote to my publisher after *St. Judas* and said I don't know what I am going to do after this but it will be completely different. This comment, and also Robert Bly's essay on my work, has given rise to some sort of assumption that I calculated that I was going to be born again or something, that I would become a completely different person. I think that this is nonsense. There was a good essay by Mark Strand, in *Field* magazine, regarding changes in poetry. He used my work as an example and he said that the only difference, really, was that I don't rhyme so often now. I don't think that a person can change very quickly or easily. Well, there is such a thing as a conversation experience surely. William James has written formally about this in *Varieties of Religious Experience*. That change is a reality. Let me say that to change one's kind of poetry would be, in effect, to change one's life. I don't think that one can change one's life simply as an act of will. And I never wanted to. What I had hoped to do from the beginning was to continue to grow in the sense that I might go on discovering for myself new possibilities of writing.

I have written a good many prose pieces now and I did this because I liked prose and I wanted to express myself that way. I put some prose pieces in my last couple of books and sometimes these have been called poems. They are not poems. They are prose pieces. Now whether they are well written or badly written is another question. I said before, in other connections, that we sometimes have a hard time discussing writing itself in the United States because we are constantly getting bogged down in nitpicking about technical terms. The French can talk about the prose-poem and do so effectively just because they can use a phrase like that and everybody knows that people may disagree with one another about these terms. But everybody in the controversy also knows that the prose-poem is a term of convenience. They know perfectly well that Flaubert wrote prose and that Baudelaire wrote in verse, and was a poet. With this distinction, then, they are free to go on and try new combinations of things. This is what I have always hoped for myself. The trouble with it all in the United States is that sure as hell somebody's going to say, now which is it, prose or poetry?

Yvor Winters said a valuable thing in this respect. He said, poetry is written in verse whereas prose is written in prose. That is a help because I think it allows us to drop the nitpicking and then go on and try to see what the writing in question is. Then we can try to determine whether or not there is a way to understand it and, finally, to undertake the extremely difficult task of determining whether it is any good or not.

Good in relation to what, we may ask? Literary criticism itself, I think, ought to be as Matthew Arnold said: an effort to see the thing in itself as it really is. He went on to say it ought to be an effort to make reason and the will of God prevail. T. S. Eliot remarked that there was Arnold referring to that joint firm, Reason and the Will of God. Whether or not that particular phrase of Arnold's is useful to us still, he did see that observing the thing itself as it really is, is only the first part of the task. The further task is the more dynamic one of trying to determine whether or not the thing itself was worth doing and what effect it can have—how far it is expressive, how far it is communicative, and finally whether it is any good. This requires us, as critics, to try to truly understand whether or not there is such a thing as the good or the bad. What do we mean by that? Can we make it clear? These are terrific and serious tasks for literary criticism.

I said at one point that there can't be a good poetry without a good criticism. I did not mean that there has to be a great body of formal criticism in print. I meant that a person who is writing and reading is going to be able to write better and more truly if he tries to think about language, if he tries to imagine what his own writing is going to look like and smell like and sound like to an intelligent person of good will. These are critical efforts. Or if he tries to determine what relation he has or can have to the authors whom he, himself, genuinely considers to be great and enduring. What do I have to do with Horace? It is a question that I have to ask myself if I am a serious man. Well, I can try to understand what Horace says, many of the things that he says, for example his pieces about the art of poetry. I can try to be true to them in the immediate terms of my own work. He says valuable things. This is not to say that I have ever written anything or could write anything within a thousand miles of Horace's excellence. To know this, and to know as I do know, that the assumption of my equalling Horace, the least thing by Horace, is an illusion—this is a help to me in understanding my own limitations and my possibilities. I am a traditionalist and I think that whatever we have in our lives that matters has to do with our discovering our true relation to the past.

* * * * *

D. S.: *What good is a poem, finally?*

Wright: I don't know. A poem is good because of the pleasure that it provides us. Samuel Johnson argues in his preface to the 1765 Shakespeare that a work endures if it gives pleasure but then, very acutely, he says that there are different kinds of pleasure. Some are more frivolous and occasional. There is nothing wrong with that, except such pleasure wears out. There is a deeper pleasure we can find in trying to see the truth, by which Johnson means to imply something about the tragic complexity of life. Shall I state Johnson's remark? He says it with such force.

> Nothing can please many or please long but just representations of general nature. Particular manners can be known to few, and few only can judge how nearly they are copied. The irregular combinations of fanciful invention may delight a while by that novelty, of which the common satiety of life sends us all in quest, but the pleasure of sudden wonder are soon exhausted and the mind can only repose on the stability of truth.

Johnson is, of course, as thoroughly aware of the multiplicity of truth as Shakespeare is. But there is a difference between the truth to be found in what T. S. Eliot very brutally calls birth, copulation, and death, and what Johnson means. There is more pleasure, Johnson says, in being able to understand those tragic complexities than there is to be found, say, in concrete poetry. Thom Gunn said the same sort of thing a few years ago while reviewing a book-length poem. He said, "This must be the first full-length *Waste Land* that I have read in a couple of years."

D.S.: You have said that when your own work fails it does so because of a lack of clarity. What do you mean by clarity and why is it difficult?

Wright: I would like to write something that would be immediately and prosaically comprehensible to a reasonably intelligent reader. That is all. That is all I mean by being clear, but it is very difficult for me. This is a Horatian idea. It is the attempt to write, as one critic said once of the extraordinarily and beautifully strong writer Katherine Anne Porter, so that "every one of her effects is calculated but they never give the effect of calculation." We read a story like her "Noon Wine" and it is what we call seamless. It is almost impossible to pick that story apart and find her constructing a beginning, middle, and end. When you read the whole thing you do realize, and not just with your feelings but with your intelligence, that what you have just looked at is a living thing. It has a form. She hasn't written in bulk, never in such bulk as, say, Edward Bulwer-Lytton. And yet, her work has a certain largeness about it because it is so alive. I think that she has thought very clearly and carefully about the need to make things clear to a reasonably intelligent reader of good will. As for other kinds of readers, well there are fools in the world, and bastards.

D.S.: You said this once: "One thing a person tries to do is to discover the appropriate form for whatever he is saying." What do you mean by form?

Wright: I don't mean form in the abstract. I mean what anyone would mean when he talks about true rhetoric. I mean the proper words in the proper places. That's all. We have mentioned Robert Creeley's idea that form is no more than an extension of content. I think I follow what Creeley is saying and as far as I follow it, I think it is sound. Beyond a certain point, however, it gets confusing and starts to sound vague. It is easiest to talk about such matters when one is dealing with comic poetry because there, as Auden pointed out, the form is predominant and the joke comes out of discovering in the following of certain strict forms. This is true even when one writes a parody in free verse like that one in William Harmon's *Oxford Book of American Light Verse*, which is a wonderful parody of Whitman in long-line Whitmanesque catalog form. There is a housewife present and her husband is drunk and comes in singing, "We won't get home until the morning" and at the end of this long line, which takes about five lines of print, the husband is finally inside and the parodist says "He inebriate, chantant." And consider Whitman's great bad line, one of the great bad lines in the world, I think, and yet like some lines in Dickens only Whitman could have written it. It's this: "How plentious, how spiritual, how resume." Isn't that nice? It reminds me of Dickens. David Copperfield, after he's gotten hung over, knows that the pure Agnes Whitfield has seen him drunk, so he goes and asks her forgiveness. She forgives him and he says . . . it is just staggering. A mediocre writer could never have written this. It has the whole of Victorian taste in it. He says, "Oh Agnes, you are my good angel, beast that I am." Isn't that fine? I know it is horrible, but it has genius in it.

* * * * *

D.S.: When people speak of the change in your poems after your first two books they speak of the surrealism and often refer to "Lying in a Hammock at William Duffy's Farm in Pine Island, Minnesota" as not untypical of your change. You have said of this poem, "All I did was describe what I felt and what I saw, lying in the hammock. Shouldn't that be enough? But no, there's your American every time, goddamnit, somebody's got to draw a moral." Would you comment further?

Wright: Well, I think that the poem is a description of a mood and this kind of poem is the kind of poem that has been written for thousands of years by the Chinese poets. I can't read Chinese, but I certainly can read Soame Jenyns and Robert Paine and Witter Bynner and Arthur Wailey. And that poem, although I hope it is a description of my mood as I lay in that hammock, is clearly an imitation of that Chinese manner. It is not surrealistic. I said, at the end of that poem, "I have wasted my life "because it was what I happened to feel at that moment and as part of the mood I had while lying in the hammock. This poem made English critics angry. I have never understood what would have so infuriated them. They could say the poem was limp or that it did not have enough intellectual content. I can see that. But I hope that it did not pretend to. It just said, I am lying here in this hammock and this and that is happening.

American critics think that last line is a moral, that it is a comment which says I have wasted my life by writing iambics, or that I have wasted my life by lying in the hammock. Actually, behind everything in my general thoughts and feelings was the idea that one of the worst things in American life is waste. I think that our tendency to waste is a truly dreadful one. I have told my students that one of the most horrifying things to me is to stand, being my age, and look at a class of nineteen- and twenty-year-old people who are trying to read a passage of, say, Milton or Shakespeare and to see their faces saying it is a waste of time. They don't see how precious their lives are.

D.S.: *One of your poems is called "The Morality of Poetry" and another is called "The Idea of the Good." Can you speak of the difference between drawing a moral and the ideas implied in these titles?*

Wright: I only used the phrase "the morality of poetry" once and it is the title of that poem in *St. Judas*. What I meant there was that there are different kinds of forms in poetry which are possible and to try to write any of them well is a good thing. That is the morality of poetry, as far as I am concerned. "The Idea of the Good" is a very, very confused poem. I don't have the faintest idea what it means. I can't imagine how anyone could find a meaning in it. It is just badly written. I forget what I was thinking of at the time. I feel this way about almost everything in my book *Two Citizens*. The book is just a bust. I will never reprint it. Let me put it this way, I ought not to have published that book the way it stands. I should have taken possibly six poems in it and tried to wait a year, to see if I couldn't revise them and see what else I had. That is what I ought to have done and I didn't. I made an ass of myself. It seems to me a bad book because most of it is badly written. Obscure and self-indulgent, it talks around subjects rather than coming to terms with them. It is impossibly ragged. It is just unfinished. If I were ever going to reprint any of it, I would take maybe six poems and write them out again in long-hand and see what might happen. I would try to think about them as thoroughly as I could.

D.S.: *Do you have a specific feeling about that book's initial poem, "Ars Poetica: Some Recent Criticism"?*

Wright: It has some strong possibilities in it, but it is still confused. I am not quite sure what it means. That can be a glib answer, an evasion of responsibility, but I mean that when I go back and look at it I can't quite figure out what it is about. I called it "Some Recent Criticism" because I had in mind to write the kind of poem that could not be glibly disposed of by some reviewers and critics who were interested in facility alone. I made that conscious effort. Suddenly I called it "Ars Poetica" as if to say here is a piece of raw life. I think artistically that was a mistake, but that is what I was trying to do. I meant to introduce something that would be difficult for certain glib reviewers to solve.

D.S.: *Is it possible that in spite of your intention and present evaluation of that poem that it could have its own myth and meaning?*

Wright: If it has those I am not aware of them. I wasn't thinking of that. You can't always tell, though. You might write something and think as clearly as you can that you have said a certain thing. Then someone else will find something in it, an intelligent person of good will, and maybe he will explain to you what is really there. There is something about language that can be very surprising, and words we use—even in conversation—sometimes can have implications, very colorful ones, that we haven't been aware of consciously. We find examples of this in our public life. I really do believe that there is, in language, something like a power to heal itself, to right itself. Language is a living thing, a part of ourselves, and, as such, I think that the notion among the evangelists of the word as flesh is a very, very complex and important living idea. I am not enough of a philosopher or critic or theologian to spell it out, yet I feel it has a certain truth.

Language can convey a meaning we were not aware of. There are staggering examples of this. One of my favorite Americans, and I have a poem about his death, was Mayor Daley of Chicago. By favorite, I mean as an example. Mayor Daley used to say to his constituents such things as: If I am reelected the great city of Chicago will rise to an even higher platitude of achievement. He did not mean to say *that,* but he did say it. And the meaning is there. There is another example in New York's Mario Procacino. In earlier years Mario Procacino would emerge to run for mayor and then disappear. He had a pencil-thin moustache, black hair slicked down and parted in the middle, and somebody once said he looked like a face painted on a balloon. He did various things. Once he went to Israel and told people that he was the President of Verranzo College. Of course, there is no Verranzo College. Once when he was running for mayor he went to Harlem and met a large constituency, a big crowd. All black people. And Mario Procacino, part of whose manner was to be sort of weepy and yearning like a hack obstetrician from Martins Ferry, Ohio—oh help this woman have her baby!—said to that audience. . . . I can hardly bring myself to say this, it is so good. If it were consciously controlled, Shakespeare could have written this line, though first he would have had to create Procacino and that audience. Procacino said to that black audience: My heart is as black as yours! Now he didn't mean *that.* He didn't intend it to sound the way it sounded to that audience and to you and to me. But he said it. It is almost as if the language cried out, save me. Somebody save me. We do have a wonderful language in America and we still haven't really gotten to it. Some people have approached it.

* * * * *

D.S.: One of the changes in your poems has been a move from a formal to a more colloquial diction. It has been suggested that this is like Wordsworth's demand for a language of the common man. Is this your intention?

Wright: No. I have never been able to figure out what Words-worth means. I don't think that one can generalize about it. It de-pends on the needs of the particular poet. In the arrangement of the words I would like to be very formal but I would like the effect of having a certain ease. That is the Horatian notion. I do think any language is available to poetry. My brother, who lives in California and works for IBM, told me that they fed things into a computer out there. They got a computer to translate Keats' "Ode to a Nightin-gale." It was nutty. But in itself, it seemed to me to make a wonderful woozy kind of poem. They translated it into other terms. They tried to clarify it. I remember Ransom reading the "Ode on Melancholy" and saying "Nor suffer thy pale forehead to be kissed by night-shade." Ransom pointed out that in the Oxford English Dictionary one of the meanings of nightshade is a night-walking prostitute. Well, the computer would get some of that made clear.

D.S.: Do you consider that there is any distinction to be made between the way you have used the image in poems and the way delineated by the Imagist poets?

Wright: I do not understand any such distinction. I am simply trying to write as clearly as I can. Sometimes I use figures of speech and sometimes I don't. I do not operate according to a set of principles or manifestos.

D.S.: You have referred frequently to the musical quality of poems. Granting that each ear may perceive this music differently, can you say what you mean by the music of poetry?

Wright: It is first of all the movement of language. This includes pauses and everything meant by timing. There is the ac-tual sound of the words, the syllables in relation to one another. And there is something beyond that which moves literally toward the condition of music. One thing that has pleased me very much is that there are at least five composers who have set things of mine to music. It has pleased me that professional musicians would find that quality in my poems.

D.S.: Can you speak of the relationship of timing to form?

Wright: Yes. Auden says it is often the timing, especially, the rhymes, that will dictate the meaning. He says that Byron sud-denly became aware of this and became a great poet in "Beppo," that wonderful piece about Venice. Also in *Don Juan*.

D.S.: Is the speaker of your poems an artificial, or created, speaker? Or is it the actual James Wright?

Wright: Sometimes it is an artificial voice and sometimes it is a direct voice. There are some poems that I have written which are more like dramatic monologues in the sense that Browning conceived of that form. Sometimes I have simply made things up. Sometimes people have called me a confessional poet. I don't see that. I feel perfectly free to make up something that never happened to me. There is not a point to point reference between the events of my books and the events of my life. Not at all. I have said that I regarded writing poetry as a curse, but that remark was a silly affectation. With me, to be as realistic as I can, I would say that writing poetry has been what one could reasonably call a neurotic compulsion. I have not made that much money from it. It is not that useful. To some extent, it has made me notorious. Notoriety makes me extremely uncomfortable. This sounds like an affectation, too, but honest to God it is not. Poetry is not a curse. Often it is a pleasure to write but I think that I have written, as I say, sort of neurotically. I have gone on writing because it has made me feel, from time to time, more emotionally safe.

D.S.: What do you mean by the remark that "the value of a poet's life is going to depend on the truth of the language and the truth of his life"?

Wright: That is another pompous remark. I don't know what it means. It reminds me of Robert Benchley's maxim from the Chinese. He says, "It is rather to be chosen than great riches, unless I have omitted something from the quotation." A remark like mine is, I think, hot air. It sort of sounds nice though. We don't have to be bullied by our own asinine remarks that have got into print.

D.S.: Do you construct your books in a certain way? Do you think of a poem or a book as having a statemental or communicative function?

Wright: Yes, I do think of the construction in a certain way. Frost said somewhere, I have forgotten where, that if there are twenty-five poems in a book, the book itself ought to be the twenty-sixth poem. That is, in presenting a group of poems in the hope that someone will read them, one ought to be aware of a relation between the poems as well as of inner relations that exist in the individual poems. It is an idea of shapeliness that appeals to me. There are blossoms all over *To a Blossoming Pear Tree,* my latest book. And I think that this book is more tightly organized than any of my previous books. Whether or not it comes through that way, I don't know. This is what I felt, anyway.

As for the second half of your question, I think that the kind of thing that a person writes will depend partly on his own interests and concerns as a human being. Those things will come out in his poems inevitably. In the poem called "To a Blossoming Pear Tree" I am talking about addressing the beauty of Nature, which is nonhuman. It suggests to me sometimes the perfection of things and I envy this perfection of things, or at least this nonhumanity, precisely because it is not involved in the sometimes very painful mess of being human. Yet I say at the end of the poem that this is what I have to be, human. Human life is a mess. This is something I wanted to say, and I said it.

JOHN HAINES

The Hole in the Bucket

. . . so poetry is arrested in its development if it remains an
unmeaning play of fancy without relevance to the ideals and
purposes of life. In that relevance lies its highest power.

Santayana

American poetry lacks ideas. Like all large statements, this one
covers a lot of ground and leaves plenty of room for error. I make it
if for no other reason than to see what response I can provoke. But
there are other reasons at hand, chiefly my dissatisfaction with the
thinness, sameness, and dullness of so many contemporary poems.
Our poems are characteristically occasional, and I do not mean by
this that they are all written for or about occasions. Williams, after
all, wrote many of his poems out of everyday encounters with
things and persons; so did Stevens. Most poets do this. But I mean
that the poems are generated by a sporadic and shallow response to
things, and not within the context of a unified outlook on life.

This may be a way of saying that we have no major poets at this
time. I myself would not be so foolish as to assert that. It has,
however, been said not only that this is the case, but that we
shouldn't expect things to be different. The statement may be true,
but I feel dissatisfied with it. The notion that this is a time for the
small and plentiful poet and not for the major talent seems to limit
beforehand the possibilities. It is as if some of us wished to shrink
the world to our own size since we cannot grow enough to equal it.

When hundreds of poems in magazine after magazine and in
book after book reveal the same casual, happenstance character,
the same self-limited frame of reference, the art of poetry itself
may be called into question. What use is such an art beyond mere
self-entertainment for the few? And without inclusive, authentic
ideas it can't be otherwise.

By "idea" I mean, among other things, some kind of conviction
about the world and the place of poetry in it. It is an insight, let's
say, that makes of experience and perception a particular way of
seeing: what we sometimes call the poet's "vision." The insight may
come as a sudden revelation, but it is more likely to be achieved
slowly as a result of simply living and responding to things in the
world, of reading and thinking, and of the daily work of writing
poems and thinking about writing poems. After a while, if one is

lucky, some pattern emerges; the substance of one's efforts begins to be clear. The process is all one piece, one way of being. And the value of the idea, once it is formed, is that it furnishes the means by which, in a world lacking unity, all that the poet sees and feels has meaning. Things fall into place. Every writer of poems seeks to accomplish something like this in single poems, or it seems to me that we would not write them at all. The task is to go beyond the single lucky poem, or even the single gift of a volume, and by a vigorous kind of self-exploration and a "prodigious search of appearances"* develop and extend the meaning of the insight. We no longer have at hand the unifying outlook on life common to all which society may once have provided its artists and citizens; but every poet who aspires to more than occasional composition must sooner or later create the idea for himself, the personal myth, much as Stevens attempted to do with his theory of the imagination. The idea itself can be criticized, but the effort needs to be made.

All the work we value most from the past sixty or seventy years was nourished by ideas. Ideas are present and abundant in Yeats and Eliot, in Pound, in Stevens, in Jeffers, and in Lawrence, to name but a few. And those poets of the same period who now seem to us to be "minor" are precisely those in whose work ideas are either weak or commonplace, or do not exist at all. Mark Van Doren's poems, for example, show that it is possible to write graceful and often interesting poems without strong ideas. This doesn't mean that the work of such poets has no permanent value: only that we must look elsewhere for the most authentic voice of the period.

Even a casual reading of modern poetry in Spanish would lead one to a similar conclusion. In Unamuno, in Machado, in Jimenez, and in Paz, the fire of the idea, the passion of it, lights up the best poems. The same is true of much contemporary European poetry in our time. Here and there in contemporary American poetry the conviction rises, where it does not freeze into dogmatism or mere gesture, only to sink again. The merest appearance of it, and the excitement it generates, seems to me to provide sufficient evidence for what I am saying.

Possession of an idea, of a conviction about human history, rescues a poet like Edwin Muir from mediocrity. In Muir's case the idea was formed in early childhood out of a series of clear glimpses into the original order of things. His memory of these, and his slowly maturing belief in the symbolic truth of dreams, and in what he called the "fable" of human life—the Fall and journey out of Eden toward some eventual reconciliation—allowed him to write

---

*Wallace Stevens.

late in life a poem like "The Horses" in which his vision is complete. Actually, Muir is remarkable for his fidelity to his vision and for the steady growth in his power of utterance.

Williams is another poet in whom an important idea began to form relatively early. We speak a new language on this continent, one no longer English, and some means of measuring this language as verse must be invented if we are to have the poetry we need. The slow clarification of this idea can be traced in Williams's work. Whatever the ultimate value of the idea, it allowed, in fact made necessary, his continued growth as a poet.

Even though an idea may appear to have negative qualities, as is sometimes the case in the work of Robinson Jeffers, behind the apparent negation can be seen the positive figure of life-enhancement. Most genuine poets have understood that one great quality of art, and it may be its most important quality, is that it enhances life for us. In more common terms, it gives us something to look up to. Things are changed, made visible in another, or ideal light; they are removed from the ordinary and become part of some very old, interior story in which we recognize something of ourselves. Poetry can hardly do this successfully when the emotion and thought generated in the words halts at the boundaries of the poem. The task, then, is to make connections, to invest the "I" of the poem with significance beyond the ordinary, to make of one's own predicament a universal case. Or to state it another way, it is to allow something besides the self to occupy the poem, to matter as much as the self. And this requires, beyond insight, honesty and imagination, two qualities not always in good supply.

Having valid ideas about poetry implies having a keen regard for poetry itself. For this a certain shifting of attention may be necessary, away from personality and career, or an abandonment of ambition in the narrow sense of it. But it also requires a sure awareness that poetry has been written for thousands of years by men and women in all sorts of places and circumstances. It is still an art; and the individual brings to this art what gifts and insights he or she possesses.

All our competence with words and with verses, with images and metaphors, asks for substance and purpose if poetry is not to be a slightly superior form of amusement. It must become more serious and more profoundly involved with the life of its time. And should anyone think I am being merely cranky, I would like to quote one of my favorite remarks by Wallace Stevens, written in a letter in 1946 and still valid: "If people are to become dependent on poetry for any of the fundamental satisfactions, poetry must have an increasingly intellectual scope and power. This is a time for the highest poetry. We never understood the world less than we do now nor, as we understand it, liked it less. We never wanted to understand it more or needed to like it more."

It may not be true that poetry requires criticism in order to be written. The poems will appear when it is time for them and not otherwise. Nevertheless, lack of serious ideas about poetry implies an absence of criticism. There are two kinds of criticism. One of them is the sort that defines and places works of the past. It tells, as well as it can, something of where we have been, what we have been, and what we have done. At its most abundant (and dull), this is the sort that endlessly sifts and classifies the past; it is essentially an academic activity, one that keeps literary scholars eternally occupied. The second and much rarer sort attempts to define the conditions for the art of the present—what we want poetry to be for us now and tomorrow. This is the kind written by Pound and by Williams, sometimes by Lawrence, and by a few others. It often conveys a sense of urgency, of necessity. The best criticism accomplishes a double task: it both defines the past and attempts to describe the present and future possibility. Of this kind we have had very little for a generation or more. The literary journals are filled with commentators, but the commentaries in most cases amount to little more than book reviewing and trivial shop-talk—the eternal and boring "nuts and bolts" of most "craft" essays. I will except from this description Robert Bly, whose erratic but often daring pieces scattered in many journals over the past dozen years or more have done as much as anything to fill a considerable void. Donald Hall should also be mentioned for the intelligence of his numerous contributions on contemporary poets and poetry.

The main value of criticism is that it provides a space in which creation can take place, a clearing in the imagination. I have been reading Octavio Paz recently, and have been greatly attracted to his far-ranging, often daring speculations on literature and society. This large-minded thinking about poetry and language, about literature and tradition, and about creative life generally, is precisely what we are lacking. And for Paz, criticism offers a way not only into a particular work, but into the process itself. Criticism and creation are one, a total experience, and are not antagonistic at all. It is the condition of thought that is important. Gossip and classification, the two extremes of most literary discussion, do not create understanding, which is surely a major function of intelligent criticism. And to provide us with the kind of understanding we need, criticism should try to work itself clear of a reliance on what some people have conveniently called "the network"—those few who can be expected to listen. They are important, but poetry is, as Paz reminds us, "the search for others, the discovery of otherness."

And he speaks of poetry as a fundamental restoration of community; poetry is essentially social, and has always been so.

There are decent, competent poems written today, many of them. They seem good; it is hard to find fault with them in detail. Few of the poems, however, remain in one's mind. They are poems that convey a certain information or mood, a few images, but which read once and understood offer little to return to. They seem meant to be replaced next week or next quarter by others very much like them. If I am at all right about this, it is not preposterous to argue that it is related to what we find in society at large. Everything we are accustomed to having and using is meant to be replaced next season by a new, slightly modified model, one often described as containing startling and revolutionary changes. In fact, it is naive to think that we aren't all affected in many, hardly suspected ways by the planned obsolescence of the material environment. Even human relationships seem to have taken on the same, dismaying character.

There is about contemporary poems generally a lack of resonance beyond the page and beyond the self that speaks the poem. For some time I have thought that this might be due partly to the flatness of statement we have grown used to in verse. Our poetry discarded some time ago much of the musical element in verse: regularity of meter, rhyme, and all the little memory aids once so common to poetry. We have grown used to seeing a poem as print, as object on the page, and have lost to some extent the ability to hear, not only the poem as a figure in time, but also the spaces and silences between the words and the syllables where so much can be said.

But there is more to it than this. We have somehow fallen into the notion that one's individual experience in the world is sufficient material to make poetry out of. It is easy to see why so many prefer to think so. We mistrust the received ideas of the past, whether they are stated as philosophy and political theory or are embodied in artistic forms. The mistrust is inevitable, I suppose, since so many of the ideas seem to have failed us when we needed them most. Moreover, the ideas have for the most part not been lived and tested, but inherited as literature, as course material, something to be taught in the classroom and unrelated to everyday life. So we prefer to rely on the illusion of our personal experience, on what can be seen and touched by the individual. This may in fact be a useful way to begin life, but it is not quite enough for poetry.

What makes a poem significant? What makes it memorable? Passion and thought, emotionally charged language, fresh imagery, surprising use of metaphor . . . yes. But also, I think, the very sure sense that the moment we enter the world of the poem we are participating in another episode of the myth-journey of humankind; that a voice has taken up the tale once more. The individual experience as related or presented in the poem renews our deep, implicit faith in that greater experience. A poem remains with us to the extent that it allows us to feel that we are listening to a voice at once contemporary and ancient. This makes all the difference. Innovations in style, strange, disordered syntax, unusual images, idiomatic explosions—these soon pass, or are means to an end. Only that remains which touches us in our deepest, most enduring self. Behind every word is the memory of another, spoken a thousand times; in the intonation of the voice, in the rise and fall of the syllables, memory does its work and reconciles the poet and the reader to a world difficult and strange.

What I have just said may seem ill-defined, but it is directly related to our misuse of, or lack of regard for, the past, what is loosely called "the tradition." I am continually surprised by the number of people in poetry workshops who have read little or no poetry beyond that written during the past five or ten years. Many of them do not read poetry regularly at all, and cannot recognize a familiar passage from Wordsworth, Yeats, Frost, or even Williams. On the other hand, they have perhaps read Creeley and Olson, Plath and Sexton, Hugo and Goldbarth, and a few far lesser people. They are more apt to have read hundreds of recent poems written by younger people influenced by these poets. At worst, they are content to read only each other.

I think this tendency is mistaken. The more one thinks about it, the more mistaken it appears to be. That younger poets should be influenced only by their near or immediate contemporaries seems a very strange notion, and it imposes a serious limitation on the possibilities for growth. Should anyone read Robert Bly, W. S. Merwin, or James Wright, you would think that person would also want to seek out and read the poets *they* learned from. Otherwise, how could anyone come to a firm conclusion about the later work? As Pound used to say, if you really want to learn about an art, you will do best to go back to the earliest things you can find and begin there. Moreover, if there is some quality missing in contemporary work, some defect in it, imitating it will only compound the trouble.

It is amazing to me that anyone with a serious commitment to poetry would not want to seek out the whole of it, to read as much of it as he or she can lay hands on, and to learn from its many forms and voices. Contrary to what many people appear to think, the "tradition" is not something outworn, an empty scaffolding kept more or less intact by English departments, but a living and useful system of values.

One of the strengths of poetry in Spanish in our time is that it has not lost contact with the past. Quevedo and Góngora are still living presences for poets in Spain and South America, as they were for Lorca and others of his generation. Paz has some interesting things to say about this.

> Instead of being a succession of names, works and tendencies, the tradition would be converted into a system of significant relationships: a language. The poetry of Góngora would not be simply something that happened after Garcilaso and before Ruben Darío, but a text related dynamically with other texts.... The importance of Quevedo is not exhausted in his work or the conceptualism of the 17th century: we find the sense of his words more fully in some poems of Vallejo, even when, naturally, what the Peruvian says is not identical with what Quevedo said. [*Claude Levi-Strauss: An Introduction* (New York: Dell, 1974), P. 148]

Elsewhere Paz speaks of historical contexts, saying that they do not serve as examples, but as stimuli. They awaken creative imagination and open up the possibilities of new combinations.

C. M. Bowra, in an essay prefacing *An Anthology of Mexican Poetry* (edited by Octavio Paz, translated by Samuel Beckett [Bloomington, Ind.: Indiana University Press, 1958]), has this to say:

> Traditions are delicate organisms and if they are treated too roughly they cease to do their right work. So if poetry breaks too violently with the past and conducts experiments in too reckless a spirit, it may well hurt itself. Indeed it is difficult not to think that something of this kind has happened in our own time, which has surely been rich in talent but has not quite produced the poetry demanded or deserved by our circumstances.

I suppose Bowra could be criticized for holding too conservative an attitude regarding tradition, but I find his remarks worth thinking about. In significant contrast to his and Paz's beliefs, North American poetry in the past several decades seems to have been marked by a continual burning of bridges, destruction of all links with the past. The result: no past, no tradition, no roots, and finally, perhaps, no poetry.

Our belief in historical continuity has broken down. In the words of someone reviewing a recent Indian history of the American West, " . . . we really don't know who we are, or where we have come from, or what we have done, or why." The meaning of our existence is in doubt. Our confusion takes many forms, and uncertainty about artistic values is only one of them. Beyond literature itself, we can expect to see any number of efforts toward political and economic renovation. We can also look for a revival of traditional religion with the animosities and mistaken boundaries that have warped it through the centuries. And these attempts will have increasingly a spirit of futility and exasperation as we come to feel their inadequacy. People will be turning anywhere for understanding and for solutions. And therein lies a great danger: the search for a rescuer, a hero who will lead us out of our predicament. In the political world this sort of person is not difficult to imagine; we have met him several times before in this century. When the order inherent in social and political structures begins to fail, what we are left with, as Jeffers saw and a hundred fallen kingdoms bear witness to, is power and the struggle for it.

One likely response to this state of things would be mindlessness—an inability or refusal to think at all except in immediate, pragmatic, and self-serving terms. The absence of intelligence in much contemporary writing, the widespread reliance on gut-reaction and crude forms, seems to say that many people have already taken this road and are satisfied to remain on it.

"Our minds are possessed by three mysteries: where we came from, where we are going, and since we are not alone, but members of a countless family, how we should live with one another." This statement of a theme by Edwin Muir seems to me still valid. It evokes for me something of the ancient high seriousness of poetry and storytelling, of instruction in life and death and the continuity of values. It seems to me to be consistent with a remark by Stevens that we can never have great poetry unless we believe that poetry serves great ends. That belief would lie at the heart of our practice of poetry, affecting everything that we do.

Poetry may regain its significance in this country when, in addition to resolving some of the difficulties outlined above, it becomes, as it has in other times and places, a less comfortable occupation; when the writing and publishing of a book of poems will be, as Stevens once described it, "a damned serious matter." This means, of course that, among other things, it will not be written or spoken where there are no others, but where an audience listens and believes.

DAVID IGNATOW

The Necessity of the Personal

"Forget all rules, forget all restrictions, as to taste, as to what ought to be said," wrote William Carlos Williams in an article, "How to Write," published in 1936.

> Write for the pleasure of it—whether slowly or fast—every form of resistance to a complete release should be abandoned. For today we know the meaning of depth, it is a primitive profundity of the personality that must be touched if what we do is to have it. The faculties untied, proceed backward through the night of our unconscious past. It goes down to the ritualistic, amoral past of the race, to fetish, to dream, to wherever the "genius" of the particular writer finds itself able to go.

Whether Williams's statement is or is not the direct cause, the proliferation of personal styles in American poetry today is unprecedented in scope and variety. It is virtually impossible to give a complete description without overlooking something new gestating in obscurity at that moment. Clearly, Williams's dictum, together with the more revolutionary impulse of that day, has had its effect upon the vast majority of American poets. In this talk, I shall limit my description to certain outstanding developments, without prejudice toward those others of equal importance that must be omitted for lack of space, or more to the point, because to describe them would actually parallel, at least in principle, those already described. At any rate, the theme of this talk, while it arises from this extraordinary diversity, is in my effort to go beyond that for an understanding of its significance for poetry as a whole.

To make a point by contrast, I begin with a discussion of the classical or traditional as practiced today. It has the grudging respect of the nonconformists for the stubbornness with which it is pursued by a small but steady island of poets, each of undoubted integrity in his or her chosen traditional mode. About that, it may even be said that it has served as a useful reference point of departure for others in the school of Williams and beyond. Of those continuing to identify with the classical forms and meters, I would name Anthony Hecht and Richard Wilbur among the most skillful and original. Their originality stems precisely from their adaptation of contemporary themes and tones to the demands of their particular imposed forms. I think it is a brave attempt to bridge an unbridgeable gulf. In their poems, the modern sensibility of horror, anger, and divisiveness has been given the formal dignity of an assumed order in things. Let me read you one poem by Anthony Hecht that illustrates this. It is titled, " 'It Out-Herods Herod. Pray You Avoid It.' "—a quotation from an Elizabethan play.

Tonight my children hunch
Toward their Western, and are glad
As, with a Sunday punch,
The Good casts out the Bad.

And in their fairy tales
The warty giant and witch
Get sealed in doorless jails
And the match-girl strikes it rich.

I've made myself a drink.
The giant and witch are set
To bust out of the clink
When my children have gone to bed.

All frequencies are loud
With signals of despair;
In flash and morse they crowd
The rondure of the air.

Their very fund of strength,
Satan, bestrides the globe;
He stalks its breadth and length
And finds out even Job.

Yet by quite other laws
My children make their case;
Half God, half Santa Claus,
But with my voice and face,

A hero comes to save
The poorman, beggarman, thief,
And make the world behave
And put an end to grief.

And that their sleep be sound
I say this childermas
Who could not, at one time,
Have saved them from the gas.

Here is a poem of almost total cynicism and despair, yet Hecht finds
it possible to seek for resolution in technical requirements alone, in
that the poem by tradition must be rounded off. The prayer in the
last stanza can only be construed as a premeditated token of helpless-
ness. Yet all is well defined and orderly as a poem. The logic in life,
death, and inhumanity relies upon the fulfillment of form. It is
poetry, in a sense, that has run through its life already. It lacks confi-
dence in any but the merest show of civilization, its outward form. It
is the abandonment of self in confrontation with the giant odds, yet
in its use of the traditional imposed form would demonstrate the
continued steadfastness and viability of the past for the present. I
can sympathize with this effort for what it is, an effort to make do. It
is the marginal approach to life for many of us who lack anything else
to rely on or with which to identify. Events are taken as they come in
the helplessness to do anything about it. Hecht's poetry reflects this
spirit, with a certain saving elegance. In their open, free forms, the
vast majority of American poets take enormous risks with the psy-
che. Endless traps confront them, as Williams himself warned and as
he experienced in his own continuous experimentation. The open
form, the do-your-own-thing, he would often write, looks so simple
and straightforward and so easily achieved through the mere abraca-
dabra of words and sentences, arbitrarily, it would seem, out of one's
hat. I shall take up this point again further on, in the conclusion to
this talk. Before going on to other styles, however, I would like to
note that Richard Wilbur, in the last poems of his I've read, appears
as an exceptional instance of a traditional poet making the unusual
effort to emerge in the direction of surrealism in free form.

At the extreme opposite pole of the Hecht poem is the single
word poem of Aram Saroyan. This style originates in the dada
movement of the post-World War I years, which, as with Williams,
had the aim of overthrowing the fixed and regulated in the arts. In
the case of dada, the aim was limited to presentations of the incon-
gruous and the accidental, that which was incommunicable by the
traditional rules of apprehension in a particular art. A Saroyan
poem, for example, could be simply the word "IS" in the middle of
a page. You might want to bring to it your past training and experi-
ence in poetry to assess the word as a poem, but Saroyan would
reject and ridicule your presumption to judge his poem on the basis
of your past training. It is *now* and it needs an entirely new ap-
proach, born of *now*, he would charge. You too are *now*, in all your

confusions and urges and unformed ideas. You are IS. Williams would agree absolutely with this position, but would go on doing his own thing.

Between the extremes of dada and of formalism, and somehow absorbing the influences of both, is the poetry of Robert Creeley, one distinguished example. I would characterize his work as deeply *present* in tone. The language moves sparingly, almost discretely, as if the words were without connection each to each, filled with their own hesitance and tentativeness. This affecting poetry is a paradigm of the modern dilemma of our failure in relationships, and yet, as poetry, never lacks communication, especially in theme. At the conclusion of a particular poem, a kind of formality emerges, the inner personal dignity shaped by the movement and resolution of Creeley's thoughts. It's a poetry that has inspired a generation of younger poets to follow in its path.

A Reason

Each gesture
is a common one, a
black dog, crying, a
man, crying.

All alike, people
or things grow
fixed with what
happens to them.

I throw a stone.
It hits a wall,
it hits a dog,
it hits a child—

my sentimental
names for years
and years ago, from
something I've not become.

If I look
in the mirror,
the wall, I
see myself.

If I try
to do better
and better, I
do the same thing.

Let me hit you.
Will it hurt.
Your face is hurt
all the same.

To the left of Creeley, stylistically, is the poetry of Robert Bly. Here is work charged with huge awakening dreams, archetypal in character. It was meant that way. Like Creeley's work, it too looks for hidden or missing links to one's identity, but in the applied Jungian mode of the collective unconscious. Here is one recent example.

Two Together

You open your mouth, I put my tongue in,
And this universe-thing begins!
Our tongues together are two seagulls whirling
        high above the Great Lakes,
Two jellyfish floating under a Norwegian moon!

Suddenly we are with the fallen leaves
        blowing along the soaked roads,
My hand closes so firmly around you
And I feel the sea rising and falling
        as I go ashore—

We are whirling together
        head down through oceans of space,
We are two turtles with wings,
We roll like tumbleweeds through the mother-air
        hurrying through the universe.

It's as mysterious after being read as before. It is wild and exciting, and yet its robust images and sounds are an assurance to us and to the poet of their beauty and goodness. Notice that the images are markedly discrete, one from the other, the connections left for the reader to make through overtones that arise in reading one image after the other. The principle is the same as that used by Creeley, and by Saroyan *in extremis,* but as language far exceeds anything that Creeley or Saroyan would attempt—or for that matter, even Williams, who advocated a primitive return. Bly's work has attracted an increasingly large following among new and more established poets in search of a way out—for example—of the negative humanism of Anthony Hecht's poetry.

We come next to the pattern poetry of Richard Kostelanetz, one of the more attractive poets in this style. It is related to the one word poem of Aram Saroyan, but Kostelanetz seeks to enhance and enlarge upon the word by shaping it on paper according to its actual signification. For example, the word DISINTEGRATION is shown in successive stages of disintegration on the page. In effect, it nullifies the point of Saroyan's method and is actually a restatement of a style of writing as ancient as the earliest extant writing discovered. In practice, though, it derives from the Chinese ideogram introduced into American poetry by Ezra Pound. The Kostelanetz poem is also intimately connected with the very popular trend called concrete poetry. Kostelanetz would rather not call his work concrete, but it does have affinities, at least in principle. For example, in the word concrete itself, each letter could be shown on the page carved out of a huge block of masonry.

I'd like now to describe several styles that have grown principally out of their relationship to the conversational and to discourse. In a highly specialized sense, they are influenced by Williams's style, but Whitman is at the root of these developments—for Williams also. I refer first to the witty anecdotal poetry of Paul Blackburn. This hardly expresses the range of information, scholarly and experiential, that goes into these graceful lines. Blackburn is one of the leading authorities on Provençal poetry and thinking, but his own poetry is filled with daily intimate concerns, and their flavor of adventure and delight. Next in the poetry deriving from the art of the conversational is the para-ritual writing of Armand Schwerner. In his poems, the use of the conversational on all levels, fine, coarse, and explosive, is a deliberate effort to evoke an image of primitive man, man exposed to all the hazards of nature and to his own mystery. It is man conceived of in the beginning of his awareness, and his language projects just those primal confusions, awes, terrors, wonders, joys, and dawning insights, though not the physical deprivations and degradations to which he was then subject. This poetry probably is the farthest extension yet of Williams's dictum of the primitive, as it is basically oral poetry, but it has its sophistications and an ironical sense to it also. Schwerner's chief work, titled *The Tablets*, is among other things a parody, if not an absolute burlesque, of scholarly, intellectual presumptiveness. An authority in anthropological research also serves as the butt. Schwerner is ridiculing the sort of detachment from reality, the so-called objectivity in academic communities, against which Williams fought so vigorously during his lifetime. This, though, is only one phase of *The Tablets,* and a means to a much more embracing, earthy celebration of life, at times wildly funny, more often embarrassing to our own hypocritical conditions.

We come next to the nonsequential Gertrude-Stein-like poetry of John Ashbery and Jerome Rothenberg, in which the phrases and sentences in common use among us are literally torn apart and placed in arbitrary relationships to one another, without regard to the intent of their original use. Now neither of these poets has any direct, perceptible relationship to the work or ideas of Williams or Whitman, and their poetry would seem to be the very opposite. Williams, in calling for a return to the primitive and unknowable in his poems, maintained the clarity of his surfaces. For Rothenberg and Ashbery, this clarity is the obstacle to their purposes. For example, the following passages from a sequence called "Sightings" by Jerome Rothenberg. A dot separates each sentence, and each sentence is on a line by itself, with the object of creating a silent pause between each. I will read the whole of "Sightings I."

He hides his heart.
.
A precious arrangement of glass and flowers.
.
They have made a covenant between them, the
circumstance of being tried.
.
Who will signal you?
.
It doesn't open to their touch though some
wait where it rests.
.
Try sleep.
.
The emblem perhaps of a herd of elephants—as signal
for a change of weather.
.
Animal.
.
A pigeon dreaming of red flowers.

In this sequence, Rothenberg would induce us to see new possibilities in ordinary sentences through an arrangement among them never before contemplated, with the purpose of lifting the ordinary and expected to a hitherto unexplored dimension of experience. It returns to the nonrational in us and rejects the cause and effect portrayal of reality to which we have been conditioned. Rothenberg's poems would replace this reality with an existence to him infinitely more complex and true than has been projected in the linear logic of our sciences and philosophies. Ultimately, the world of the subjective, the dark, the unformed and unpredictable to which he is urging us, is what he would name as the one certifiable reality in us all.

Among others writing from this perspective is David Antin. His wry manipulations expose the absurdity of relying on language itself for our grasp of reality. Jackson MacLow can be placed in relationship to Antin for his use of random techniques. This method employs words arbitrarily through chance selections from—for example—a dictionary opened with the eyes closed. In a poem published by MacLow in issue number 4–5 of the magazine *Some/Thing*, he has assembled a whole series of words, including nouns, adjectives, verbs, and participles, each through an intricate reasoning process derived from a musical score by Beethoven, *Bagatelle in B Minor, Op. 126*. Among those words and participles are "plate," "yearning," "generally," "generals," "felt," "platter." The poem is divided into seventy-two sections to correspond to the seventy-two measures in the Presto section of *Bagatelle*.

1. The plate?
   A plate.

2. The plate ("a" plate?)
   generally
   felt like a "plate": generally?
   Generally.

3. Forty plates yearning,
   in general, for generals,
   yearning for forty
   generals, plateless generals,
   or ones who plateless felt.

4. If plateless, the generals felt
   (& generally,
   they felt, those generals, "plateless")
   was the generals' yearning
   felt?

This is not altogether a spoof of language and meaning. In fact, very wittily, the play on these random words has produced a comment on a particular point of view, and it may be concluded from the above that words can be made to say whatever you wish them to say, which falls in line with Antin's inferences, but the accidental and the incongruous of the dada movement are the keystones to this method. The results, though, are very different from the original plan. MacLow is saying something with which we can communicate instantly through our training and experience in past literatures. The difference from the past traditions is that MacLow is allowing himself full freedom of his mind to go where it will, in full confidence of the final results. The unconscious comes into play here equally with the unconscious of Robert Bly or Armand Schwerner, but of the order of MacLow's temperament and momentary disposition. The poem is actually metaphysical in tone and intent. I know I am raising questions in your minds by making such a flat statement about a revered intellectual tradition in connection with MacLow's ostensible confusion. I shall take up these questions along with others as the conclusion to my talk. I do want to go on to several more kinds of poetry circulating widely in this country, and having reputation outside the country too. Before going on, though, I want to comment briefly on the poetry of John Ashbery, who shares in the principles of Rothenberg, Antin, and MacLow, but enters a darkening area of experience, truly impenetrable and frightening in its most concentrated form. Here is a short poem in illustration.

Last Month

No changes of support—only
Patches of gray, here where sunlight fell.
The house seems heavier
Now that they have gone away.
In fact it emptied in record time.
When the flat table used to result
A match recedes, slowly, into the night.
The academy of the future is
Opening its doors and willing
The fruitless sunlight streams into domes,
The chairs piled high with books and papers.

The sedate one is this month's skittish one
Confirming the property that,
A timeless value, has changed hands.
And you could have a new automobile
Ping pong set and garage, but the thief
Stole everything like a miracle.
In his book there was a picture of treason only
And in the garden, cries and colors.

Note that the linear thinking here, beyond the first few sentences, suddenly and inextricably veers off to give one a disoriented sense. It's as if one had been deliberately led down a path to enter a sudden maze, from which one is never to extricate oneself. The tone of self-assurance with which the poem proceeds in its baffling text becomes ominous for our own state of mind. Ashbery has a significant following among poets of a surrealist disposition in their own work.

A rather charming kind of poetry being "made" today, partaking of dada principles and the Williams free form, is that of the "found" poem. Here the poet takes a word, a sentence, a whole paragraph from magazines, books, newspapers, and advertising matter, without discernible relationship among them, and puts them together on a single page according to his or her insight into them as a group. All together, they say something different to us from their original purpose in print. It is a poet discovering possibilities for the sake of possibility. In other words, he is exercising his poetic talent for metaphor, relating the unrelated in unexpected, illuminating ways.

I am going to conclude this part of my talk by limiting myself to a group of the more notable styles that have caught on in this country and can be found in many anthologies and magazines. I am referring to a group of poets directly affected by Williams's own style. Its effect upon the poet is marked, though each poet's voice is distinctly his or her own. In this regard, Denise Levertov's work holds a central position. Confronting observed phenomena, she penetrates to their spiritual significance for her, much in accordance with Williams's own practice. Charles Reznikoff's objective presentations are straightforward comments upon themselves through subtle arrangements of their details. There is the intellectual dance among the parts by Louis Zukofsky, especially in his chief later work *A*, that is still in progress. There is George Oppen's definitive power and Harvey Shapiro's depths of somberness and elegiac control; the nature poetry of Gary Snyder, the jazz prosody of Ted Joans, the black folk idiom of Lucille Clifton, the city ironies of David Henderson, the jeremiads of LeRoi Jones, the exuberant metaphors of Simon Perchik. The poetry of Allen Ginsberg, Robert Lowell, Galway Kinnell, Louis Simpson, John Berryman, and W. S. Merwin, to name a few of the more prominent, has been described and discussed knowingly and at length elsewhere by others—some of these poets also owing a debt to Williams, others hardly so. But everyone in this vast, ever proliferating diversification serves to emphasize over and over the deeply subjective phenomenon among us called poetry, and all of it, by tacit understanding among the poets themselves, accepted as poetry.

How could this be, we ask, with each poet so much himself, uniquely different in makeup and point of view from the others? I am talking about the open, free form and the dada influence in their infinite variety. For the reader alone it could be a baffling experience, leading him to contrary and conflicting opinions about poems vastly different from each other. Obviously, this tacit understanding among the poets is in rejection of any objective criterion for poetry. But do we actually have an objective criterion? This is the question I have raised in my discussion of the numerous styles developed by poets with roots in the dada and free form movements.

There is no objective criterion for the judgment of poetry. An Anthony Hecht might insist on a technical basis for his own grounds, but as we have seen, these grounds have been rejected by American poets as a whole, among whom we can count national prize winners, university professors, and poets with international reputation. There is no objective criterion as such for the judgment of the truly contemporary poem, certainly not in the traditional sense that a poem must adhere to a set of rules before it can be judged for the proficiency of its conduct. How then can we examine the work being done in the name of poetry? How can we praise that which is done? Are we in a dilemma? What criterion are we using in praising the poets today and encouraging them in their efforts? For me, the question simply returns to the first underlying principle in modern poetry since before T. S. Eliot, and in agreement with him—precisely the principle which puts Eliot and Williams in secret affinity with each other. This is the principle stated by Williams in his 1936 article, from which I have already quoted, "How to Write," and which, unquestionably, was not an original discovery with him either, given the intellectual climate of the 1920s in which he matured.

The subjective is all that is real for the person, meaning each and every one of us. In the poem, it is the expression of one's reality, something we must respect at once. There is no contravening another person's sense of himself and his world. We must accept it on his terms, though we need not accept it for ourselves. But this is not an impasse in the art of poetry. It is actually a fantastic discovery of unlimited possibilities. Men and women have discovered themselves as individuals, and that this sense of individuality is something shared among them as a way of life. Paradoxically, it is a way of life that leads to community. In affirming themselves, they affirm all the others. It is the discovery of free relationships within community. But how do we derive poetry from this discovery? Poetry, as I see it, is formed by the terms with which the person sees himself. These are terms embodied in his poems. They are the terms by which he lives and by which his poems must gain their authenticity, first of all. They are terms as they originate in and flow from insights into his life; and this is no different from what Wallace Stevens, a contemporary of Williams and a friend, has said in his book, *Ideas of Order*—to paraphrase, What the imagination does with the reality we are is the reality we live by. Let me quote the last six lines of a poem, "The Truth," by Pablo Neruda, the greatest of the South American poets, and counted among the greatest in the world.

> speak your secret in secret;
> and to truth: never withhold what you know
> lest you harden the truth in a lie.
>
> I am no one's establishment. I administer
> nothing: it suffices to cherish
> the equivocal cut of my song.

Doesn't this remind you of Whitman? Well, Neruda has named Whitman as the father of his inspiration from the very start. No doubt, the point I have raised as to the authenticity and wholeness of modern poetry is complicated, but its principles are clear: they are rooted in being. As individuals, we live unto ourselves. This has been forced on us by our divided and conflicting culture. As poets, then, we affirm ourselves as persons. As with everyone else, it is vitally important that we know who we are and where we are in a society that is in constant motion and counter motion. To be caught up in this conflict without a firm grasp of oneself is to invite destruction, indiscriminate and impersonal. This is what each of us refuses to let happen, and so the poet, reacting in like manner, makes that effort to be identified with himself and others. He does it with the poem. He sets himself apart from his society and its maelstrom in the poem. He distinguishes himself from the threatening chaos with the poem that says who he is, what he is thinking. The reader finds a distinct life style in the work, a sense of self separate from and in relation to the environment. The poet cannot be confused with anyone else. He has absorbed his time and place, and yet retains his own identity. It is the affirmation of being. It is the principle of free form.

This is the mind of the serious poet, and it separates him decisively from all previous traditions in the history of his art. It has links with the dada movement but goes beyond it in affirming once more an order to things—but in one's own being. It affirms the power and uniqueness of the person. It emphasizes the individual as judge of his own acts, including his art. It forces others to look upon his acts and his art in terms of his own making. At the same time, it makes the poet responsible for the integrity of his poems in terms of his being. This is the principle by which the contemporary poem may be judged for its value as a poem, in my view. It is consistent with the autonomy of the person as poet and makes both reader and writer search out, each for himself, that inner coherence which is the mark of the free form.

As a principle, it is not easy to live up to steadily for the poet, nor is it any easier for the reader to apply, for all his patience and empathy with the poet and his poems. A tragic example of such a relationship was the one between Ralph Waldo Emerson and Walt Whitman. It is to Whitman that we owe this principle of the autonomy of the poet, but Emerson in his later years found it impossible to accept, after having hailed Whitman in the early years as the genius he was looking for in American letters. Whitman in his later poems had become even more explicitly himself, to Emerson's horror. In 1876, compiling a comprehensive anthology of American poets then writing, Emerson deliberately left out Whitman. Through all of Emerson's complaints about him ran the recurrent one about Whitman's supposedly obscene self-exposure in the later poems, against all canons of society. Whitman refused to accommodate himself to those canons by cutting or omitting the offensive poems, and Emerson disowned him. Today there is even less room than before for accommodation. First of all, we have discovered that we ourselves are this society and, as such, we cannot compromise without bringing disaster upon ourselves and the country which is ours. We must persevere and maintain ourselves on this high level of commitment. We no longer have a choice. As poets, we are making our own destiny. It no longer can be imposed on us from outside, as in the past. Influences there will always be, but to be used at our discretion. There once was a call among American critics for that epic poet who would tell the story of this country straight and whole. That story is being told now, poet by poet, a clear, loud, and very powerful truth.

1971

LOUIS SIMPSON

Reflections on Narrative Poetry

Why tell stories in lines of verse? Isn't prose a more suitable medium?

It would be, if poets only had ideas and wished to convey them. But feeling is more urgent, and their feelings are expressed by the movement of lines. In poetry the form, more than the idea, creates the emotion we feel when we read the poem.

In everything else poets share the concerns of the writer of prose, and may indeed learn more about writing narrative poems from the novelist than from other poets, for in the past two hundred years it has been the novelist whose labor it was to imitate life, while the poet prided himself on his originality, his remoteness from the everyday. "Life" was the business of the middle class and the novelists who entertained it.

As a result, poetry has been impoverished. In the theory of poetry held by Poe and his French translators, poetry is lyrical and intense, the reflection of an unearthly beauty. Many people believe that poetry is a language we do not speak, and that the best poetry is that which we are least able to understand.

I wish to discuss another kind of poetry, that which undertakes to be an imitation of life. The aim of the narrative poet is the same as for the writer of prose fiction: to interpret experience, with the difference I have mentioned: his writing will move in measure. And this measure evokes a harmony that seems apart from life. I say "seems" because it would be impossible to prove that it exists. Readers of poetry, however, feel it. This harmony is what poetry is, as distinct from prose.

Let us learn from the novelist, however, how to deal with the world, for it is his specialty. We may learn from Chekhov, and Conrad, and Joyce . . . and a hundred other writers of fiction. I see no reason that a poet should not take notes, as prose writers do, or write out his story first in prose. I believe that Yeats sometimes worked in this way.

I once read an interview with a poet in which she spoke contemptuously of "subject-seeking" poets. It was Charles Olson's teaching, I believe, that the poet should not have a subject but should put himself into a dynamic relationship with the environment, and poetry would rise out of this. But when I read the books of the poet who was so down on subject-seekers, I found that her own poems always had a subject. In fact, she could be all too explicit, writing about her family or writing poems with a political message. Either she was deceived about the nature of her writing or felt that she could dispense with the rule she had made for others.

There are kinds of poetry that seem visionary, having little resemblance to life. But even these rely on images, and the images, however farfetched, have points of contact with our experience. The room envisioned by Rimbaud at the bottom of a lake is still a room. But I shall not insist on the point. Let us admit that there are kinds of poetry that are not representations of life. This does not concern us: we are speaking of narrative poetry. This has to do with actions and scenes. The action may be subtle, the scene barely sketched, but the aim is to move the reader, and to increase understanding, by touching the springs of nature.

But it is not enough to hold a mirror up to nature. As Henry James says in the preface to *The Spoils of Poynton*, "Life has no direct sense whatever for the subject and is capable, luckily for us, of nothing but splendid waste. Hence the opportunity for the sublime economy of art."

So you take what you need and rearrange it, and you invent. Invention is supposed to be the sine qua non of the so-called creative arts. It is what people usually mean when they use the word "imagination." The poet, says Longinus, thinks that he sees what he describes, and so is able to place it before the eyes of the reader.

Yes, of course. But I wonder how useful this description is to the man who does the job? It may actually do more harm than good, by urging the writer to strain his powers of invention. Rather than try to work himself up to a pitch of imagination, the poet would do well to discover what is there, in the subject. Let him immerse himself in the scene and wait for something to happen . . . the right, true thing.

"There can be," says James, "evidently, only one logic for these things; there can be for [the writer] only one truth and one direction—the quarter in which his subject most completely expresses itself."

So you choose the direction that has the most to offer. Some writers, however, are unwilling to go so far. It is instructive to take up a book of poems and see, with every poem, which direction the poet has chosen to take. Some poets take the easiest direction, an ending that will please most people. The sad thing about these poets is that they don't please anyone very much: for all their attempts to be good-natured the public will desert them for some poet whose writing is obscure and who seems to despise them. The mob does not admire those who flatter it—at any rate, not for long. They know they are only a mob and reserve their admiration for those who tell them so.

One day you were stopped on the street corner by an old panhandler. While the lights were changing and people scurrying by, he told you his story.

He served in Mexico with "Black Jack" Pershing, over forty years ago. He had a wife who was unfaithful. One day he followed her and confronted her with it. "Baby," he said, "I'm wise to you and the lieutenant."

A few days later you wrote a poem about it, trying to describe a Mexican landscape and evoke the atmosphere. But something was missing.

It was not until you asked yourself why you were interested that the story began to move. The account of his following touched upon some unease in your soul. The rest was merely scaffolding: you were not interested in the landscape or the history of the time. But the tale of jealousy affected you . . . you could imagine yourself in his shoes.

But though poetry rises out of feeling, the poem is not just personal. You could put yourself in the old man's shoes . . . you saw yourself following a woman through a lane in the dust and heat. But, and this is my point, you *saw* . . . you were a character in the story. Your feelings had been separated from yourself. You were therefore able to make them move in one direction or another. You were writing a poem to be read by others, not just getting a feeling out of your system.

Storytelling is an impersonal kind of art, even when the story appears to be about oneself. The "I" who appears in the poem is a dramatic character. "Je est un *autre*."

In recent years there was talk of "confessional poetry." Robert Lowell and Sylvia Plath, among others, were said to be confessional poets—that is, to be writing directly about their lives. But when we read the poems in *Life Studies* and *Ariel* we find that the incidents they relate have been shaped so as to make a point. The protagonist is seen as on a stage. In confessional poetry, on the other hand, there is no drama. The drama is not in the poem but outside it, in a life we cannot share.

I would advise the poet to be as objective about himself as possible. In this way you will not be locked into the treadmill of your own personal history, treading the same stairs again and again.

For twenty years there has been an outpouring of subjective art. There was a generation that believed that poetry should be nothing more than an expression of the poet's feelings. "Why talk about art? Be sincere and tell it like it is."

That was an unhappy generation. They could never advance beyond themselves. It is ironic that, at the same time that they were abolishing art, they complained of a lack of understanding. For art is a key to understanding.

Everyone has feelings—indeed it is impossible not to feel. But we need to understand one another. Scripture tells us that all the ways of a man are right in his own eyes but the Lord pondereth the hearts. The ways of the poet James Merrill must surely be right in his own eyes, and I cannot explain my aversion to his style except as an aversion to the personality it presents. The style is the man.

> Tap on the door and in strolls Robert Morse,
> Closest of summer friends in Stonington.
> (The others are his Isabel, of course,
>
> And Grace and Eleanor—to think what fun
> We've had throughout the years on Water Street . . .)
> He, if no more the youthful fifty-one
>
> Of that first season, is no less the complete
> Amateur. Fugue by fugue Bach's honeycomb
> Drips from his wrist—then, whoops! the Dolly Suite.

What else can one possibly say on this subject? There is one thing: one can say, as an absolute rule, that poets must not use words loosely.

When I was a young man I wrote a poem in which I said that poetry had made me "nearly poor." I showed this to a friend, himself a writer, and he advised me to change "nearly poor" to "poor"—it would be more striking. I kept the line as it was, and never again did I pay attention to anything this critic had to say. A man who does not know the difference between being nearly poor and being poor, or who is willing to disregard it in order to make a better-sounding line, is not to be trusted. A man like that would say anything.

Since we have moved away from standard forms, the movement of the line, also, depends on the movement of the poet's soul, how he feels, and thinks, and breathes. As late as the 1950s American poets were expected to write in meter and rhyme. And a few years ago there was talk of songwriters' bringing about a renaissance of rhyme. But there has been no talk of this lately. Most American poets write free verse. This may fall into groups of lines that make a repeating pattern, but the pattern is still irregular. I do not know of any poet who writes in regular forms—meter, stanza, and rhyme— with the assurance of Robert Lowell and Richard Wilbur thirty years ago.

I believe that we shall continue to write free verse of one kind and another, and that it is possible to write a sustained narrative in free verse just as effectively as though it were written in hexameters or the meters used by Walter Scott. The long narrative poem by Patrick Kavanagh titled "The Great Hunger" is a case in point. It moves just as well as writing in rhyme and meter, and, moreover, echoes the speech of a modern world, which meter and rhyme cannot.

I can see no reason for writing in the old forms of verse. Finding the form for the poem as one writes is half the joy of poetry.

Poets try to think of new images. But it does not matter whether the image be new or old—what matters is that it be true. Poets who think that by producing farfetched images they are changing our consciousness are doing nothing of the kind. One comes to expect the unexpected.

As the painter Magritte points out, everyone is familiar with a bird in a cage. Anyone can visualize a fish in a cage, or a shoe. But these images, though they are curious, are, unfortunately, arbitrary and accidental. If you wish to surprise, alarm, and alert the reader on the deeper levels of consciousness, visualize a large egg in the cage.

"There exists a secret affinity between certain images; it holds equally for the objects represented by those images."

One writes, refusing temptations, sailing past the siren voices. Are the lines about morphology really necessary? What worked for another may not work for you. All sorts of ideas come into a writer's head, but only some are in keeping with his nature, his way of saying a thing.

Imagine that you are reading your poem aloud, and that two or three people whose intelligence you respect are sitting in the audience. If you say something banal, or try to conceal a poverty of thought in a cloud of verbiage, you will see them yawn, their eyes beginning to close.

If you visualize an audience you won't go in for merely descriptive writing. It was description that killed the narrative poem in the nineteenth century. Think of the long poems of Tennyson or Swinburne. What was it the Victorians found in all that scenery? Perhaps it had something to do with sex. The shopkeepers who ruled Western Europe and, later, the United States, couldn't tolerate talk of sex in their houses. But the woods were loaded with naked bums and flying feet.

Since movies were invented we have had no time for descriptions of scenery and for long drawn-out transitions. Nor for the working-out of an obvious plot. And still this kind of poetry continues to be written. The history of the conquistadors and wagon trains are favorite subjects. Sometimes these volumes are handsomely bound—American publishers are incurable optimists, they hope for another *John Brown's Body,* but what they are more likely to get is the equivalent of the Thanksgiving play, with scenes of the Pilgrim Fathers—the parts being taken by members of the town council—Red Indians, the minister and the minister's wife, and the farmhand and his girl. It ends with bringing on a cow and baskets heaped with corn and pumpkins. Perhaps this is what people have in mind when they warn us of the danger of having a subject.

I have been reading an article on prose fiction in which the writer says that, without anyone's noticing, we have entered upon a new period of realism. I believe this to be true, and true of poetry as well.

"Most artists and critics," said Susan Sontag, writing in the sixties, "have discarded the theory of art as representation of an outer reality in favor of art as subjective expression."

Critics define movements in art just as they come to an end. For twenty years we have been reading poetry that expressed the personal feelings and opinions of the poet. The movement is exhausted—this is apparent in the visual arts as well as poetry and fiction. People long for understanding and a community of some kind.

The word "realism" can be misleading. I do not mean reporting, but writing that penetrates beneath the surface to currents of feeling and thought. Not Champfleury but Flaubert.

I do not know a better way to explain my ideas than by showing how I have applied them. I shall therefore end with a poem.

The images have the affinities Magritte speaks of, though I do not think I should point them out—to do so would take away the pleasure of reading, for myself as well as the reader. I may point out, however, that realism allows for fantastic images and ideas . . . but they have a reason for being. The landscape that suddenly appears in the poem . . . the old man sitting with his back to the wall, the woman who appears in a doorway . . . are in the mind of one of the characters.

TESS GALLAGHER

The Poem as Time Machine

Once, at an auction in upstate New York, I watched two men carry a mahogany box with a crank handle onto the lawn. One of the men turned the lever until he was satisfied and then put a large black disk into the box and opened the front of the box so the little doors, spread wide, made the whole contraption seem as though it might fly away. But instead, a chorus of voices, recorded many years before, scratched and muted by all that intervening time and space, drifted out over the crowd.

Before anyone in our group knew what I was doing, I had signaled my way to ownership and the two men were approaching us carrying the Victrola, its record still turning above their heads.

In hearing the phonograph I had not forgotten life in the jet age; in fact, the simultaneity of jets and hand-wound phonographs had only amplified my amazement with both inventions. A few months before, I had been in Iowa; then in hours I was in New York. The morning of the auction I had spoken by telephone with my parents on the West Coast. That night I would watch a TV news reporter in Egypt, another in Israel. Still, all these inventions for transcending time and distance had not kept me from the original magic of the phonograph music. I did not exclaim: "See how they used to do it," but rather: "Voices out of a flat disk, human voices singing out of a mahogany box!" I was like an astronaut dropped suddenly into my own moment.

I remember the day my father came home from the neighbors' in 1949 and said they had a radio with talking pictures. It was his way of explaining television to us in terms of what he knew: radio. Several years later I would sit on the rug with half a dozen neighborhood kids at the house down the block, watching Flash Gordon and advertisements for Buster Brown shoes.

Such early space-travel films may have marked my first encounter with the idea of time machines, those phone booths with the capacity to transport one into encounters with Napoleon or to propel one ahead into dilemmas on distant planets. I was six or seven years old and already leading a double life as an imagined horse disguised as a young girl. I had long brown hair and a young friend named Koene Rasanen who suffered from the same delusions, which were, oddly, tolerated by our parents. There were several ridges behind my house which our horse-selves delighted in. Some of my freest moments still exist in those images of myself standing silhouetted on the highest knoll, pawing with one foot, tossing my thick pony mane and neighing for my friend with such authority that a real horse pastured down the block began to answer me.

To be called to the house to run errands or peel potatoes for dinner was to suffer a temporary malfunction of the time machine. Adults were those creatures who had suffered permanent malfunctions. If you neighed at them, they put it down to a sexual phase, or took it as a practical cue to shop for a horse.

When I got my first horse, at age ten, it was strangely unsatisfying. Already that exchange of the real object for the imagined embodiment had begun to disinherit me. I hadn't wanted a horse to ride, I had wanted to *be* a horse, and had, in the nearest human proximity, managed it.

Flash Gordon never became a horse by stepping into a time machine, but he could choose any one of countless masquerades at crucial moments in history or in the futures he hoped to outsmart. The whole idea of past or future being accessible at the push of a button seemed so natural to me as a child that I have been waiting for science to catch up to the idea ever since.

In the meantime, there have been a few wonderful gimmicks— Polaroid cameras and even Polaroid movie cameras: instruments built to surprise the moment by reproducing it as close to its occurrence as possible, thereby extending the past-as-present, a spectator's present at that. So we have Mother tying the bow in Polly's hair. And if we like, we can run the film backward and untie Polly's hair. We have then an ongoing past as a spectator's present.

With the country in a state of constant mobility, we depend more than ever on telephones to keep friends who have been left behind at the last outpost. We can be in immediate touch. Two disparate people living in the "now" may hook up across the miles, talking their pasts into the present up to that point where the pie is burning in the oven or where someone has knocked on the door. We may hurtle the body through space into exotic places on jets. It costs a lot *not* to be where you're expected to be . . . that trip you took to get away from the familiar faces, those phone calls you charged to make up for having forgotten those people who are truly living too far away to be held constantly in mind. Already we are shaking ghosts like shaking hands, meeting ourselves as hasbeens where we stand.

I can still see Mark Strand shuffling the poems on his knees in a classroom in Seattle, Washington, in 1970 and saying in that ironic, ghost-ship voice of his: "Time, that's the *only* problem."

Octavio Paz defined the poet's time as "living for each day; and living it, simultaneously, in two contradictory ways: as if it were endless and as if it would end right now." Stanley Kunitz has written a poem entitled "Change," which gives this dual sense of impermanence and the desire to be eternal. He also includes memory as it comments upon the present moment, often painfully.

> Dissolving in the chemic vat
> Of time, man (gristle and fat),
> Corrupting on a rock in space
> That crumbles, lifts his impermanent face
> To watch the stars, his brain locked tight
> Against the tall revolving night.
> Yet is he neither here nor there
> Because the mind moves everywhere;
> And he is neither now or then
> Because tomorrow comes again
> Foreshadowed, and the ragged wing
> Of yesterday's remembering
> Cuts sharply the immediate moon;
> Nor is he always: late and soon
> Becoming, never being, till
> Becoming is a being still.
>
> Here, Now, and Always, man would be
> Inviolate eternally:
> This is his spirit's trinity.

Always, as a maker of poems, I have been witness to the images, have been led by the poem as it speaks into and with itself and opens out of its contradictions to engage the reader. But the reader is also the maker of the poem as it lives again in his consciousness, his needs, his reception, and even his denials. The poem is in a state of perpetual formation and disintegration. It is not at the mercy of pure subjectivity, but, as Ortega y Gasset would say, it is "the intersection of the different points of view." This, then, brings about a succession of interpretations of which no single one, even that of the poet, is the definitive one. In this way the poem enters and *becomes* time. It becomes, as Paz phrases it, "the space that is energy itself, not a container but an engenderer, a catalytic arena open on all sides to the past, on all sides to the future."

This conception of time as an atmosphere, as the "now" of the poem, which Paz calls "the Historical Now" or "the Archetypal Now," is what I would like to call "the point of all possibilities." By this I mean the point at which anything that has happened to me, or any past that I can encourage to enrich my own vision, is allowed to intersect with a present moment, as in a creation, as in a poem. And its regrets or expectations or promises or failures or any supposition I can bring to it may give significance to this moment which is the language moving in and out of my life and my life as it meets and enters the lives of others.

"Poems," says Paz, "search for the you." In America we begin to ask who will colonize the "I," that island of cannibals, of separations, of endings and be-alls, of my-turn, or better-than-you, of privilege and sweat-of-the-brow rectitude, of I own this and you own that, homeland of the civilized heartbreak where, if you leave, I shall get along anyway, I shall do perfectly well without you. There are others and others and you will not be one of them, where if your coat were drowning, I would not save it. No, the "I" without its search for the "you"—either by implication as the "I" in each of us or in a direct reaching toward the other—this "I," whose reaching *in* is not at the same time a reaching *out,* is like a character in a novel who is running on empty. We cannot long be interested in its roadside reveries, its monologues with the vast interiors. Even if you are speaking to a "you" that will not listen, it is better than no "you" at all. This includes the "you" that is the self, of course, but as "other." We remember Yeats speaking endlessly to Maud Gonne; Emily Dickinson talking to Death as if to a suitor; Hamlet confiding in a skull; Colette, who, when her mother died, saw no reason to stop writing letters to her.

The time of the "I" is expanded when it considers the "you," and perhaps the time the poem makes allows us to find courage for the risks yet to be taken in our "walking-around" lives. The poem not only makes time, it *is* time; it is made of time as is the bee who dances out the directions that are and are not the map of a place, but the remembering of a way back to the flower feast that belongs to others, to the hive, and to the very moment in which that way is given.

I have, in a poem, called a man back from the dead if he has not answered me fully in life. Yeats, in "He Wishes His Beloved Were Dead," even rushes ahead of a death to gain the right urgency in which he might be granted forgiveness.

> Were you but lying cold and dead,
> And lights were paling out of the West,
> You would come hither, and bend your head,
> And I would lay my head on your breast;
> And you would murmur tender words,

Forgiving me, because you were dead:
Nor would you rise and hasten away,
Though you have the will of the wild birds,
But know your hair was bound and wound
About the stars and moon and sun.

The time of the poem is not linear, is not the time of "this happened, then this, then this," though I may speak in that way until I am followed and the language leads me out of its use into its possibilities. No one is buried so deeply in the past that he may not enter the moment of the poem, the point of all possibilities where the words give breath, in a reimagining. If the language of commerce is a parade, then the language of the poem is that of a hive where one may be stung into recognition by words that have the power to create images strong enough to change our own lives as we imagine and live them. The poet between poems is like a child called into the house to peel potatoes for supper. The time of the house is enigma to him. He cannot wait to be out the door again. *Time Is a River without Banks* is the title of Chagall's painting of the winged fish flying through the air above the river. The fish is playing a fiddle above a clock which flies with it. In order to indicate the river there are houses and lovers and the reflections of houses. The lovers are not looking up. They are in love and at the point of all possibilities. They have transcended time, which is all around them like the unheard music of the fiddle.

It is the poet who refuses to believe in time as a container, who rushes into the closed room of time, who plunges through the bay window and slashes a hand across the harp, even if what results is not music so much as a passionate desecration of a moment, which, like the photograph in its effort to fix us, excludes us from our own past. The poet is always the enemy of the photograph. If she talks about her own appearance in the group smiling on the porch, she will inch her thumb into the lens to indicate that she has escaped. She will assault the image with words, changing the bride's dress into a cascade of petals. She will make sure the train pulls away from the platform.

The poem as time machine works in an opposite way from the time machine as used in H. G. Wells. In the latter, one is sent out like a lonely projectile into time past or future, casting the present into a future or a past. The poem, on the other hand, is like a magnet which draws into it events and beings from all possible past, present, and future contexts of the speaker. It is a vortex of associative phenomena. "A baby is crying. / In the swaddling-pages / a baby," says Bill Knott. " 'Don't cry. No Solomon's sword can / divide you from the sky. / You are one. Fly.' " We move from baby to swaddling-pages to the threat of Solomon's sword dividing the baby not from itself but from the sky, then to the baby metamorphosed into the sky itself and told to fly. We remain in the present moment of the crying baby, but we are in touch with babies past; the baby Jesus in swaddling clothes, the baby who is being fought over by two women, each claiming to be its mother. And beyond this, we are given the possibility of flight, of a nature that is as indivisible as sky.

In poem-time, the present *accompanies* memory and eventuality; it is not left behind, since the very activity of the words generates the poem's own present no matter what tense the poet uses. The poem's activity in the consciousness of the reader is a present-time event which may, nevertheless, draw on his past, his expectations and hopes.

> All lives that has lived;
> So much is certain.

When Yeats says this in his "Quarrel in Old Age," it is more than salutary. It is an acknowledgment that the past is not a burial ground but a living fiber that informs and questions what is and will be.

I sit in a Montana café having a meal with my mother, who is visiting from Washington State. Suddenly she remembers a time when she was beautiful, when she had the power of beauty. I realize I never knew her in that time, though often she still acts from it, as from some secret legacy. I see that I have failed to make her know her present beauty, so she must return endlessly to that past—a reservoir. Even as I see her, I see myself, my own aging. I walk with her into "the one color / of the snow—before us, the close houses, / the brave and wondering lights of the houses." It has been snowing during our meal, and the houses have been transformed by a covering of snow, as though time in the form of snow has softened all contours, has fallen down about us deep enough, white enough, to put everything on the same plane spatially and temporally. The girlhood beauty of my mother accompanies us as we leave, gives the houses their brave and wondering lights, causes them to drift in a white sea under the covering of night.

Perhaps it is our very forgetting that allows these past images significance. If we remembered constantly, the time-fabric of our lives would remain whole and we would have no need of the poem to re-involve us in what was part of what is and may be.

"Forget! Forget it to know it," Robert Penn Warren says in his poem "Memory Forgotten."

How long
Has your mother been dead? Or did you, much older,

Lie in the tall grass and, motionless, watch
The single white fleck of cloud forever crossing the
blue—. . . .

How much do we forget that is ourselves—

Nothing too small to make a difference,
And in the forgetting to make it all more true?

That liquid note from the thicket afar—oh, hear!
What is it you cannot remember that is so true?

So Warren connects forgetting with what we feel to be true, the smell or the sound from afar that, if we knew its significance, would give us back some essential part of ourselves. He makes forgetting a positive accident, like the money found in a coat you hadn't worn for months, an accidental payload. The truth that we are is bound up with our partiality, our inability to hold everything of ourselves in memory as we go. Every time we remember some forgotten moment in a way that illuminates the present or causes the present to mediate some past, then the boundaries we thought were there between past, present, and future dissolve, if only for the time that is the poem.

It is believed that in the infant's first consciousness of the events and objects passing before him, he does not separate himself from them, but experiences his own identity simply as an endless stream of stimuli. His response to events is not so much toward as *in* them. The infant is immersed in objects, and their time in space continues with him, is infinite.

The Hindus have a name for this continuing or fourth dimension of "being across time." It is called the *Linga-Sharira*, that which remains the same in us though our cells change completely every seven years and we are not in fact the same in body that we were. Part of what the poem does is to restore us to consciousness of the *Linga-Sharira* which continues through change and which is immeasurable.

The poem, because it takes place at the point of all possibilities, in that it can intersect with all past, present, and future expectations, is able to accommodate this fourth dimension, the "something else" of the *Linga-Sharira*, which allows us to change yet to remain the same through time. "The same," in this instance, means as in an overview, so the total life is seen at the same instant as any one point of the life and we may say, This is she as she is, was, and will be.

Proust reminds us that "perhaps the immobility of things that surround us is forced upon them by our conviction that they are themselves, and not anything else, and by the immobility of our conception of them." The past and future are linked to our apartness, our identity as beings cut off from this original immersion in a time without succession. In that time, the time of the infant, there were no landmarks apart from us to signal our departure or arrival, our movement toward or away; no forgetting or remembering was then possible.

Even the stopped moment of a photograph paradoxically releases its figures by holding them because the actual change, the movement away from the stilled moment, has already taken place without us, outside the frame of the photograph, and the moment we see ourselves so stilled, we know we have also moved on. This is the sadness of the photograph: knowing, even as you look, it is not like this, though it was. You stand in the "was" of the present moment and you die a little with the photograph.

Octavio Paz speaks of the poetic experience as one which allows us to deny succession, the death factor. "Succession," he says, "becomes pure present. . . . The poem is mediation: thanks to it, original time, father of the times, becomes incarnate in an instant." The poem then represents an *overflowing* of time, the instant in which we see time stopped without its "ceasing to flow." It overflows itself, and we have the sensation of having gone beyond ourselves.

"Poetry," says Paz, "is nothing but time, rhythm perpetually creative." In the time of the poem we are held, not as the photograph holds, but as in a simultaneity of recognitions which wake us up in the middle of our lives. The poem causes an expansion of the "now." Archibald MacLeish's "Epistle to Be Left in the Earth" is a poem which expands the "now" by including the speaker's and the reader's deaths as encountered by those who live after.

> . . . It is colder now
>   there are many stars
>   we are drifting
> North by the Great Bear
>   the leaves are falling
> The water is stone in the scooped rocks
>   to southward
> Red sun grey air
>   the crows are
> Slow on their crooked wings
>   the jays have left us
> Long since we passed the flares of Orion

Each man believes in his heart he will die
Many have written last thoughts and last letters
None know if our deaths are now or forever
None know if this wandering earth will be found

We lie down and the snow covers our garments
I pray you
                    you (if any open this writing)
Make in your mouths the words that were our names.

Part of the recent popularity of the writing of poems in prisons,
grade schools, poetry workshops in universities, and the wards of
mental clinics has developed from the sense that we are traveling
too fast through a time which has fewer and fewer of the future-
maintaining structures with which we grew up. I mean the struc-
tures of marriage, of the family, of the job as a fulfillment of one's
selfhood. These allowed one to look ahead into the near and far
future of one's life with some expectation of continuity, which is a
part of one's future-sense. We now have serial marriages, separa-
tions between parent and child, as well as jobs that come and go as
technology fluctuates even more crazily to accommodate a product-
oriented society.

It may be that the poem is an anachronism of being-oriented
impulses. It is an anachronism because it reminds us ironically that
we stand at the point of all possibilities yet feel helpless before the
collapse of the future-sustaining emblems of our lives. This has
reduced us to life in an instantaneous "now." The time of the poem
answers this more and more by allowing an expansion of the "now."
It allows consequence to disparate and contradictory elements in a
life. The "I," reduced to insignificance in most spheres of contem-
porary society, is again able to inhabit a small arena of its own
making. It returns us, from the captivities of what we do and make,
to who we *are*.

When the "now" expands, it includes before and after. The
poem reminds us that the past is not only that which happened
but also that which *could* have happened but did not. The future,
says Ouspensky, in a similar way, holds not only that which will
be, but everything that *may* be. He reminds us that if eternity ex-
ists at all, every moment is eternal. Eternal time is perpendicular
at each instant to successionary time, which is time as we *misper-
ceive* it. An example of an unrealized future enacted in poem is
Gene Derwood's "Elegy," where we read that the boy "lamentably
drowned in his eighteenth year" will not fulfill the expectations
of adulthood:

Never will you take bride to happy bed,
Who lay awash in water yet no laving
Needed, so pure so young for sudden leaving.

All time is *during*. That is why it is so hard to exist in the present. Already we are speeding ahead so fast we can only look back to see where we have been. I once said to a group of students that the poet is like a tuba player in a house on fire. Crucial events surround him, threatening to devour, while he makes inappropriate music with an instrument that cannot help causing its serious manipulator to look ridiculous.

This speeding up of the time-sense in contemporary life, through the technology of mobility and through the disintegrative nature of human relationships, has affected the language of the poem as a time-enacting mechanism. The poem has begun to move in simple sentences, in actions and images more than in ideas, to speak intensely about the relationship of one person to another, to attempt to locate its subject matter or its speaker, if only during the time of the poem, very specifically at 142d Street on July 23, 1971. Many contemporary poems have opted for the present tense and a great suspicion has fallen over the past and future tenses. If they are used at all, they are converted into a present happening in order to insure immediacy. The sentences are simple perhaps because this slows the time-sense down and makes the language more manageable. Though some wonderful poems are being written with this pacing, I am often nostalgic for a more extended motion. It is no secret that the contemporary reader has begun to balk at the periodic sentence. The atrophy of even short-term recall in America has caused the mind to resist holding complex verbal structures. When my Irish musician friend tells me of singers who can sing hundreds of songs that have been passed on to them, I see how far we have come from this kind of memory.

The poem as time machine has inherited a heavy responsibility from these strains on the language and on the human figure's diminishing stature among its self-perpetuating creations. The poem is expected to tell us, not that we're immortal, but simply that we exist as anything at all except contingencies. It has the old obligations to carry experience memorably in the language, but with few of the formal structures to aid memory. Its voices have become a chorus of one, the personal "I" venturing as far as the patio or the boathouse. But as regards man's relation to time, the poem has shown itself valiant. I am no longer envious of Flash Gordon and his time machine. The poem is the place where the past and future can be seen at once without forsaking the present.

In a poem I consecrate all that forgotten life through memory, cast like a light on my life and the lives of others. The poet is the Lazarus of the poem, rising up with it. In the time of the poem it is still possible to find courage for the present moment. The life imagined in the poem has been known to affect the speaker, the reader, their sense of what can be salvaged or abandoned in a life. However, if we are like the blind man whose reality in the instant of "now" ends at the tip of his stick as he walks along the cliff, we must still believe in falling. The poem, for all its bounty, is a construct, and though the words in it may give the fiercest light, we cannot live there. Poems are excursions into belief and doubt, often simultaneously.

Mostly we are with the child peeling potatoes at the kitchen sink. We are too short for the view out the window except when we stand on the kitchen chair, which we are not supposed to do, but which we do. The time in the poem can be as useful as a kitchen chair, helping us to be the right size in a world that is always built for others. If I did not grow up to be a horse, I will not hold it against my life. I could not think fast enough to keep my two-leggedness from setting in. Still, I know there is a young girl in me who remembers the language of horses. She is with me in the time of the poem.

With all the modern time-savers, we have no better machine for the reinvention of time than the poem. I would not trade my least-loved poem for a Polaroid snapshot. The real time-savers are those that accommodate the mind, the heart, and the spirit at once.

JOHN LOGAN

On Poets and Poetry Today

(1971)

Poets and poetry today. Yes, but where is poetry itself? Or as Cummings might ask, "Who is poetry, anyway?" Poetry is existentially first among the great genres because, thinking of poetry as lyric contrasted to tragic or epic and agreeing with Yeats that out of our quarrels with ourselves we make poetry, we can say that this thing, poetry, is the expression in literature of the narrowest or first circle of encounter, the circle of one's self, whereas tragedy is the expression of encounter with the immediate community, the community of family, and the epic is the expression of encounter with the larger community of the nation or the race. Under this view the novel is a mixed form of poetry which may be primarily lyric as in Proust, primarily tragic as in Dostoevsky and Faulkner, or primarily epic as in Tolstoy. But given this manner of definition, with its increasingly large circles of encounter, one expects the larger circles to include the smaller, so that one anticipates in tragedy certain lyric moments (as in Claudius's monologue at prayer in *Hamlet*) and one expects in epic both the lyric moment (as in Achilles' soliloquy by the sea) as well as certain tragic figurings (as that of Achilles and Patroclus in the *Iliad*).

The question arises rather naturally why lyric poets die so young—i.e., why they do not survive to surmount tragic encounters and reach the larger circle of epic involvements (or, as we might say, political involvement): Keats, Shelley, Byron, Hart Crane, Dylan Thomas, the latter remaining a little longer, Rimbaud a little less long, having abandoned as a teenager any powerful production of words and surviving only to write domestic or business letters.

I would like to expand my definitions in a different direction to include comedy in order to say what I think about it. There are two tragic moments allied to levels of personal maturity or (looked at from inside the hero) as rites of passage: the tragedy of the young man, of Hamlet to Oedipus Rex who moves from young manhood to maturity, and the tragedy of the older man, of Lear or Oedipus at Colonus (or in a certain reading of Willy Loman) who moves from maturity to sanctity or *superior* manhood. The first is a movement embracing life as the fulfillment of youth and the other is a movement embracing death as a fulfillment of life. Oedipus must leave Thebes in order to make himself available to other states. Christ must leave us locally, he says, in order to be really with us. Hamlet died for us.

Between these two tragic moments lies comedy, which is the moment of wedding, as in *Twelfth Night,* comedy par excellence, where three couples marry at the close or in *Ulysses* which ends with Molly Bloom's powerful yea-saying to the idea of renewed honeymoon. It is at the moment of wedding where the young tragic problem is solved: the encounter with the family is reconciled by our stepping out of the family we are born into in order to found our own. But this healing action involves love and love must be learned. The source of tragic conflict is ambivalence, and the problem of learning to love is the problem of learning to exorcise the ambivalence in one's relationship with another. Language enters the discussion at this point because we are all stutterers in the face of love; all of us then are country bumpkins who must learn to speak, to utter our love without ambivalence. Thus all of us, as poor lovers, identify with the mute or inarticulate heroes, the Benjys, the jongleurs, the lonely hunters of the heart. "We fog bound people are all stammerers," O'Neill says.

The final moment of inarticulation is the moment of silence, the moment of late tragedy, as the other inarticulation is the moment of young tragedy. In the later inarticulateness one hears this: "Be still and know that I am God." It is the silence of Hamlet (who moves so swiftly from the one tragic moment to the other, combining the acceptance of life with the acceptance of death) as opposed to the self-castrating silence of Iago. "*Wovon man nicht sprechen kann darüber müss man schweigen.*"[1] As distinct from these two moments of inarticulation, the very first such moment, of which I shall speak later, is that of infancy. To say a paradox: Man's inarticulations mark the joints in his life.

Now as it is practically impossible to rid ourselves utterly of ambivalence, so at the time of wedding we still stutter and the comedy is imperfect; thus tragicomedy is the most existential dramatic form, the one closest to the truth of the human situation, and Beckett knew acutely what he was about when he used this genre.

"I suppose the easiest part of the production of art is the suffering," I have written elsewhere. "Artists have not minded pain so long as they keep it from killing them and get their work done: so

---

1. Wittgenstein, "Whereof man cannot speak of this he must remain silent." (All notes in this essay are by John Logan.)

long as the mad man, the beast and the angel Dylan Thomas found inside himself or the boy, the man and the woman James Joyce found in himself, did not crack the china skull in which they sprouted so dangerously together."[2]

But many poets have chosen death rather than to continue their work, and some poets (I have mentioned Rimbaud) have been able to survive only if they did not write but committed instead the symbolic castration of the murder of the gift, the excision of power in themselves. The trauma of continued life for a poet is, I believe, allied to the problem of continuing to build what we call "the body of work" a man forms. The word body ("corpus") is important. One of my colleagues at State University of New York[3] has found that Sylvia Plath's work shows a fantasy of building the body of the father, the Colossus of her title—that her poems are fragments of this body and that her suicide coincides with the inability to continue such work. This exactly corroborates for the female poet what I have suggested for the male lyric poet: that he builds in his work the body of his mother—that he wishes to give birth to her as she has done for him. In building the body of the parent of the opposite sex through his work the poet establishes a sexual relationship with his own work and dramatizes at the lyric level (the battle with himself, that is) the tragic battle (the battle with the parent). Thus he plays out within himself the primal scene, one part of himself taking the feminine role another the masculine. It is because of this fact—that one forms a body with his poetry—that we must demand of poetry a surface of sensual beauty.[4] The poet must conjure the vision of the mother and he must make her sing to him (and, in narrative poetry, tell him "a story").

The fact that so many lyric poets die young, or, in Dante's phrase, "midway through life" (Hart Crane was nearly 33) suggests that they cannot duplicate in their work the lower half of the mother's body, the part that *takes* as well as giving with the upper part. A poet who survives may find himself like Yeats writing poetry which is more sexually oriented in his later years. I find it significant here that one's breaking into syntax, an advance which makes poetry possible, comes about rather suddenly as another acquaintance of mine has found,[5] in connection with attempts to deal with the separation from the mother before the age of one.

---

2. See "Dylan Thomas and the Ark of Art" in this volume.
3. Murray Schwartz. The title of Sylvia Plath's first book of poems was *The Colossus*.
4. In my opinion the poets who most show this in my time are James Wright, Galway Kinnell, and Robert Bly.
5. David Bleich

Separated from the breast, the poet begins to rebuild that portion of the mother's body with the mouthing of his poetry, having already as a child rebuilt her face in another way into that of his dolls or his toy animals. But oftentimes the poet would rather die than face the sexuality of the mother (and hence, of the parents together), which keeps him separated from her in the tragic fashion. He chooses death over the tragic encounter, remaining a lyric poet, holding onto his melancholy for dear life, as it were, and falling far short of the true comic moment, the moment of wedding free of ambivalence [the wedding which on the other hand is so often also the wake (as in Shakespeare, Joyce, and Faulkner)].

This concern of the poet with the mother's body, as I see it, helps me to understand why the poetry of the New York School is so unfeeling. Whether Kenneth Koch writes about "The Pleasures of Peace" or whether he writes about "Sleeping with Women," all feeling is leveled, and one is left with brilliant ratiocination and with a bastard comedy which has somehow short-circuited the moment of the truly comic, the moment, I repeat, of wedding. Perhaps we laugh at this poetry for the same reason we laugh at jokes, because we are spared the expenditure of energy necessary to deal with anxieties roused by feelings, and this excess of energy can emerge in the smile. It is easy to see why Koch is such a great teacher of children. There is no body of the mother and no scene of the parents in New York School poetry and so this poetry shows its kinship with abstract painting, which it grew up with. Abstract painting has got rid of the human figure and thus got rid of erotic feeling, for Kenneth Clark has pointed out that there is erotic feeling present at the base of the use of the nude in painting. All figures painted (once undressed in the eyes of the beholder) lead to the nude and hence to the primal scene. The audience as voyeur is spared sexual anxiety in abstract painting. However, it is a self-defeating movement for, as Plato pointed out in the *Meno*, where there is color there shape goes also, and wherever there is shape, I add, there lurks finally (to "rorshock" us) the figure of the parent and its display in the primal scene. The figure finds its way back into pop art and pop poetry only through the elaboration of the child's comic strip (I now see "comic strip" as an unconscious pun) with its curious pointillist composition which visualizes the minute bullets the TV gun shoots us with to form its images. Or again pop art (should I call it mom art also?) elevates to totem status the baked goods and the cans of the kitchen or tubes of the bathroom and so uses figures which hide again the parents and their scene together.

As painting shows erotic concern at its root (a painter paints with the brush of his penis said D. H. Lawrence) so does poetry both at the fantasy level of the body of the work and also at the level of immediate presence, for in poetry there is always breath, the breath of the mouth, and behind it of moist, hidden organs, with their enactment of expulsions. To use an earlier myth, one might say that every breathing of a poem is an expulsion from the garden of Eden, which by the poem's content and by its ritual rhythms, its yearnings, tries to dramatize our return to that Garden. Here, however, I am more directly concerned with genital expulsion out of the mouth—I am more concerned with the displacement upwards from that "other mouth" which the man and woman know, and with the expelling itself, which, looked at from the masculine point of view, is ejaculation, while looked at from the feminine it is giving birth.[6]

The aggressive poetry of hatred, or warmongering or antiwarmongering, of racism or antiracism tries to hide behind the skirts of the poet's mouth to say that the poet is only masculine (and this whether the mouth speaks feminist content or not). I am not saying there is no place in poetry for militancy, the politically persuasive, the feminist or the masculinist. I am saying that what makes something *poetry* in the first place is its musical quarrel with the self, its lyricism. Without that there *is* no poetry though there may well be something else. David Ray once asked me to write a poem about the Hungarian Revolution and I told him all my poetry was about the Hungarian Revolution. "Out of our quarrels with others we make rhetoric," Yeats said. "And out of our quarrels with ourselves we make Poetry." "The spiritual combat," Rimbaud told us, "is more bloody than any human battle." And he should know for he died a slow death of it. Some poets brandish their swords to make us forget they are using words and that words are of the mouth, of the mother, and to make us forget that poetry is learned first as a way of separating from the mother's breast, as a way of realizing, through the pain of weaning, the radical separateness, the identity indeed, of the self. So Robert Bly in his "Deep Image" poetry, as it is sometimes called, writes brilliant, strong poetry of the war (against it to be sure) as in "The Teeth Mother Naked at Last" but reminds us in discussion that the true job of the poet is to lead the masculine, aggressive function back a certain way toward the wings of the feminine function. (I may say here that I am mildly suspicious of how successful Bly's aesthetic is at exorcizing the aggressive element, for in an essay he speaks of "dipping down into the unconscious" when this active procedure can in fact scarcely work. One does not dip down into the unconscious, one finds a method of allowing it to well up into one's poem.)

---

6. As an image common to male and female, it might be seen as displaced anal activity.

To return, when I spoke of the poet's leading "the masculine aggressive function back a certain way toward the wings of the feminine function," I was not basically using a theatrical image, but I might do that: The poet comes out on the stage in the masculine light of day, under the sun, sometimes too much "I, the sun," indeed having emerged from the dark belly of Jonah's whale onto the shore or, in my present image, having just emerged from the wings. But he must return there, to the belly or the wings, in order to recoup and nourish himself so that he can nourish us, feed us bread, not stones.

Returning from the wings onto the stage, the poet may well lead his brothers, the members of his school, and one thinks first here of the school coming out of the shadow of Black Mountain. I may say that this celebration of brothers, too, is a way of short-circuiting the tragic encounter with the parents, with their primal scene and their judgmental function. One needn't deal with the parents if one keeps in touch primarily with the brothers. In so far as paternal figures are relevant for the Black Mountain group, they indeed seem more maternal or matriarchal than patriarchal, even though they may be sexually male (Olson and Williams); for there is more concern in this group with its members being of the same earth than with a judgmental hierarchy of first and second sons or daughters. But I am particularly concerned here with the following fact: In showing us what good brothers and sisters they are the Black Mountain poets deny the *fight* with the brothers. Now Melanie Klein in her analysis of youngsters has found that sibling battles dramatize the primal scene. The Black Mountain poets thus deny their involvement in that. I know that fraternity is more important, for instance, to Duncan than hierarchy, for when I wrote him in 1961 or 1962 at the time of the beginning of my poetry magazine *Choice* and asked him for poems (having stated that I did not believe in schools because schools tended to elevate lesser talents in the same swim and to ignore greater talents not in the same swim), Robert replied that he did not agree with the policy of printing the best wherever you could find it and thought it much more important to print members of a group. I also know that fraternity is very important not only to the Black Mountain poets as such but to the San Francisco beat poets as well, who constantly talk about one another in their poems and have their pictures taken and published together. The two schools often overlap and give readings or workshops together. I remember a wonderful quotation from Ginsberg who was being interviewed in San Francisco after he, Creeley, Levertov, and Duncan had given a workshop together in Vancouver. "Mr. Ginsberg," asked the interviewer, "I understand you and Miss Levertov and Mr. Duncan taught the craft of verse up at UBC in

Vancouver." "No," said Ginsberg, "Denise and Robert and I did not teach the craft of verse. We were all emotionally bankrupt and went around weeping and asking our students for love."

He is right about that. We must love one another or die, said Auden, and before him a character in *Brothers Karamazov*. Poets say they want everybody to love everybody but they (we) mainly want you the audience to care about us, and so we do what we can to make you feel that we care about you. The poet is an anonymous lover, I believe, and his poetry is an anonymous reaching out, which occasionally becomes personal—when there are those present who care to listen. At the personal moment a mysterious thing happens which reminds us of magic, and hence of the power of Orpheus: the loneliness each of us feels locked inside his own skin, and the anonymous reaching each of us does, therefore, becomes a *bond* and hence we are neither alone nor anonymous in the same sense as we were before.

I for my part am a loner, not a member of a school. I want to help others discover their own voices in workshops and I want others upon hearing my work to hear their own voices echoing inside themselves.

Does this allow me to say I have escaped the flight from the primal scene somehow? That I have faced it and stood alone, having earned the right to wear a necklace of "the bad mother's" teeth, having come away from them unbidden and unbitten? Or that I have watched the primal scene untraumatized and have been enabled to move on without the support of sisters and brothers? I might wish it did, but in fact it does not, for in some ways I am jealous of the brotherhoods of poets, which do not number me among them. And as a loner reaching out to you the audience with the long penis of my tongue of poems, showering the sperm of my syllables (like the asperges of water of the priest or the rice thrown at weddings) and breathing on you with the passion of my warm breath, I have only recently learned to look at you as you are looking at me. (It is easier for me to imagine that I am an exhibitionist in the spotlight than that I am a voyeur, which is probably closer to the truth, wanting to peer into the curtained windows of your inmost heart to see what I may be fertilizing there.) In other words I too displace the battle of the primal scene and in still another way: for it takes place between you and me which is (in my terms) more tragic than lyric, for it is the displacement of relationships from my own parents and siblings, with whom I am not at ease. Why do we so much fear that primal scene? Why do poets go to such great lengths (my phrase) to displace, dramatize and (right word) *embody* it? Perhaps because otherwise we would have to see that we are gods: that we have the power and thus the responsibility to give life or to withhold it, to love or to murder, engender or destroy. Though this be true for poet and nonpoet alike, the poet feels it especially: for, unable to account for the gift he possesses, he has already begun to suspect for this other reason that he may be a god. Such anointment, such mixed blessing brings special, powerful guilt. As I have said in another place and still deeply believe and repeat: "It's not the skeleton in the closet we are afraid of, it's the god."

III. Poetry and Ambition ✑
    Poets on the Academy and Literary Industry

DONALD HALL

Poetry and Ambition

1. I see no reason to spend your life writing poems unless your goal is to write great poems.

An ambitious project—but sensible, I think. And it seems to me that contemporary American poetry is afflicted by modesty of ambition—a modesty, alas, genuine . . . if sometimes accompanied by vast pretense. Of course the great majority of contemporary poems, in any era, will always be bad or mediocre. (Our time may well be characterized by more mediocrity and less badness.) But if failure is constant the types of failure vary, and the qualities and habits of our society specify the manners and the methods of our failure. I think that we fail in part because we lack serious ambition.

2. If I recommend ambition, I do not mean to suggest that it is easy or pleasurable. "I would sooner fail," said Keats at twenty-two, "than not be among the greatest." When he died three years later he believed in his despair that he had done nothing, the poet of "Ode to a Nightingale" convinced that his name was "writ in water." But he was mistaken, he was mistaken. . . . If I praise the ambition that drove Keats, I do not mean to suggest that it will ever be rewarded. We never know the value of our own work, and everything reasonable leads us to doubt it: for we can be certain that few contemporaries will be read in a hundred years. To desire to write poems that endure—we undertake such a goal certain of two things: that in all likelihood we will fail, and that if we succeed we will never know it.

Every now and then I meet someone certain of personal greatness. I want to pat this person on the shoulder and mutter comforting words: "Things will get better! You won't always feel so depressed! Cheer up!"

But I just called high ambition sensible. If our goal in life is to remain content, *no* ambition is sensible. . . . If our goal is to write poetry, the only way we are likely to be *any* good is to try to be as great as the best.

3. But for some people it seems ambitious merely to set up as a poet, merely to write and to publish. Publication stands in for achievement—as everyone knows, universities and grant-givers take publication as achievement—but to accept such a substitution is modest indeed, for publication is cheap and easy. In this country we publish more poems (in books and magazines) and more poets read more poems aloud at more poetry readings than ever before; the increase in thirty years has been tenfold.

So what? Many of these poems are often *readable*, charming, funny, touching, sometimes even intelligent. But they are usually brief, they resemble each other, they are anecdotal, they do not extend themselves, they make no great claims, they connect small things to other small things. Ambitious poems require a certain length for magnitude; one need not mention monuments like *The Canterbury Tales, The Faerie Queen, Paradise Lost,* or *The Prelude.* "Epithalamion," "Lycidas," and "Ode: Intimations of Immortality" are sufficiently extended, not to mention "The Garden" or "Out of the Cradle." Not to mention the poet like Yeats whose briefer works make great connections.

I do not complain that we find ourselves incapable of such achievement; I complain that we seem not even to entertain the desire.

4. Where Shakespeare used "ambitious" of Macbeth we would say "over-ambitious"; Milton used "ambition" for the unscrupulous overreaching of Satan; the word describes a deadly sin like "pride." Now when I call Milton "ambitious" I use the modern word, mellowed and washed of its darkness. This amelioration reflects capitalism's investment in social mobility. In more hierarchal times pursuit of honor might require revolutionary social change, or murder; but Protestantism and capitalism celebrate the desire to rise.

Milton and Shakespeare, like Homer, acknowledge the desire to make words that live forever: ambitious enough, and fit to the O.E.D.'s first definition of "ambition" as "eager desire of honor"— which will do for poets and warriors, courtiers and architects, diplomats, Members of Parliament, and Kings. Desire need not imply drudgery. Hard work enters the definition at least with Milton, who is ready "To scorn delights, and live laborious days," to discover fame, "the spur, that last infirmity of noble minds." We note the infirmity who note that fame results only from laborious days' attendance upon a task of some magnitude: when Milton invoked the Heavenly Muse's "aid to my adventurous song," he wanted merely to "justify the ways of God to men."

If the word "ambitious" has mellowed, "fame" has deteriorated enough to require a moment's thought. For us, fame tends to mean

Johnny Carson and *People* magazine. For Keats as for Milton, for Hector as for Gilgamesh, it meant something like universal and enduring love for the deed done or the song sung. The idea is more classic than Christian, and the poet not only seeks it but confers it. Who knows Achilles' valor but for Homer's tongue? But in the 1980s—after centuries of cheap printing, after the spread of mere literacy and the decline of qualified literacy, after the loss of history and the historical sense, after television has become mother of us all—we have seen the decline of fame until we use it now as Andy Warhol uses it, as the mere quantitative distribution of images. . . . We have a culture crowded with people who are famous for being famous.

5. True ambition in a poet seeks fame in the old sense, to make words that live forever. If even to entertain such ambition reveals monstrous egotism, let me argue that the common alternative is petty egotism that spends itself in small competitiveness, that measures its success by quantity of publication, by blurbs on jackets, by small achievement: to be the best poet in the workshop, to be published by Knopf, to win the Pulitzer or the Nobel. . . . The grander goal is to be as good as Dante.

Let me hypothesize the developmental stages of the poet.

At twelve, say, the American poet-to-be is afflicted with generalized ambition. (Robert Frost wanted to be a baseball pitcher and a United States senator: Oliver Wendell Holmes said that *nothing* was so commonplace as the desire to appear remarkable; the desire may be common but it is at least essential.) At sixteen the poet reads Whitman and Homer and wants to be immortal. Alas, at twenty-four the same poet wants to be in the *New Yorker*. . . .

There is an early stage when the poem becomes more important than the poet; one can see it as a transition from the lesser egotism to the greater. At the stage of lesser egotism, the poet keeps a bad line or an inferior word or image because *that's the way it was: that's what really happened.* At this stage the frail ego of the author takes precedence over art. The poet must develop, past this silliness, to the stage where the poem is altered for its own sake, to make it better art, not for the sake of its maker's feelings but because decent art is the goal. Then the poem lives at some distance from its creator's little daily emotions; it can take on its own character in the mysterious place of satisfying shapes and shapely utterance. The poem freed from its precarious utility as ego's appendage may possibly fly into the sky and become a star permanent in the night air.

Yet, alas, when the poet tastes a little fame, a little praise. . . .

Sometimes the poet who has passed this developmental stage will forget duty to the art of poetry and again serve the petty egotism of the self. . . .

Nothing is learned once that does not need learning again. The poet whose ambition is unlimited at sixteen and petty at twenty-four may turn unlimited at thirty-five and regress at fifty. But if everyone suffers from interest, everyone may pursue disinterest.

Then there is a possible further stage: when the poet becomes an instrument or agency of art, the poem freed from the poet's ego may entertain the possibility of grandeur. And this grandeur, by a familiar paradox, may turn itself an apparent 180 degrees to tell the truth. Only when the poem turns wholly away from the petty ego, only when its internal structure fully serves art's delicious purposes, may it serve to reveal and envision. "Man can *embody* truth"—said Yeats; I add the italic—"he cannot *know* it." Embodiment is art and artfulness.

When Yeats was just south of fifty he wrote that he "sought an image not a book." Many aging poets leave the book behind to search for the diagram, and write no more poetry than Michael Robartes who drew geometrical shapes in the sand. The turn toward wisdom—toward gathering the whole world into a book—often leaves poetry behind as a frivolity. And though these prophets may delight in abstract revelation, we cannot follow them into knowing, who followed their earlier embodiments. . . . Yeats's soul knew an appetite for invisibility—the temptation of many—but the man remained composite, and although he sought and found a vision he continued to write a book.

6. We find our models of ambition mostly from reading.

We develop the notion of art from our reading. When we call the poem more important than ourselves, it is not that we have confidence in *our* ability to write it; we believe in *poetry*. We look daily at the great monuments of old accomplishment and we desire to add to their number, to make poems in homage to poems. Old poems that we continue to read and love become the standard we try to live up to. These poems, internalized, criticize our own work. These old poems become our Muse, our encouragement to song and our discouragement of comparison.

Therefore it is essential for poets, all the time, to read and reread the great ones. Some lucky poets make their living by publicly reacquainting themselves in the classroom with the great poems of the language. Alas, many poets now teach nothing but creative writing, read nothing but the words of children . . . (I will return to this subject).

It is also true that many would-be poets lack respect for learning. How strange that the old ones read books. . . . Keats stopped school when he was fifteen or so; but he translated the *Aeneid* in order to study it and worked over Dante in Italian and daily sat at the feet of Spenser, Shakespeare, and Milton. ("Keats studied the old poets every day / Instead of picking up his M.F.A.") Ben Jonson was learned and in his cups looked down at Shakespeare's relative ignorance of ancient languages—but Shakespeare learned more language and literature at his Stratford grammar school than we acquire in twenty years of schooling. Whitman read and educated himself with vigor; Eliot and Pound continued their studies after stints of graduate school.

On the other hand, we play records all night and write unambitious poems. Even talented young poets—saturated in S'ung, suffused in Sufi—know nothing of Bishop King's "Exequy." The syntax and sounds of one's own tongue, and that tongue's four-hundred-year-old ancestors, give us more than all the classics of all the world in translation.

But to struggle to read the great poems of another language—*in* the language—that is another thing. We are the first generation of poets not to study Latin; not to read Dante in Italian. Thus the puniness of our unambitious syntax and limited vocabulary.

When we have read the great poems we can study as well the lives of the poets. It is useful, in the pursuit of models, to read the lives and letters of the poets whose work we love. Keats's letters, heaven knows.

7. In all societies there is a template to which its institutions conform, whether or not the institutions instigate products or activities that suit such a pattern. In the Middle Ages the Church provided the model, and guilds and secret societies erected their colleges of cardinals. Today the American industrial corporation provides the template, and the university models itself on General Motors. Corporations exist to create or discover consumers' desires and fulfill them with something that satisfies briefly and needs frequent repetition. CBS provides television as Gillette supplies disposable razors—and, alas, the universities turn out degree-holders equally disposable; and the major publishers of New York City (most of them less profitable annexes of conglomerates peddling soap, beer, and paper towels) provide disposable masterpieces.

The United States invented mass quick-consumption and we are very good at it. We are not famous for making Ferraris and Rolls Royces; we are famous for the people's car, the Model T, the Model A—"transportation," as we call it: the particular abstracted into the utilitarian generality—and two in every garage. Quality is all very well but it is *not* democratic; if we insist on hand-building Rolls Royces most of us will walk to work. Democracy demands the interchangeable part and the worker on the production line; Thomas Jefferson may have had other notions but de Tocqueville was our prophet. Or take American cuisine: it has never added a sauce to the world's palate, but our fast-food industry overruns the planet.

Thus: Our poems, in their charming and interchangeable quantity, do not presume to the status of "Lycidas"—for that would be elitist and un-American. We write and publish the McPoem—*ten billion served*—which becomes our contribution to the history of literature as the Model T is our contribution to a history which runs from bare feet past elephant and rickshaw to the vehicles of space. Pull in any time day or night, park by the busload, and the McPoem waits on the steam shelf for us, wrapped and protected, indistinguishable, undistinguished, and reliable—the good old McPoem identical from coast to coast and in all the little towns between, subject to the quality control of the least common denominator.

And every year, Ronald McDonald takes the Pulitzer.

To produce the McPoem, institutions must enforce patterns, institutions within institutions, all subject to the same glorious dominance of unconscious economic determinism, template and formula of consumerism.

The McPoem is the product of the workshops of Hamburger University.

8. But before we look into the workshop, with its training program for junior poets, let us take a look at models provided by poetic heroes of the American present. The university does not invent the stereotypes; it provides technology for mass reproduction of a model created elsewhere.

Question: If you manufacture Pac-Man, or a car called Mustang, and everyone suddenly wants to buy what you make, how do you respond? Answer: You add shifts, pay overtime, and expand the plant in order to saturate the market with your product. . . . You make your product as quickly as you can manufacture it; notions of quality control do not disturb your dreams.

When Robert Lowell was young he wrote slowly and painfully and very well. On his wonderful Library of Congress LP, before he recites his early poem about "Falling Asleep over the Aeneid," he tells how the poem began when he tried translating Virgil but produced only eighty lines in six months, which he found disheartening. Five years elapsed between his Pulitzer book *Lord Weary's Castle*, which was the announcement of his genius, and its underrated successor *The Mills of the Kavanaughs.* Then there were eight more years before the abrupt innovation of *Life Studies. For the Union Dead* was spotty, *Near the Ocean* spottier, and then the rot set in.

Now, no man should be hanged for losing his gift, most especially a man who suffered as Lowell did. But one can, I think, feel annoyed when quality plunges as quantity multiplies: Lowell published six bad books of poems in those disastrous last eight years of his life.

(I say "bad books" and would go to the stake over the judgment, but let me hasten to acknowledge that each of these dreadful collections—dead metaphor, flat rhythm, narcissistic self-exploitation—was celebrated by leading critics on the front page of the *Times* and the *New York Review of Books* as the greatest yet of uniformly great emanations of great poetical greatness, greatly achieved. . . . But one wastes one's time in indignation. Taste is always a fool.)

John Berryman wrote with difficult concentration his difficult, concentrated *Mistress Bradstreet;* then he eked out 77 *Dream Songs.* Alas, after the success of this product he mass-produced *His Toy His Dream His Rest,* 308 further dream songs—quick improvisations of self-imitation, which is the true identity of the famous "voice" accorded late Berryman-Lowell. Now Robert Penn Warren, our current grand old man, accumulates another long book of poems every year or so, repeating himself instead of rewriting the same poem until it is right—hurry, hurry, hurry—and the publishing tribe celebrates these sentimental, crude, trite products of our industrial culture.

Not all poets overproduce in a response to eminence: Elizabeth Bishop never went on overtime; T. S. Eliot wrote bad plays at the end of his life, but never watered the soup of his poems; nor did Williams nor Stevens nor Pound. Of course everyone writes some inferior work—but these poets did not gush out bad poems late in their lives when they were famous and the market required more products for selling.

Mind you, the workshops of Hamburger University turned out cheap, ersatz Bishop, Eliot, Williams, Stevens, and Pound. All you want. . . .

9. Horace, when he wrote the *Arts Poetica,* recommended that poets keep their poems home for ten years; don't let them go, don't publish them until you have kept them around for ten years: by that time, they ought to stop moving on you; by that time, you ought to have them right. Sensible advice, I think—but difficult to follow. When Pope wrote "An Essay on Criticism" seventeen hundred years after Horace, he cut the waiting time in half, suggesting

that poets keep their poems for five years before publication. Henry Adams said something about acceleration, mounting his complaint in 1912; some would say that acceleration has accelerated in the seventy years since. By this time, I would be grateful—and published poetry would be better—if people kept their poems home for eighteen months.

Poems have become as instant as coffee or onion soup mix. One of our eminent critics compared Lowell's last book to the work of Horace, although some of its poems were dated the year of publication. Anyone editing a magazine receives poems dated the day of the postmark. When a poet types and submits a poem just composed (or even shows it to spouse or friend) the poet cuts off from the poem the possibility of growth and change; I suspect that the poet *wishes* to forestall the possibilities of growth and change, though of course without acknowledging the wish.

If Robert Lowell, John Berryman, and Robert Penn Warren publish without allowing for revision or self-criticism, how can we expect a twenty-four-year-old in Manhattan to wait five years—or eighteen months? With these famous men as models, how should we blame the young poet who boasts in a brochure of over four hundred poems published in the last five years? Or the publisher, advertising a book, who brags that his poet has published twelve books in ten years? Or the workshop teacher who meets a colleague on a crosswalk and buffs the back of his fingernails against his tweed as he proclaims that, over the last two years, he has averaged "placing" two poems a week?

10. Abolish the M.F.A.! What a ringing slogan for a new Cato: *Iowa delenda est!*

The workshop schools us to produce the McPoem, which is "a mold in plaster, / Made with no loss of time," with no waste of effort, with no strenuous questioning as to merit. If we attend a workshop we must bring something to class or we do not contribute. What kind of workshop could Horace have contributed to, if he kept his poems to himself for ten years? No, we will not admit Horace and Pope to our workshops, for they will just sit there, holding their own work, claiming it is not ready, acting superior, a bunch of *elitists*. . . .

When we use a metaphor, it is useful to make inquiries of it. I have already compared the workshop to a fast-food franchise, to a Ford assembly line. . . . Or should we compare Creative Writing 401 to a sweatshop where women sew shirts at an illegally low wage? Probably the metaphor refers to none of the above, because the workshop is rarely a place for starting and finishing poems; it is a place for repairing them. The poetry workshop resembles a garage to which we bring incomplete or malfunctioning homemade machines for diagnosis and repair. Here is the homemade airplane for which the crazed inventor forgot to provide wings; here is the internal combustion engine all finished except that it lacks a carburetor; here is the rowboat without oarlocks, the ladder without rungs, the motorcycle without wheels. We advance our nonfunctional machine into a circle of other apprentice inventors and one or two senior Edisons. "Very good," they say; "it *almost* flies. . . . How about, uh . . . how about *wings*?" Or, "Let me just show you how to build a carburetor. . . ."

Whatever we bring to this place, we bring it too soon. The weekly meetings of the workshop serve the haste of our culture. When we bring a new poem to the workshop, anxious for praise, others' voices enter the poem's metabolism before it is mature, distorting its possible growth and change. "It's only when you get far enough away from your work to begin to be critical of it yourself"—Robert Frost said—"that anyone else's criticism can be tolerable. . . ." Bring to class only, he said, "old and cold things. . . ." Nothing is old and cold until it has gone through months of drafts. Therefore workshopping is intrinsically impossible.

It is from workshops that American poets learn to enjoy the embarrassment of publication—too soon, too soon—because *making public* is a condition of workshopping. This publication exposes oneself to one's fellow-poets only—a condition of which poets are perpetually accused and frequently guilty. We learn to write poems that will please not the Muse but our contemporaries, thus poems that resemble our contemporaries' poems—thus the recipe for the McPoem. . . . If we learn one thing else, we learn to publish promiscuously; these premature ejaculations count on number and frequency to counterbalance ineptitude.

Poets who stay outside the circle of peers—like Whitman, who did not go to Harvard; like Dickinson for whom there was no tradition; like Robert Frost, who dropped out of two colleges to make his own way—these poets take Homer for their peer. To quote Frost again: "The thing is to write better and better poems. Setting our heart when we're too young on getting our poems appreciated lands us in the politics of poetry which is death." Agreeing with these words from Frost's dour middle-age, we need to add: and "setting our heart" when we are old "on getting our poems appreciated" lands us in the same place.

11. At the same time, it's a big country. . . .

Most poets need the conversation of other poets. They do not need mentors; they need friends, critics, people to argue with. It is no accident that Wordsworth, Coleridge, and Southey were friends when they were young; if Pound, H.D., and William Carlos Williams had not known each other when young, would they have become William Carlos Williams, H.D., and Pound? There have been some lone wolves but not many. The history of poetry is a history of friendships and rivalries, not only with the dead great ones but with the living young. My four years at Harvard overlapped with the undergraduates Frank O'Hara, Adrienne Rich, John Ashbery, Robert Bly, Peter Davison, L. E. Sissman, and Kenneth Koch. (At the same time Galway Kinnell and W. S. Merwin attended Princeton.) I do not assert that we resembled a sewing circle, that we often helped each other overtly, or even that we *liked* each other. I do assert that we were lucky to have each other around for purposes of conversation.

We were not in workshops; we were merely attending college. Where else in this country would we have met each other? In France there is an answer to this question and it is Paris. Europe goes in for capital cities. Although England is less centralized than France or Romania, London is more capital than New York, San Francisco, or Washington. While the French poet can discover the intellectual life of his times at a café, the American requires a degree program. The workshop is the institutionalized café.

The American problem of geographical isolation is real. Any remote place may be the site of poetry—imagined, remembered, or lived in—but for almost every poet it is necessary to live in exile before returning home—an exile rich in conflict and confirmation. Central New Hampshire or the Olympic Peninsula or Cincinnati or the soybean plains of western Minnesota or the lower East Side may shine at the center of our work and our lives; but if we never leave these places we are not likely to grow up enough to do the work. There is a terrible poignancy in the talented artist who fears to leave home—defined as a place *first* to leave and *then* to return to.

So the workshop answers the need for a café. But I called it the *institutionalized* café, and it differs from the Parisian version by instituting requirements and by hiring and paying mentors. Workshop mentors even make assignments: "Write a persona poem in the voice of a dead ancestor." "Make a poem containing these ten words in this order with as many other words as you wish." "Write a poem without adjectives, or without prepositions, or without content. . . ." These formulas, everyone says, are a lot of fun. . . . They also reduce poetry to a parlor game; they trivialize and make safe-seeming the real terrors of real art. This reduction-by-formula is not accidental. We play these games *in order* to reduce poetry to a parlor game. Games serve to democratize, to soften, and to standardize; they are repellent. Although in theory work-shops serve a useful purpose in gathering young artists together, workshop practices enforce the McPoem.

This is your contrary assignment: Be as good a poet as George Herbert. Take as long as you wish.

12. I mentioned earlier the disastrous separation, in many universi-ties, of creative writing and literature. There are people writing poetry—teaching poetry, studying poetry—who find reading *aca-demic*. Such a sentence sounds like a satiric invention; alas, it is objective reporting.

Our culture rewards specialization. It is absurd that we erect a barrier between one who reads and one who writes, but it is an absurdity with a history. It is absurd because in our writing our standards derive from what we have read, and its history reaches back to the ancient war between the poets and the philosophers, exemplified in Plato's "Ion" as the philosopher condescends to the rhapsode. In the thirties poets like Ransom, Tate, and Winters entered the academy under sufferance, condescended to. Tate and Winters especially made themselves academically rigorous. They secured the beachheads; the army of their grandchildren occupies the country: often grandsons and daughters who write books but do not read them.

The separation of the literature department from the writing department is a disaster; for poet, for scholar, and for student. The poet may prolong adolescence into retirement by dealing only with the products of infant brains. (If the poet, as in some schools, teaches literature, but only to writing students, the effect is better but not much better. The temptation exists then to teach literature as craft or trade; Americans don't need anyone teaching them trade.) The scholars of the department, institutionally separated from the contemporary, are encouraged to ignore it. In the ideal relationship, writers play gadfly to scholars, and scholars help writ-ers connect to the body of past literature. Students lose the writer's special contribution to the study of literature. Everybody loses.

13. It is commonplace that, in the English and American tradition, critic and poet are the same person—from Campion to Pound, from Sidney to Eliot. This tradition started with controversies be-tween poets over the propriety of rhyme and English meter, and with poets' defense of poetry against Puritan attack. It flourished, serving many purposes, through Dryden, Johnson, Coleridge, Wordsworth, Keats in his letters, Shelley, Arnold. . . . Although cer-tain poets have left no criticism, there are *no* first-rate critics in the English tradition who are not also poets—except for Hazlitt. The

poet and the critic have been almost continuous, as if writing poetry and thinking about it were not discrete activities.

When Roman Jakobson—great linguist, Harvard professor—was approached some years ago with the suggestion that Vladimir Nabokov might be appointed professor of Slavic, Jakobson was skeptical; he had nothing against elephants, he said, but he would not appoint one professor of zoology.

Oh, dear.

The analogy compares the elegant and stylish Nabokov—novelist in various languages, lepidopterist, lecturer, and critic—to the great, gray, hulking pachyderm, intellectually noted *only* for memory. . . . By jokes and analogies we reveal ourselves. Jakobson condescends to Nabokov—just as Plato patted little Ion on his head, just as Sartre makes charitable exception for poets in *What is Literature?*, just as men have traditionally condescended to women and imperialists to natives. The points are clear: (1) "Artists are closer to nature than thinkers; they are more instinctive, more emotional; they are childlike." (2) "Artists like bright colors; artists have a natural sense of rhythm; artists screw all the time." (3) "Don't misunderstand. We *like* artists . . . in their place, which is in the zoo, or at any rate outside the Republic, or at any rate outside tenured ranks."

(One must admit, I suppose, that poets often find themselves in tenured ranks these days. But increasingly they enter by the zoo entrance, which in our universities is the department of creative writing.)

Formalism, with its dream of finite measurement, is a beautiful arrogance, a fantasy of materialism. When we find what's to measure and measure it, we should understand style-as-fingerprint, quantifying characteristic phonemic sequence . . . or whatever. But it seems likely that we will continue to intuit qualities, like degrees of intensity, for which objective measure is impossible. Then hardnoses will claim that only the measurable exists—which is why hard-nose usually means soft-head.

Once I audited a course of Jakobson's, for which I am grateful; the old formalist discoursed on comparative prosody, witty and energetic and learned, giving verbatim examples from Urdu and fifty other languages, exemplifying the multiplicity of countable noise. The journey was marvelous, the marvel diminished only a little by its terminus. The last lecture, pointed to for some weeks, turned out to be a demonstration, from an objective and untraditional approach, of how to scan (and the scansion was fine, and it was the way one scanned the poem when one was sixteen) of Edgar Poe's "The Raven."

14. A product of the creative writing industry is the writerly news-letter which concerns itself with publications, grants, and jobs—and with nothing serious. If poets meeting each other in 1941 discussed how much they were paid a line, now they trade informa-tion about grants; left wing and right united; to be Establishment is to have received an N.E.A. grant; to be anti-Establishment is to denounce the N.E.A. as a conspiracy. . . . Like Republicans and Democrats, all belong to the same capitalist party.

Poets and Writers publishes *Coda* (now *Poets and Writers*), with chatty articles about self-publication, with lists of contests and awards. It resembles not so much a trade journal as a hobbyist's bulletin, unrelievedly cheerful, relentlessly trivial. The same or-ganization issues the telephone book, *A Directory of American Poets,* "Names and addresses of 1,500 poets. . . ." The same organization offers T-shirts and bookbags labeled "Poets and Writers."

Associated Writing Programs publishes *A.W.P. Newsletter,* which includes one article each issue—often a talk addressed to an A.W.P. meeting—and adds helpful business aids: The December, 1982, issue includes advice on "The 'Well Written' Letter of Application," lists of magazines requesting material ("The editors state they are looking for 'straightforward but not inartistic work' "), lists of grants and awards ("The annual HARRY SMITH BOOK AWARD is given by COSMEP to . . ."), and notices of A.W.P. competitions and conventions. . . .

Really, these newsletters provide illusion; for jobs and grants go to the eminent people. As we all know, eminence is arithmetical: it derives from the number of units published times the prestige of the places of publication. People hiring or granting do not judge quality—it's so subjective!—but anyone can multiply units by the prestige index and come off with the *product.* Eminence also brings readings. Can we go uncorrupted by such knowledge? I am asked to introduce a young poet's volume; the publisher will pay the going rate; but I did not know that there was a going rate. . . . Even blurbs on jackets are commodities. They are exchanged for pam-phlets, for readings; reciprocal blurbs are only the most obvious exchanges. . . .

15. Sigh.

If it seems hopeless, one has only to look up in perfect silence at the stars . . . and it *does* help to remember that poems are the stars, not poets. Of most help is to remember that it is possible for people to take hold of themselves and become better by thinking. It is also necessary, alas, to *continue* to take hold of ourselves—if we are to pursue the true ambition of poetry. Our disinterest must discover that last week's nobility was really covert rottenness, etcetera. One is never free and clear; one must work continually to sustain, to recover. . . .

When Keats in his letters praised disinterestedness—his favorite moral idea, destroyed when it is misused as a synonym for lethargy (on the same day I found it misused in the *New York Times, Inside Sports,* and the *American Poetry Review*)—he lectured himself because he feared that he would lose it. (Lectures loud with moral advice are always self-addressed.) No one is guiltless of temptation, but it is possible to resist temptation. When Keats worried over his reputation, over insults from Haydon or the *Quarterly,* over Shelley's condescension or Wordsworth's neglect, he reminded himself to cultivate disinterest; to avoid distraction and to keep his eye on the true goal, which was to become one of the English Poets.

Yeats is responsible for a number of the stars in the sky, and when we read his letters we find that the young man was an extraordinary trimmer—soliciting reviews from Oscar Wilde and flattering Katherine Tynan, older and more established on the Celtic turf. One of the O.E.D.'s definitions of ambition, after "eager desire of honor," is "personal solicitation of honor." When he wrote, "I seek an image not a book," he acknowledged that as a young man he had sought a book indeed. None of us, beseeching Doubleday or Pittsburgh, has ever sought with greater fervor.

And Whitman reviewed himself, and Roethke campaigned for praise like a legislator at the state fair, and Frost buttered Untermeyer on both sides. . . . (Therefore let us abjure the old saw that self-promotion and empire-building mean bad poetry. Most entrepreneurs are bad poets—but then, so are most poets.) Self-promotion remains a side issue of poetry and ambition. It *can* reflect a greed or covetousness which displaces the grand ambition—the kind of covetousness which looks on the life lived only as a source of poems; "I got a poem out of it." Or it can show only the trivial side of someone who, on other occasions, makes great art. At any rate, we should spend our time worrying not about other people's bad characters, but our own.

Finally, of course, I speak of nothing except the modest topic: How shall we lead our lives? I think of a man I admire as much as anyone, the English sculptor Henry Moore, eighty-four as I write these notes, eighty when I spoke with him last. "Now that you are eighty," I asked him, "would you tell me the secret of life?" Being a confident and eloquent Yorkshireman, Moore would not deny my request. He told me:

"The greatest good luck in life, for *anybody,* is to have something that means *everything* to you . . . to do what you want to do, and to find that people will pay you for doing it . . . *if* it's unattainable. It's no good having an objective that's attainable! That's the big thing: you have an ideal, an objective, and that objective is unreachable. . . ."

16. There is no audit we can perform on ourselves, to assure that we work with proper ambition. Obviously it helps to be careful; to revise, to take time, to put the poem away; to pursue distance in the hope of objective measure. We know that the poem, to satisfy ambition's goals, must not express mere personal feeling or opinion—as the moment's McPoem does. It must by its language make art's new object. We must try to hold ourselves to the mark; we must not write to publish or to prevail. Repeated scrutiny is the only method general enough for recommending. . . .

And of course repeated scrutiny is not foolproof; and we will fool ourselves. Nor can the hours we work provide an index of ambition or seriousness. Although Henry Moore laughs at artists who work only an hour or two a day, he acknowledges that sculptors can carve sixteen hours at a stretch for years on end—tap-tap-tap on stone— and remain lazy. We can revise our poems five hundred times; we can lock poems in their rooms for ten years—and remain modest in our endeavor. On the other hand, anyone casting a glance over biography or literary history must acknowledge: Some great poems have come without noticeable labor.

But as I speak I confuse realms. Ambition is not a quality of the poem but of the poet. Failure and achievement belong to the poet, and if our goal remains unattainable, then failure must be standard. To pursue the unattainable for eighty-five years, like Henry Moore, may imply a certain temperament. . . . If there is no method of work that we can rely on, maybe at least we can encourage in ourselves a temperament that is not easily satisfied. Sometime when we are discouraged with our own work, we may notice that even the great poems, the sources and the standards, seem inadequate: "Ode to a Nightingale" feels too limited in scope, "Out of the Cradle" too sloppy, "To His Coy Mistress" too neat, and "Among Schoolchildren" padded. . . .

Maybe ambition is appropriately unattainable when we acknowledge: *No poem is so great as we demand that poetry be.*

ROBERT FRANCIS

Four Pot Shots at Poetry

Be Brutal

A friend comes with poems to be criticized. "Be brutal," he says. "Be ruthless. Tear them apart."

You smile and take the poems in your hand. Be brutal? Somehow you never feel brutal toward a poem, even when it obviously deserves brutality. Toward a human being, perhaps, now and then, but not toward a poem. It lies there on the page so helpless to defend itself, so at your mercy. After all, it is only a few inoffensive words put together in a certain way.

No, you could never be really brutal with a poem. And you suspect that he knows you couldn't. What he really wants and hopes is that you will love his poems and praise them. But he wants to keep as far as possible from seeming to. He wants your praise to surprise him. He wants to say he didn't think the poems were very good himself. Ideally he himself would like to be brutal while you triumphantly defend his poems. "Be brutal," he says.

Pulling yourself together, you resolve to be helpful, tactful, and honest, all at the same time. You recall the critics of *your* poetry who were only honest. Particularly one man who lit his pipe and took a puff and said, "The trouble with this poem—" And took another puff and said, "The trouble with this poem—" And took another puff and said, "The trouble with this poem—"

So you ask your friend if he would be willing to leave the poems with you for a day or two. You want to brood over them.

"Okay," he says. "But be brutal."

Defense of Poetry

I knew a poet once who defended poetry. He defended poetry as he would have defended womanhood on the highway at night. Actually he did more than defend poetry, he defended individual poems. Thus he went beyond Shelley and Sidney who were content to defend poetry in general and in the abstract. One might almost say there never was a poem this poet wouldn't defend. None was too poor or frail for him to champion. Frailty rather than beauty it must have often been that roused his chivalry.

If a slip of a high-school girl wrote an "Ode to Spring," this poet instantly became protective. Any poem, any poem at all, by the fact of its being a poem was precious and therefore precarious.

He was a rare bird. Possibly no one today feels and acts just as he did.

Certainly not I. I would say that a poem worth defending needs no defense and a poem needing defense is not worth defending. I would say it is not our business to defend poetry but the business of poetry to defend us.

Teacher

When I look back at the poetry teaching I have done or tried to do, I see it in the form of a round pie cut in six sections.

The first slice is what I told them that they already knew. This generally pleased them since it made them feel like advanced students.

The second slice is what I told them that they could have found out just as well or better from books. What, for instance, is a sestina?

The third slice is what I told them that they refused to accept. I could see it on their faces, and later I saw the evidence in their writing.

The fourth slice is what I told them that they were willing to accept and may have thought they accepted but couldn't accept since they couldn't fully understand. This also I saw in their faces and in their work. Here, no doubt, I was mostly to blame.

The fifth slice is what I told them that they discounted as whimsey or something simply to fill up time. After all, I was being paid to talk.

The sixth slice is what I didn't tell them, for I didn't try to tell them all I knew. Deliberately I kept back something—a few professional secrets, a magic formula or two.

So my pie is all used up and what teaching have I done?

Yet we always had a good time in class. Drawn together by a common interest and pursuit, we enjoyed one another's company. Especially we enjoyed laughing together.

It Really Isn't

It isn't expensive to be a poet. A pencil and piece of paper are all the equipment needed to get started. Homer managed with less.

A pencil or pen and a few pieces of paper. Then an envelope or two and some postage stamps.

Pencil or pen or typewriter. A portable typewriter isn't expensive if you can make one last a lifetime.

You may fancy writing in an Italian villa or a French château, but the poems you write there will be no more immortal than those written in your bedroom at home.

Nor do you need very much of that most precious of all items, time. Odds and ends will do. Evenings, early mornings, noon hours. Sundays, holidays, and when you sprain your ankle.

It's quite otherwise with a painter. Paints, brushes, and canvases cost money, and a painter can't very well paint in his bedroom. Still less could a sculptor sculpt in a bedroom. An architect may need a whole suite of rooms in an office building. And as for the composer, what can he do without a grand piano and somewhere to play it?

No, if a poet can support himself he can support his poetry. If he can keep himself fed, his poems won't starve.

So, when you come right down to brass tacks, a poet doesn't really need the aid, assistance, subsidy, and support that munificent philanthropy stands ready to grant him. In this, isn't he lucky?

If you insist on giving him something, say, a free year in Rome, it may turn out that what you have chiefly done is to add to his baggage.

DIANE WAKOSKI

Poetry as the Dialogue
We All Hope Someone Is Listening To

Who can a poet be? What can he be to a world which does not read poetry? What is his craft, when no two poets writing today can get together on their definitions of what constitutes a poem, to say nothing of what constitutes a good poem? Is a poet an artist; a philosopher; or someone who has lived and written about a passionate and adventurous life? Can it mean anything to be a poet when we live in a world where *only* poets read poetry? What is the function of a poem if, as most poets declare, poetry is not popular entertainment?

Permit me. Let me talk about these concerns. They are not academic questions for me, as I call myself a poet, and daily have to look at myself and wonder if my life can have any meaning at all. And while I have never given in to my urges to believe that cooking a meal or going to the most perfunctory job, to say nothing of being in the medical profession and saving people's lives, is a more meaningful activity than writing poetry, it is a battle with an angel, or devil, which leaves me black and blue every day; and not necessarily proud that I have won.

Frank Norris wrote crude, serious, cynical novels of the nineteenth century which portray the American sensibilities and their origins better than any psychology or sociology textbook ever could. I just finished reading a tedious book by Norris called *The Octopus* which I probably would not have finished had I not been on summer vacation in a foreign country where one is lucky to find any book in English at all, especially if you require five or six a week. But I am glad I stuck it out because it forced me once again to face the meanings of being a poet, the limitations of poetry, and the question of how any poet is to think of these things in his own mind. It also presented a picture to me that I know well, but need my face shoved into occasionally, of what nonpoets think of poetry and poets. That means about ninety-nine percent of all people.

I suppose you've all read the novel, but perhaps you read it as a portrait of the great impersonal crushing force of big business on little men, the railroad versus the wheat farmers, and of the great insensitivity of the rich as opposed to the oppressive evil that the victimized poor are driven to. There are sentimental scenes like the one in which pages alternate with scenes of a millionaire's dinner party and a German immigrant mother and her baby starving to death on the streets of San Francisco, having been driven out of their farm home by the railroad which has also killed their husband-father and protector. But for me the novel spoke much less melodramatically, or more interestingly, of its protagonist, Presley, who is, in the midst of all this wheat and railroads, a poet. Presley has apparently come from a rich family, though we never find out where his money comes from; but he lives a carefree life, belongs to the right clubs, has gone to the university, and is considered an equal by all the rich businessmen who people the novel. By the way, to be rich in this novel is to *allow* you to be virtuous. The poor are always driven to evil. A terrifying view, if true. Anyway, our poet has the possibility of being a virtuous man because he is rich, though not sullied with any of the shenanigans of the other rich men who had to wheel and deal to get and keep their money.

Anyway, Presley during the novel's pages is living on the ranch in the San Joaquin Valley with the most wheat. He is friendly with the millionaire family who owns it, and comes to stay as a guest because he wants to write an epic. The great epic of the West. Unfortunately, he keeps getting sidetracked by his anger at the railroad for their attempts to ruin the lives of these western farmers. So he wanders around and finally is inspired to write an angry poem about the exploitation of the wheat farmers and workers by the railroad. He reads it to his friend, the wandering shepherd (who incidentally has been to college too, so you know that he's got something going for him), who immediately rises out of his own troubles—a murdered girlfriend—and proclaims the piece "a great poem." Reassured that he is at last cooking for immortality, Presley swears that he will not take any money for this poem (natural virtue), that he wants to help the people, and sends it off to the biggest newspaper in San Francisco (whose editor just happens to know that he is a friend of every wealthy society member in San Francisco and belongs to the best club), which prints it on a separate page with its own art work. Everyone talks about it and other newspapers reprint it. It is called "The Toilers" and soon literary magazines start writing about its passionate genius and a publisher even gives him a contract to publish a book of poems (*The Toilers and Other Poems*). I am sure if Robert Bly or Yevgeny Yevtushenko read *The Octopus,* they would be in seventh heaven thinking of a great poem which could stir the masses and then be taken up by the literary establishment and touted as great poetry.

By the way, the literary establishment in *The Octopus* is represented by two women. Mrs. Derrick is the wife of the rich wheat farmer with whom Presley lives. She never lifts a hand; she never eats dinner with the men when they talk politics. She reads slim volumes of verse and little magazines with her cat, Princess Nathalie, on her lap, and feels her life is wasted because she wants to be in Rome or Venice and has never been. Mrs. Cedarquist is the San Francisco wife, independently wealthy before marriage, of a twice-over millionaire (he therefore is extra virtuous and is presented as the nicest guy in the book) who espouses causes and has a drawing room famous for always housing the newest poet, the currently popular composer, the new psychic palm reader from India, the current protégée of Mary Baker Eddy, or a lecturer on the classics from Germany. She thinks poetry is "divine" and is always raising money for charity bazaars and sponsoring new magazines. While Mrs. Derrick is simply a quiet, useless, sad woman, Mrs. Cedarquist is presented as a loud fool. A bumbler who needs the sense of something being fashionable before she could know enough to like it.

These two women and the proletariat press represent the readers of poetry, the latter only under certain favorable circumstances where a poem can say what an editorial could not say without getting sued for libel or having big business cut the editor out of his job. Yes, it seems then that the poem printed in the newspaper served mainly to make Presley famous with the little reviews; for, being represented by effete people like Mrs. Derrick, they long to think of themselves as embracing something which is both aesthetic and useful. The sad result of the printing of "The Toilers" in the newspaper is to lead Presley to get up during a political meeting where his friend and host Derrick is crucified and deliver an impassioned oration against big business with a lot of Marxist jargon that everyone in the hall applauds and no one understands. In other words, even his so-called political and therefore useful poem is in no way useful either to his friends or to all the farmers who are being destroyed by the railroad. In the end, he suffers as all poets do from some nervous malady, and after being interviewed by the chief owner of the railroads and patted on the head for writing poetry and told that political poetry is useless because people don't see that all history is made by itself and little men only interfere with it, do not cause it, goes off on a voyage to India for his health on a ship owned by Cedarquist, the twice-over millionaire whose wife patronizes the arts. He stands on the ship, having seen six men, two of whom were close friends, shot down by the railroad and killed, one man driven to robbery and manslaughter because he was cheated by the railroad, two families illegally ruined financially because the railroad controlled the courts, his patron Derrick driven insane by one man in the railroad who connived against him, a pretty girl lost to prostitution, and her mother and sister dying of starvation. Yes, he stands on the ship and meditates:

> Falseness dies, injustice and oppression in the end of everything fade and vanish away. Greed, cruelty, selfishness and inhumanity are short-lived; the individual suffers, but the race gones on. Annixter dies, but in a far-distant corner of the world a thousand lives are saved. The larger view always and through all shams, all wickedness, discovers the Truth that will, in the end prevail, and all things, surely, inevitably, resistlessly work together for good. [p. 438]

I bring up this book now and have so lengthily described Presley because it brought to the fore every feeling I have had about the contradictions and problems of poems, poets, and poetry.

First of all: the problem of audience. Do we have only two choices, the effete and foolish, or the ignorant who think we are going to help them change injustice? Do we want fools to call us wise? Do we seriously think a poem can unravel the tangles that have created a bad political situation and make people stop acting for their own profits and, instead, act for the good of others? It seems to me, those two alternatives describe English or European poetry as opposed to Socialist-realist concepts of poetry. American poetry has found a third alternative and it is a variation of the European. Here, poets read poetry. We think of ourselves not as the effete Mrs. Derrick or the foolish rich Mrs. Cedarquist, but rather as the wise Presleys reading our own poems. A friend writes to me in a letter:

> I guess I don't feel there is much of an audience, period. Smatterings in the universities, and outside them. My readers are mostly poets and a few student-age people who use my work to try and pull themselves out of hell. I don't think of that as an *audience*. The spiritual auditorium is dark with a few tortured ghosts up front and in the rear. Norman Mailer has an audience.

Being an optimist, I have devised a way of looking at the audience of poets for poetry as not such a bad thing, given that we are educating thousands of young people to write poetry and to feel that writing does mean something in terms of their own identities and ways of life, and consequently maybe those who read and write poetry are not so cutoff from the world at all. Except that this concept makes poetry into a pastime rather than a real activity and it de-emphasizes the craftsman aspect of the art and makes it into a hobby. Most of us would rather give up poetry forever than have our writing considered our hobbies. So we are back to the problem of where to find an audience. Why don't doctors, lawyers, engineers, or other artists read poetry as they read novels, books of history, philosophy, or other literary books? Is poetry really just somebody's hobby, in their eyes?

And this leads me to the question of who can a poet be if most people simply think that writing poetry is what sensitive people do in their spare time? I have always maintained that you may not call yourself a poet. The title is one you have to earn, and when the world calls you a poet, then you are entitled to it. But the world called Ogden Nash and Edgar Guest poets and will continue to do so much longer than it will call me or Galway Kinnell or Jerome Rothenberg poets. Something is wrong. That's where all the confusion lies. That's why we honor things like the National Book Award or the Pulitzer Prize or the Bollingen Award or Guggenheim grants or publication by big publishers. Even though we know that you never will win a Yale Younger Poets award if you do not know the judge and that many people who do win such awards are cronies, still it gives us something to hang on to, some sense that there is a profession, a craft, more than a hobby involved. When Presley's poem, "The Toilers," is taken up by the literary magazines, this signals the fact that the poem is not mere editorial rhetoric but rather has literary merit as well as passion. In *The Octopus*, neither literary merit nor passion seems to mean anything much, for if Presley were not rich already he could not have either the time to live the observing life he does or the money to pay his club dues, or even be a virtuous person. Norris's view of the poet is an utterly condemnatory view in any realistic terms. And I am afraid that Norris sees the poet in precisely the way almost everyone today who doesn't write poetry sees him. It has been the very mistaken notion of a number of poets in the past seven or eight years that we can wipe away that view of the poet by ourselves becoming political activists and trying to make the world a better place to live in. But most of these poets have mainly risen to antiwar, or black, or women's lib platforms and delivered in some cases good poems and in other cases very bad ones and done nothing to change anything, just as when Presley addressed the assembly everyone applauded but not only did he not cause any useful action, Norris is even more condemnatory, for he does not allow Presley even to feel he has *moved* the audience:

> Weak, shaking, scarcely knowing what he was about, he descended from the stage. A prolonged explosion of applause followed, the Opera House roaring to the roof, men cheering, stamping, waving their hats. But it was not intelligent applause. Instinctively as he

made his way out, Presley knew that, after all, he had not once held the hearts of his audience. He had talked as he would have written; for all his scorn of literature, he had been literary. The men who listened to him, ranchers, country people, store-keepers, attentive though they were, were not once sympathetic. Vaguely they had felt that here was something which other men—more educated—would possibly consider eloquent. They applauded vociferously but per-functorily, in order to appear to understand.

Presley, for all his love of the people, saw clearly for one moment that he was an outsider to their minds. He had not helped them nor their cause in the least; he never would. [p. 370]

The alienated position of the poet is powerfully presented by Norris in this novel because he shows Presley living with the rich, himself rich, wanting to write about the "real" world or "the people" and himself being a man of learning whose favorite author is Homer (whose work he doesn't consider "literary," as poems published in little magazines are "literary"), yet claiming he does not like "literature" because to him literature is what women like Mrs. Derrick spend all day reading. He is neither a working man nor willing to be aesthete. He wants the impossible. And I do not see any of us in the world of contemporary poetry as any different from Presley. Then who is the poet? And who can be his readers? If the poet is an intelligent man who practices a craft which is writing, then his readers would presumably have to be other intelligent men, though not necessarily writers, simply people who know some-thing about the craft of writing. But then we encounter the prob-lem of definitions of poetry so that we can intelligently talk about the craftmanship of the poem.

In the contemporary poetry scene, the old division between Apol-lonian and Dionysian poetry is almost a battleground. But it is a kind of cold war, since supposedly those two kinds of poetry are not at war but should simply be two ways of approaching poetry. A few years ago a sad exchange of letters was published in the *New York Times* book review section, between Ginsberg and Howard, arguing over National Book Award candidates—Ginsberg arguing that Corso should win because he was a poet of passion and genius (Dionysian?) and Howard that Van Duyn should win because she was a poet of intelligence and craft (Apollonian?) and both of them forgetting that theoretically those were both possibilities for great poetry, not two little ideas which had to fight against each other like starlings trying for the same food.

And I remember a sad article by Denise Levertov in the early 1960s which claimed that there were poets who wrote out of need and poets who wrote out of desire, and of course there was a condemnation of the philistines who wrote out of such a base thing as desire (Apollonian?) and devotion for the inspired geniuses who wrote because they need to (Dionysian?). The problem became, how do you distinguish between need and desire, for some of the most cerebral poetry, such as Creeley's which by those definitions should be classified as the poetry of desire, was precisely the sort of poetry she was championing as the poetry of need. Is there anyone who writes who does not need to? Who does so from any spurious motive, as he would run his grocery business for profit or write advertising because he was paid to? Every poet needs to do what he does, surely? And what poet, worth that designation, ignores the desire to make a good poem, to find the best words, metaphors, and images to construct his poem? Poets have been yelling "Need," "Desire," or "Genius," "Craft" at one another for the last fifty years. A war where no war ever needed to be. Different approaches to the same things—a good life for all, a beautiful poem the goal.

In your own heart, if you are a poet, you know which of your poems came out of the blood of your life, and you also know that you worked hardest to make them your most beautiful poems too, because they meant so much to you. No critic needs to tell you when you are writing something powerful. But that requires honesty, and that is not an easy quality to possess about oneself. It is fairly easy to be honest about others compared to the process of really admitting to yourself what is going on in your own head. And perhaps that is the resolution to my argument here: that a poet is someone dedicated to inventing and writing in the most beautiful way he can an honest picture of the world he sees. He must create his own audience and that may mean settling for a very few. It certainly means culling and culling from those who say they read and those who say they write. It means redefining every day, and honestly, what it is you have done (no matter how small) and what it is you would like to try to do. It means honestly reading other poetry and honestly rejecting your own when it does not mean anything. Poetry, then, is not philosophy or entertainment but a kind of philosopher's stone which allows many possibilities. Its greatest power is to make you see both how necessary your own life is, and yet, despite that necessity, its relative unimportance. The poet as a social figure is a sad one, for he is a man who lives for his inner worth and somehow expects others to see inner worth as outer manifestation. Most of all the poet is his own poems, and we all know that ultimately very few will read them. I cherish for myself, though, the belief that the few who read them are not the Mrs. Derricks and Mrs. Cedarquists of the world but other serious people who feel the poem is somehow the extension of life—that part of all of us which allows us to reflect and mediate after the fact of life.

I think the most serious consideration for *all* poets writing today is to acknowledge that poetry is an art, a craft, and that twentieth-century poetry has many forms that were never created or thought of before. This means acknowledging both the Apollonian and Dionysian. It means recognizing the fact that it takes someone who knows about poetry to recognize and care for good poetry, and consequently that probably most of us will be one another's readers. This means making ourselves good readers as well as dedicated writers. It means, somehow, seeing all the possibilities. It probably also means (and this is true of all good art today) viewing the world as an individual, in a compelling personal way, rather than seeing the world as any member of a class—a rich man, a poor man, a working man, a black, a pacifist, a woman. A poet is a man who puts the richest part of himself on the page and is willing to spend his life learning the craft required to do that. If he does not do that, his work will seem effete and meaningless even to those few of us who read poetry with the same passion we have for writing it. Norris presents Presley as a failure not because of his wealth and the consequent separation he has from the emotions of real people, but because he allows himself the fantasy that he can write about something because it is important even if it doesn't affect his own life. And because like all the other rich men in the novel Presley has an illusion of power, in his case the conviction that *his* words could change the world, fix up its miseries. Poetry is the weakest and smallest voice, thus the most poignant and beautiful when heard. Poetry comes when you have no other power. Then you do not ask silly academic questions like, what does it mean to be a poet? You simply write the most compelling poems you can and hope that somewhere someone will be listening. Why? Because to speak is to have something to say. But it only takes two people for a conversation, and poets must remember that. The poem must speak to someone or it is silly. It is talking to yourself in the kitchen. But if it speaks to one person, then it is a poem. We all hope, of course, that many others will be listening in.

JOHN FREDERICK NIMS

The Greatest English Lyric?
A New Reading of Joe E. Skilmer's "Therese"

Genuine revolutions in literary taste and theory occur on an average only once every seven generations; therefore it is a source of satisfaction to have myself piloted what may be the most shattering reappraisal in our literature. I am referring—as the world of letters now knows well—to the discovery (made about the time that flying saucers began to be widely observed here and abroad) of that core of inner *is*-ness in the poetry of the long misread, long underrated Joburt Eggson Skilmer, or Joe E. Skilmer as he himself signed his poems. Slighted by serious readers for what seemed the facility of his technique and the pious banality of his thought—especially as shown in the poem known as "Trees"—Skilmer was in reality the perpetrator of an existentialist hoax on a public that prided itself on knowing what was genuine.

For years, many of us had been dissatisfied with the reading generally accorded this remarkable poem—the kind of official reading that provoked academic guffaws in a thousand classrooms. "There is more here than meets thee, eye," I would murmur to myself, teased by a host of ambiguities, of velleities that never quite came clear. It was a question of tone. Perhaps my first breakthrough came when I heard Professor Wrugson O. Muttson reading a line from Pound's "The River-Merchant's Wife: A Letter":

> At fourteen I married my Lord you.

Muttson read the line as if it expressed wifely devotion. But it was obvious to me, as to any especially sensitive reader, that Pound intended the line to be heavily ironic, and that the "tone" might better be represented by something like

> At fourteen I married (my Lord!) *you?*

My trouble had been that I was ventriloquizing, putting my own voice into the poem, instead of letting it *read itself to me*. Do not read poems—this became my principle—be read to by them. This approach led to a number of discoveries, of which possibly the most earth-shaking was my article proving that Hamlet's famous soliloquy is not about suicide at all but about his meteorological and alchemical experiments with a number of test tubes (the "retorts" he is famous for), of which the tube lettered "E" seemed the most promising if the most vexatious:

> Tube "E" or not tube "E"—that is the quest, chum.
> Weather? 'Tis no blur in the mind

But this reading, now officially adopted in the best textual editions, is too well known to need further quotation. I have also found my method of "deep reading" fruitful in the perusal of several thousand lines of *Paradise Lost,* and I suspect that our whole literature will have to be reread in the light of it. However: it was on the basis of this strict principle that I returned to Skilmer's great love poem to Therese Murk of Peoria. Called simply "Therese," or "T'rese," it had too long been thought of as having something to do with "trees"! The misconception arose from Skilmer's supreme irony; he had all too successfully "achieved an overlay," as he liked to say when speaking of the technique of poetry. That is, by a triumph of art he had given a shallow surface glaze, a pretty spindrift, to the profound abysses of the poem—a glaze so *trompe-l'oeil* that many were never able to see beneath it. What the public had been doing was reading only the "overlay" instead of what he called the "substruct," and what they settled for was something miserably like this:

> I think that I shall never see
> A poem lovely as a tree.
>
> A tree whose hungry mouth is pressed
> Upon the earth's sweet flowing breast.
>
> Upon whose bosom snow has lain,
> And intimately lives with rain.
>
> A tree that looks at God all day,
> And lifts her leafy arms to pray.
>
> A tree that may in summer wear
> A nest of robins in her hair.
>
> Poems are made by fools like me,
> But only God can make a tree.

Sheer banality! (and how far short of Skilmer's own noble definition of a poem as "a shimmering spitball flung into the great catcher's-mitt of eternity.") But the poem's *inner*ness, which my researches have arrived at, is another thing entirely. What I mean to do here is demonstrate the "substruct," unit by unit, explicating where I can, though it is doubtful that any reader, or group of readers, will ever arrive at an adequate notion of the riches hidden in this most wonderful of poems.

1.

> *I* think? That I shall never, see!
> Up, owe 'em love. Leah's a tree.

Probably not since John Donne's "For Godsake hold your tongue, and let me love" has a poem opened with such explosive élan. "*I* think?" he rages; and in that fury is a ringing refusal to see life merely in terms of the "cogitations" that have amazed lesser poets. Here the whole Eliotic tradition of intellectualized verse is swept cleanly away forever—an achievement the more remarkable inasmuch as that tradition had not yet come into being. But few poets have had antennae so sensitive, been so unfailing a Tiresias (Therese? Ah yes!) in divining the yet-to-come. Crass indeed is the reader who fails to sense, in the proemial words, the poet's curling lip, or who fails to note the hoot of scorn in the derisive "see" that concludes the line with a vulgarity ah how *voulu*! Almost blatant, this effect; and yet, beneath the brassy fanfare, what delicate counterpoint of grammatical woodwinds in the antiphony of declarative mood to interrogative, an antiphony that becomes harangue when we feel it in terms of the inner dialogue, the colloquy of a soul tormented by an age when all values have turned moot. Yet, as always in Skilmer, violence tempered with amenity: instead of the scowling "will" of resolution, only the disclaiming modesty of that simple "shall."

The second line, opening with courage and defiance, can but deepen the stated theme. "Up!" (cf. the Italian "Su! coraggio!") as the poet, confronting the inenarrable chaos of his world, lifts himself from that slough of despond by the Muses' very bootstrap. Don't *give* love away, he exhorts himself; don't wanton away so rare a substance on the all and sundry. *Owe* them love; do not pay when payment is despised. How much terser these moving words than such romantic maundering as

> When I was one-and-twenty
> I heard a wise man say,
> "Give crowns and pounds and guineas
> But not your heart away . . ."

But—oh marvel of art—again the tight-lipped acerbity is softened by one of the loveliest transitions in all poetry. After the corrosive cynicism of the opening, the gentle evocation of biblical woman-hood fuses, as in Dante, with the mythology of the ancient world, in a line that sums up the fugacity of all things mortal. "Leah's a tree" indeed; Leah has *become* a tree, has escaped from the aggressor's pursuit, from the weary wheel of being. When Skilmer says "Leah" he is of course thinking of Daphne—the names have three letters (if no more) in common; our poet works by preference in that hallowed *three*, perhaps more meaningfully here than elsewhere, since in his sturdy American dialect *Therese* and *threes* would have been pronounced alike. It is no accident that the number of lines in the poem (12) is easily divisible by three, with none left over. Charac-teristic too of Skilmer's esemplastic knack is this grafting of image onto image; it is wholly natural that in thinking of the Ovidian Daphne he should conceive of her *a lo divino*—see her not as some mincing pagan, but aureate in the scriptural halo that Dante too looped like lassos of tinsel round her.

2.

A tree—who's hung? Greymouth is pressed
Upon the earth-Swede, Flo Ingbrest.

A tree is indeed a tree, embodies as nothing else the very essence of the arboreal. An image of the world's green beauty—but no less an emblem of its horror. Skilmer's panoramic imagination sees the tree as a death-image, a very gallows with its dismal fruit. Painstak-ing Dantists ("In our age," the poet dourly quipped, "there are no painless Dantists") may well see here the influence of Dante's Wood of the Suicides.

We have learned little about Flo Ingbrest—Florence C. Ingbrest of 1222 Stitt Street, Des Moines. Her very address is known only because it was found tattooed on the left hip of a sailor washed ashore at Tampa after the great hurricane of '23. It is clear that Miss Ingbrest meant much to the poet, who saw in this simple Swedish girl a power participating so fully in the chthonic matriarchal atavism of the dark earth itself that he calls her simply his "earth-Swede." Her earthy affections, however, were soon alienated by the vague and sinister figure the poet calls Greymouth, a misty shape ominous as any of the ghosts that slink nameless through the early Eliot. Though much research has been done on the unknown Greymouth, little has been ascertained. Dr. Woggs Clurth, basing his argument soundly on the morpheme "rey" in Greymouth, has proposed that he was really Watson King of Canton, the affable rapist; Dr.

Phemister Slurk, dispensing with what he derides as "evidence," has suggested that he represents Warren G. Harding, an Ohio politico of the twenties. Cavillings all: Greymouth, whosoever he may have "been" in the world we think of as real, now, through Skilmer's artistry, exists forever in the purlieus of the Muse—slinking, loose-lipped, drivelling, livid with his nameless vice.

3.

> Upon whose boozin's (no!) *has* lain
> Anne D'Intagh Mittley—lives wi' Thrane.

In the third stanza, sometimes insensitively printed as the fifth, the tragedy grows blacker yet. After Florence C. Ingbrest and a handful of casual flames, the poet sought solace with the Mittley sisters of Boston. Researchers have shown that there were two: Daisy (or "Diz") Mittley, and her much younger sister Anne D'Intagh. It was the younger the poet loved, but again the romance with blighted by a conniving interloper, this time the wealthy Thaddeus Thrane of Glasgow, whose nationality is slyly derided in the dialectal "wi' " for "with." The butt of frequent barbs in the Skilmer corpus, he is here dismissed with a contemptuous phrase. Though his beloved Anne lived "wi' " Thrane at the time the poem was written, Skilmer seems less troubled by this passing infidelity than by her amour with Greymouth—for Greymouth is the true antecedent of "whose." We now learn that he was a heavy drinker—and immediately the mysterious soubriquet is clear. Extensive research has established that *gris* is the common French word for *grey*. But *gris* also means *drunk*. Greymouth then is unmasked as Drunk Mouth. Indeed, so great a guzzler was Greymouth that the loyal Miss Mittley was said, by a witty metonomy (or synecdoche) to have lain not on his bosom but (with a pun that anticipates Joyce by several weeks) on his "boozin's." One almost hesitates to mention that "bosoms" too has its questionable advocates. Be that as it may, one wonders if in all literature the tragedy of four lives has been so harrowingly adumbrated? All one can conjure up for comparison is Dante's

> Siena me fè; disfecemi Maremma.

But Dante, with his five and a half words for one life, is longwinded compared with Skilmer, who averages a mere three words per head, or even less, if one counts the "wi' " as fractional diction. In this grisly aperçu, so true of all humanity, the resources of typography too are put to unexampled use, with the two-letter "no" followed by an exclamation mark that is like a spine straight with moral indignation, and enclosed in the semicircularity of parentheses, like lips rounded in incredulous refusal. But the "no" is uncompromisingly jostled by the assertive *has,* with its harsh aspirate, distorted from honest Roman type into italics, set askew from the vertical: even the letters, means the poet, have *lost their aplomb* before the moral horror. (A textual note: there are those, and their name is legion, who read "Hugh Inta Mittley" in the second line. But nothing in Skilmer's emotional history gives countenance to a suppositious passion for Anne's little brother Hugh, then three years and some months old.)

4.

A tree that *looks* it!—Gawd! Auld, eh?
And Liffs hurl eavey alms, *tout prêts.*

And so it goes. The world-weariness, the melancholy, Skilmer in the depths of his Hamlet mood, or what he himself ruefully called, in the bad German he had learned from "certain ladies" in Milwaukee, "meines Hamletische Gesauerpusskeit." Does even Hamlet, whom so many have called the "Danish Skilmer," have a line so weary, stale, flat, and unprofitable as "A tree that *looks* it"?—in which the poet accepts the humble monotony of things as they are in their weary *haecceitas,* the sad fact that they are only what they are, and so fully *look* what they are, instead of embodying the splendor of their Platonic archetypes. "The interminable pyramidal napkin," broods E. E. Cummings—but how sesquipedalian this in comparison with Skilmer's demotic oomph. And from time immemorial this nauseating sameness—old indeed, and more than old. Probably there is no more plangent understatement in the language than Skilmer's simple but despairing "auld." For the poet, unable to tear his ravaged heart from thoughts of Thrane, glumly Scotticizes: "Auld, eh?" he spits out, thereby more keenly identifying Thrane with all he most distrusts in reality. Cosmic gloom induces wide-ranging speculations: the bard's restless mind hovers around the anthropology he loved so deeply, and from what sad strata of the past he must have disinterred his pregnant and touching lines about the Liffs. A Liff, as we know now, is the baseborn son of a Riff father and a Lett mother.*

---

*So Professor Nims alleges. There are others who take a less simplistic view. "Liff," as every schoolboy knows, is the way Dubliners refer to the River Liffey, whose waves are here in reference, since one casts alms, or bread, upon the waters. It would seem that Skilmer is alluding to the future *Finnegans Wake* (Anna Livia Plurabelle) which was to be so profoundly influenced by "Therese."—ED. [F. B.]

But even a Liff, born who knows where in semi-savagery, may hurl the alms of charity (as the miserly Thrane never did), alms that shelter us like eaves from the cold and rook-delighting heaven, alms that are always ready, *tout prêts*, to relieve us. In his polyglot technique, Skilmer, as so often, again anticipates the practice of Ezra Pound, his foremost epigone: he uses the French words to imply that even the barbarous Liffs have achieved a measure of urbanity, as compared with certain uncivilized Scots he could mention. The touch of Gallic vivacity brightens, but all too briefly, the poem's Stygian verge. (Again, a textual note: some read "A tree that looks *two*," and explain it as referring to the illusory nature of perceived reality. Rubbish!).

5.

A tree . . . that Mayan summer! 'Ware
Honesta Robbins! Henna hair!

In explicating this *locus classicus* of modern poetry, it is necessary to bear in mind certain facts about the manuscripts—or "menu-scraps," as Skilmer himself wryly called them. Always a victim of poverty, the poet used to quill his sublimest ditties on the backs of labels laboriously soaked off the bottles of whiskey on which he shrewdly spent what little means the world afforded him. Thousands of these labels have survived, mute testimony to the trembling fingers that treasured them—each bearing only a few words of that great cornucopia of song he willed posterity. (There are also three labels from spaghetti cans, and one from a small can of succotash.) A study of some hundreds of manuscripts shows that Skilmer first wrote "A tree . . . that Aztec summer!"—a reference to the year he spent in Central America with an anthropological expedition. An idyllic year, possibly the happiest of his life, when his natural warmth and high spirits, so often thwarted by dingy circumstance, overflowed with an almost boyish ebullience. Arriving in early May, he had been married there three times by late June—and each time happily. Hence the little idyll about the Aztec summer, found on the manuscript *Old Overholt 202* and certain others. (The spaghetti labels have little authority.) But the definitive reading is to be found on *Heaven Hill 714:* not "Aztec" but "Mayan," a word which Skilmer pronounced with the long *a* of *May.*

"A tree . . . that Mayan summer!"—and there it is forever, the bright leaves bathed in a golden haze of old romance, lost histories. An idyll, yes—but before long Skilmer's domestic bliss was shattered. He was followed to Yucatan by Mrs. Chloe P. Robbins of Ashtabula, a steamfitter's widow. With her came her daughter, the forty-seven-year-old Honesta Lou, whom Skilmer called his "buxom nymph o' siren voice"—she was six feet two, her flaring red hair vivid with purple highlights. It is this vision of somewhat menacing loveliness that is now evoked in lines that recall Coleridge's

> Beware, beware,
> His flashing eyes! his floating hair!

With deft economy, Skilmer laments the timelessness of his plight by using the archaic " 'Ware" for "Beware."

6.

> Po' Em's our maid. 'Bye, fools! Like me,
> Butt only. Godkin may kertree!

Almost from the beginning, it was clear to a happy few that what seemed "poem" was really "Po' Em," a poor Southern girl named Emma or Emily. Her identity long eluded researchers, until Dr. Cecily P. Wunkhead, basing her argument largely on blood tests, litmus paper, and *Old Crow 1066* (and rejecting the famous "succotash reading" as spurious) proposed that the unknown Em was none other than Emily Dickinson. To show that Emily is the mouthpiece not only for New England but for all America Skilmer resorts to an amazingly simple device: he gives her a *southern* voice: probably not since Praxilla has the ethos of inner dynamic been so functionally aligned with dialectal specificity.

And why Emily Dickinson? Because she is the American Muse, ever at our side to lend a helping hand with torch on high—a servant, she, of servants of the laurel. Po' Em's our *maid,* and with our trust in her we can afford to dismiss the vulgar many, as Skilmer does with much the same testy arrogance that Yeats and Jonson flaunted. Whereas Jonson needed ten words or so in his

> Far from the wolves' dark jaw, and the black asses' hoof . . . ,

Skilmer does it in two burning words, " 'Bye, fools!" But immediately compassion returns, and he remembers that the ordinary man, just as he, is only a butt for the slings and arrows of outrageous fortune. This might have set a-moping a less resilient bard, but Skilmer recovers, to conclude with a thundering diapason of *Jubel und Ruhm* such as not even Beethoven has ever equalled: the magnificent "Godkin may kertree!" Godkin: a little god, that least of the divinities in man, godkin *may*—but how the gala vowel, long *a,* implies lyric certainty in a word which, heard by the intellect alone, might seem to allow for doubt. *May* what? He may "kertree"! It is fitting that the pinnacle of Skilmer's sublimity should glitter in this final phrase of his greatest poem. And how like him to achieve sublimity by means so simple! Here he seizes from its lexical limbo the humble prefix *ker-*, as in *kerplunk, kerplop, kerflooie*. A prefix that only once before in English had assumed nobility, in J. F. Dudley-Andover's sublime translation of Dante's

E caddi come corpo morto cade

as

I plopped kerplunk, as corpses plop kerplunk

Holding the precious *ker-* in the jeweler's forceps of his wit, Skilmer works it into a new thing entirely by fusing it with the unexpected "tree": to "kertree," to burst into flower, into foliage, nay, into very tree itself! One sees the creativity of the universe, the vital breath taking form in a great efflorescence of green, a cosmic sneeze as if the whole sweet growth of April and May, by some cinematic magic, were effected in an instant.

It is around this magical last line that scholarship itself tends oftenest to kertree. "Godkin" in particular has stimulated the finest hermeneutic acumen of our century to new Everests of perception. Professor Fiedler has explored in depth the profound viscerality of "gutkin." The Cambridge School has constructed a breathtaking new theory of the origin of tragedy on the reading "goat-kin." It is hardly surprising that "incentive psychologists" make much of "goadkin." Professor Fitts, citing γάδ- and κύων, finds a fish-dog, or dog-fish, allusion that unfortunately cannot be discussed in these pages. Nor can the suggestion of certain Welshmen, who urge an early form of "gwiddcwyngh." Professor Rákóczi is more to the point in reminding us of what careless readers might forget: "gyödzskin" is a medieval South Hungarian gypsy cant word (though hardly the most common) for a thickish wine made out of half-rotted arti-chokes: what vistas open here! Only recently Nopançópi Hópail has removed the whole question from the field of linguistic speculation to that of biographical allusion by proposing—how imaginatively!— that "godkin" is "Godkin": E. L. Godkin (1831-1902), who came to America from Ireland when twenty-five, founded *The Nation,* and was a disciple of the Bentham-Mill-Grote school of philosophy.

On the whole subject, however, no one commands more respect than Professor Fredson Bowers, whose monumental fifty-volume edition of Skilmer, *The Fourteen Poems and Certain Fragments,* is promised for 1970 by the Southeastern Arkansas Junior Teachers' College Press. As early as 1962 Professor Bowers wrote: "I wonder if you have thoroughly considered the evidence of *Old Crow 16?* In this version, possibly a trial, 'May' is capitalized and must therefore be taken as the month. If this is so, the possibility obtains that the godkin referred to is the month of May, and hence we can explain the diminutive. After all, in the month of vernal growth there is something godlike in the creative surge of the sap and the burgeoning of the chlorophyll. However, the syntax is then in question. There is perhaps no need to associate 'godkin May' with the 'butt,' even though a month that pretends to be a little god might be a butt for something. I think on the whole we are to take 'godkin May's' activities with approval, not with disapproval. If so, then I suggest that Skilmer, overcome with the wonder of vegetable love and the rites of spring, finds that normal syntax deserts him and is reduced to two paired but mutually discrete exclamations. 'Godkin May!' or: Oh the wonder of it all! And then that exclamation that sums up the plosive force of May, 'Kertree!' "

This is brilliantly reasoned and would seem to be the last word on the subject—but Professor Bowers had not yet done with it. A few years later he decided that the line had further subtleties, which he explained, in bibliographical terms, as follows: "It could be read as a series of ejaculations, rising to a climax. The lack of punctuation appropriate for this reading is of course nothing unusual with Skilmer. That is: only God-kin—the one God—He only. Then, in remembered ecstasy of that Mexican spring, May [and here Professor Bowers shows his grasp of contemporary allusion] just busting out all over, like the bursting sap, the springing leaf, in the ultimate mystical union with Nature, kertree! Thus exclamation points should be placed after each unit. I suggest these are at least alternate readings."

But perhaps these are matters beyond the power of man to determine. However it may be, Godkin may indeed kertree—but it takes a poet of supreme insight to perceive this, a poet able to wrest language from dead strata of the past and kerplunk it living in the midst of men. But explication is no substitute for the poem. Here, for the first time presented in its ur-textual splendor, is what many* would consider the greatest lyric poem of our literature:

THERESE

By Joe E. Skilmer

I think? That I shall never, see!
Up, owe 'em love. Leah's a tree.

---

*Does this include Professor Ian Watt?—ED. [F. B.]

A tree—who's hung? Greymouth is pressed
Upon the earth-Swede, Flo Ingbrest.

Upon whose boozin's (no!) *has* lain
Anne D'Intagh Mittley—lives wi' Thrane.

A tree that *looks* it!—Gawd! Auld, eh?
And Liffs hurl eavey alms, *tout prêts*.

A tree . . . that Mayan summer! 'Ware
Honesta Robbins! Henna hair!

Po' Em's our maid. 'Bye, fools! Like me,
Butt only. Godkin may kertree!

RICHARD KOSTELANETZ

The New Class

(1976)

The American Poetry Anthology (1975)—what a pretentious, encompassing title for Daniel Halpern's collection that, upon closer inspection, appears quite modest and parochial. At least sixty-five of Halpern's seventy-six contributors have, like himself, worked as college teachers—not of literature or art or history, to be sure, but of creative writing. Many of them, to judge from the biographical notes, have also received graduate degrees not in literature or something else but in "writing," often from the University of Iowa. This anthology is the end result of a hermetic system: an M.F.A editing M.F.As' poems for aspiring M.F.As to study. Its precursor in this respect is David Allan Evans' *New Voices in American Poetry* (1973), whose preface acknowledges the aim not to establish taste but to fall snugly into "courses in creative writing." Are academic "writing" positions becoming the plums (or plots) that indubitably minor poets pick?

Ever fashionable, *The Ampoant* includes black poets, Amerindian poets, one Nisei poet, but it does not include New York school poets, underground poets, avowedly gay poets, visual poets, sound poets, minimal poets, or nonsyntactic poets—absolutely none. Why? One reason that comes immediately to mind is that members of the latter groups, unlike the former, are never employed to teach creative writing. Since their work is, for now at least, academically blacklisted, it is not included here.

The book's total exclusion of "undesirables" suggests that a sort of new fascism has struck again. Only a year ago, I suggested in *The American Poetry Review* (which, curiously, exemplifies the sin), "The complete absence of [visual poetry], along with other avant-garde forms, in the poetry magazines and anthologies is one symptom of literary opportunism in its current form, impressing academics by the neglect of what they consider 'not poetry.'"

Indicatively, there is only one full-time writer here, Jim Harrison, but the choice from his work is limited to poems composed some years ago, when he was teaching creative writing, naturally. *The Ampoant* is an act of opportunistic literary politicking, whose heft (506 pages) acknowledges a new establishment whose existence I for one had not previously perceived. Tellingly, this high-priced book comes not from a quality paperbacker, anticipating modest returns, but a mass house, Avon (Hearst Corp.), whose salesmen undoubtedly envision gross sales to, you guessed it, creative writing classes. Bless 'em.

Though Halpern's preface claims "heterogeneity, in terms of form, attitude, and treatment of content," I see an editorial principle that favors not diversity but uniformity—more precisely, miniscule diversity amidst general uniformity: a soft surrealism, image-centered, stylistically prosy, unmetrical, humorless, slightly incoherent, willfully mysterious, structurally flaccid and, of necessity, attitudinally "poetic." The language of these poems is predominantly low-keyed and undistinguished, the diction stilted, the subjects trivial and the tone limp, as words march militarily from flush left-hand margins in unbroken horizontal lines, straight through conventional syntax and unemphatic line breaks to predictable periods. A quiet modesty pervades, as the book eschews encompassing visions, moralistic jeremiads, blatant confessionalism, even strong language; everything extreme is earnestly excised from *The Ampoant*. The contents are so similar that an ingenious reader could easily take lines from one poet and work them into poems by another poet.

Halpern also connects his selections to the "growing internationalism of American poetry," but none of *these* poems were published abroad (unlike more experimental American poetry, which often appears abroad). None of *these* poets relate to their European contemporaries. *These* Americans are importers of a putative European past, rather than exporters of a present American art that participates in European developments. The false claim seems concocted to cater to the American academic sweet tooth for things "European."

The Ampoant has so much prose, artificially chopped into lines of poetry, that the reader would relish some variation, even an interlude of dialect or, yes, a hackneyed rhyme. A typically prosy example comes from Halpern himself: "On the prow, / standing on red planks, / the white maiden holds / hand to temple, / faint, keening. / The fog snags the edge / of her gown, dissolves / it at the ankle, begins / for thighs, for breasts / unlike white stone, her / neck, and then her / lips like white stone." Passages like this make me wonder about the current status of the academic distinction between *poetry*, which is to say heightened language, and irredeemable *prose?* (The review you are now reading is, to my mind, prose. *The Ampoant* suggests that it might well pass as "poetry": The review / you / are now / reading is, / to my mind, prose. . . .)

Given Halpern's preference for murky prose that is difficult to

read, but easy to "teach," (and "poetic" prose as an ultimate exten-
sion of prosy "poetry"), it is scarcely surprising that, even within the
circumscribed class of poets he favors, some of the better practitio-
ners are omitted. Superior post-1934, sometime professor-poets
that come to my alphabetical mind include Dick Allen, R. H. W.
Dillard, Ray DiPalma, Charles Doria, Albert Drake, Siv Cedering
Fox, David Franks, Albert Goldbarth, John Jacob, Joe Johnson,
Laurence Lieberman, N. J. Loftus, Richard Mathews, Michael Jo-
seph Phillips, Jonathan Price, Grace Schulman, David Shapiro,
Jane Shore, Karen Swenson, Al Young. There are, no doubt, other
young poetry professors who, like these, write better poetry than
Halpern's weaker colleagues.

Theoretically, academic affiliation has nothing to do with poetic
style, but the grim uniformity of Halpern's inclusions, along with
the absence of esthetic surprises, suggests that he perceives a direct
connection. The implicit critical achievement of *The Ampoant* might
be the identification of junior academia's current period style.
However, even here Halpern sabotages his literary purposes, for
an anthology representing a certain class of once-scorned writers
(academic poets) should include only the very best work. Other-
wise, skeptical readers will think that the group as a whole is com-
pletely undistinguished, while the chosen poets will think their
literary cause betrayed. *The Ampoant* is, alas, the sort of anthology
from which the better contributors will want to disassociate them-
selves. Some of those initially blessed will recognize the kiss of
death.

Indicatively, the book's biographical notes are nearly identi-
cal, representing an implicit tribute to editorial homogenization.
Though many of the contributors' names are unfamiliar, their
"credentials" are not. The Halpern bionote usually opens with the
chosen poet's year of birth, followed by the universities at which
he or she has studied, the places in which he or she has lived,
awards received, publications edited, and colleges taught. A typi-
cal example, aside from omitting *alma mater,* is the editor's resumé
for himself:

> Daniel Halpern (1945) was born in Syracuse and grew up in Los
> Angeles and Seattle. He spent two years living in Tangier, Morocco
> [*sic*] where he began the literary magazine *Antaeus.* He has received
> various awards, including the YMHA Discovery Award in 1971, the
> Great Lakes Colleges National Book Award for his first book of
> poems, National Endowment for the Arts Fellowships, and was a
> Robert Frost Fellow at Bread Loaf. He is the editor of the American
> Poetry Series for the Ecco Press, and teaches at Princeton University
> and The New School for Social Research.

These biographical presentations are, like the book itself, colorless and earnestly ambitious, speaking not about poetry but careers. There are no quotations of purposes from the contributors, no critical commentary or even descriptive characterization from the editor. There is nothing as well about husbands, wives, or lovers. It is all so perfunctory that one suspects the presence of a machine. It is hard to remember one biographical note apart from the others; it is nearly as hard to remember individual poems. What is one to make of this fascination with professional positions (which are not poems) and with awards (which are not poems, either)?

It would be neither unflattering nor inaccurate to characterize Halpern as a remarkably sensitive and successful literary politician, whose magazine *Antaeus* has featured well-known writers who have, in turn, made Halpern's reputation as a celebrity-chaser—the Norman Podhoretz of the younger generation. (Thus, the awards and fellowships.) A young literary politician choosing this well-trod opportunistic path generally makes a point of ignoring his chronological contemporaries. In this respect, devoting *The Ampoant* to youngsters represents a creditable editorial departure for Halpern. However, since he has, in the past, exhibited so sure a sense of the real sources of professional power, I take this new anthology to be a fat acknowledgment of the literary-political preeminence of provincial professors. Indeed, at least in poetry, that group, with its magazines and small presses, might by now be more powerful than the literary-industrial complex which, though it publishes some of Halpern's own books, pays increasingly less attention to poetry. The publisher's publicity flier declares, echoing their author-editor Halpern: "Mr. Halpern has chosen the poets for this anthology without regard to 'schools of poetry', current fashion or literary cliques." What egregious nonsense. He has chosen up sides and isolated his own team. Onward, college soldiers.

It seems to me that Richard Howard, himself a master literary politician, single-handedly keeps alive an older generation of academic poets, memorialized in his critical book, *Alone in America* (1969) and his anthology, *Preferences* (1974). If Howard did not exist, let me conjecture, these poets would disappear from public view. Halpern apparently wants to serve a similar function with a younger generation of academics, becoming their Man in Manhattan, who will be amply rewarded with invitations to declaim his own poetry at backwoods universities. Typically again, Halpern, as a sensitive conservative politician, acknowledges in his preface such old-boy powerhouses as Howard Moss, Leonard Randolph, Stanley Kunitz, and Donald Hall, "without whose help the publication of this book would have been impossible." What, one wonders, is meant by "impossible"?

Back in 1957, three then-young academic poets—Donald Hall, Robert Pack, and Louis Simpson—produced *New Poets of England and America,* a paperback anthology that exploited fifties conservatism on the way to the classroom. The copy I have reads "Seventh Printing October 1962." For nearly a decade, it suggested not how poetry might be written but what sorts of poems will earn a coveted A. Though both editors and contributors to *New Poets* prospered in the academic world, the kind of metrical poetry they practiced has since disappeared from public view. Perhaps the book's success in the classroom, coupled with the general mediocrity of its inclusions, contributed to erasing this once-dominant style from the printed page.

I would wager that *The Ampoant* will have a similar, two-sided career.

Fame, Fortune, and Other
Tawdry Illusions

My name is not a household word like Drano or Kleenex. Mostly people have no particular reaction when they meet me, although you can never be sure. My gynecologist "knows who I am" because his receptionist Audrey read one of my novels, as has my accountant. However, from time to time people recognize me on the street or in odd and disconcerting circumstances like in a shopping mall when I was trying on a skirt, or another time in a restaurant when Woody and I were having a bloody if moderately quiet argument. I am not so bad about accidental recognition as I used to be. I do not try to crawl into my own pocket or pretend if I don't move a muscle or breathe, I will wake in my own bed, but I can't say I ever behave more gracefully than a sneak thief caught.

Publishing books, especially about women, brings letters that can break your heart: women losing custody of their children, women shut up in mental institutions because they rebelled against being an unpaid domestic or took a female lover, women in all shapes and colors of trouble.

> Women dyeing the air with desperation,
> women weaving like spiders from the gut
> of emptiness, women
> swollen with emotion, women with words
> piling up in the throat like fallen leaves. . . .
>   "Women of Letters"

You also get flattering letters from women as well as some men who tell you what your books have meant to them. You also receive hate mail, if you have any visible politics.

The admirers who do not give pleasure are those who call up, generally when you are sleeping or writing, making supper, entertaining friends and say, "Hello, I read your book, I happen to be in Wellfleet, and can I come over?" There is no way to satisfy such a caller. When I was younger, I was so astonished and grateful anybody had read anything of mine and liked it, I would invariably say yes. Dreadful, dreadful scenes resulted. Worse than that, whole boring evenings and days and someone who felt they had the right to invade again at will and at some point would have to be dealt with forcefully. People who want to invite themselves into your house to meet you generally are pushy and sometimes more than a little nuts, and nothing less than letting them move in or letting them have at least an arm or leg of their own will satiate a baseless hunger. The people I lived with after *Small Changes* was published put their collective foot down, saying they got nothing whatsoever out of tourists who came to gape at me. Now I make excuses, unless I know the person in some way, unless a genuine connection exists so that we can hope for two-way communication.

Every week several books and at least one manuscript arrive with requests for blurbs, criticism, help of some sort. I used to try to respond to all those requests, but I got further and further and further behind. The books I now put on a pile in terms of when they arrived (I am currently a year and eight months behind) and the manuscripts I promptly return, if the authors provided postage. I do not attempt to read manuscripts at all, unless it is for someone I know. That alone happens at least twenty-five times a year. All the books I do finally glance at or skim at least and a certain number I read, but I feel haunted, snowed in by them. I remember how long I was utterly unknown. I feel guilty, but I know rationally that if I was to read even a quarter of them, I would do nothing else; and I do not have a lot of time to read in the first place. Unlike academics, I don't have long vacations. I may take a two week vacation every couple of years, and if Woody can come with me, I will take a three or four day vacation once a year on a business trip to an interesting place. But to make a living at writing, I have to hustle and I have to work six days a week.

I travel a lot giving readings, and there the weirdness flourishes in some pockets like mold. People go through ego dances before me that I find confusing and bemusing. I do not have the middle-class patina and I am not much good at making gracious casual conversation. I like best to talk to people one on one, not necessarily about me. Women who go about giving readings are expected to act like ladies, like mommies, or like tough dykes, and I don't fit into any of those standard roles.

Joanna Russ says it's my body type and my style that gets me in trouble. Nobody tries to make her play mommy, or at least not quite as often at first glance. She's tall as the Empire State Building, lean and elegant, and dresses tailored. I am five feet four (almost), *zoftig*, and dress more or less peasanty.

I remember about 1973 or 1974, I was wearing my standard Women's Liberation Army garb, slumped way over so my boobs wouldn't jiggle too much because I wasn't supposed to wear a bra, dressed in about thirty pounds of denim, when I thought to myself, Why do I have to wear male drag to talk to and about women? I went back to skirts. I dress the way I feel good. And I always read in a dress: let there be no mistake I am a woman, proud of it.

What do people want from somebody they have heard of? It is not even, frequently, a matter of having read your work and formed expectations, for I have gone through upsetting pas-de-deux with individuals who had no idea what kind of work I produce. I was pure celebrity to them, some kind of superperson because a published writer. Of the people who have some familiarity, many are attached to one particular novel and express resentment that I do not resemble physically or in character either Miriam or Beth in *Small Changes,* or Vida in *Vida*—that I am not a native speaker of Spanish, like Consuelo in *Woman on the Edge of Time,* or a karate enthusiast like Leslie in *The High Cost of Living,* or a systems analyst like Miriam. I have had fans become hostile when I tried to explain that a novel was not autobiographical. The hostility seems to divide into those who feel put upon (I thought it was true and now I find it's just a story!) and those who suspect you're trying to keep the truth from them: all novels are thinly disguised autobiography and you're just trying to cover up being a lesbian or being a mother who has lost custody of her children, or whatever.

Readers of the poems tend to have somewhat more accurate expectations, although one of the first things always said when I get off the plane is, "I/we expected you to be taller" or "I/we expected you to be bigger." I intend to write a poem soon about being four feet tall, and then everybody will say, "Oh, but we expected you to be smaller." All microphones are preset as if everybody were five feet ten, and the podiums are sized accordingly.

Once in a while you arrive into a situation where somebody has decided beforehand you are their sex object. You land and are visited with this great rush that has nothing whatsoever to do with you, and which seems to assume you have no commitments, no attachments, but are really a figment of their sexual imagination capable of fitting right into the fantasies they have worked up. I find that so off-putting I don't even feel flattered. Mostly men do this, but sometimes women do it. There may even be the implication that they got you this real nice gig, paying more than they think you or any woman is worth, so you should thank them by rolling over belly up in their bed.

My advice to the struggling young writer is, never thank anybody sexually, and never use your body as payment or prepayment for help. Fuck only people you want, and then no matter what goes wrong and how you get clobbered emotionally, at least you will have catered to your own sexual tastes and you will not feel victimized.

You have been your own free agent and will be stronger for it. If you are honestly turned on by someone who can help you, clear sailing. But if you are a woman, you have to be especially careful you don't get known as X's girlfriend, because then you can write *The Four Quartets* and still people will say you got published because you were X's girlfriend.

Every writer has some groupies, and how you deal with them is your own decision, within the law. You can sense that a great many of them would not like you as you are, as opposed to the idealized or otherwise fictional image they are toting around; or what they offer is a come-on for expecting you are going to be for them what Joanna Russ calls a magic mommy: solve all their problems, make them happy, get them published or produced or whatever, make the world right—for them—and have no real needs of your own to be satisfied. Since writers are generally pretty needy beings, such encounters are programmed for disaster.

On the other hand, one of the possible relationships that may work out for a woman writer is a relationship with a younger person who does know who you are and what you do, and who genuinely admires that before getting to know you—but does get to know you. Such an intimacy can contain a lot less bloody gutfighting than some-body, particularly a man, your own age. Oftentimes women who have achieved some small success find that the man or woman they lived with beforehand cannot adjust to what they view as an unneces-sary fuss about somebody they knew back when. Fame loses you lovers and friends, as well as bringing people flocking closer. It does, however, make it easier to find new relationships. You can pick and choose a little. That doesn't mean you'll choose any more intelli-gently than you did when you were seventeen and still squeezing pimples or twenty-five and invisible as a grain of salt at the seashore, but you may have learned something.

Many men and many women cannot bear success even of the most limited and partial sort coming to someone they married or whose life they have been sharing. They may feel they cannot hold on to their lover with all the new competition, real or imagined. More often they resent what they feel is the shift of emphasis from themselves as center of the marriage or life, to the other person who was supposed to dance attendance on them, not to be rushing off to Paducah to give poetry readings, not be signing books, mak-ing speeches, or giving interviews.

You will, as a traveling woman, find all too often that that fuss, however minor, also infuriates local men who feel that you are after all just a cunt and they've seen better, and why isn't everyone fuss-ing about them? Similarly you will find as a traveling woman that frequently academic women in universities who may write a poem or two a year or always meant to write someday will look at you with annoyance and just about say to you, why all the attention on you? You're just a woman like me. Why should they pay you to come in here and read, lecture, pontificate?

People also commonly confuse three things quite distinct. As an American poet you can achieve a certain measure of fame, but you don't get rich and you don't acquire power. David Rockefeller is rich and David Rockefeller is powerful. Allen Ginsberg may be famous, but he doesn't own half of Venezuela or even New Jersey and he isn't consulted on the national defense budget or our policies toward South Africa. Morris the Cat enjoyed far more fame than any writer I know, but you didn't imagine him as wielding power.

Few writers are rich. If they are, maybe they inherited money. When you hear about a $100,000 paperback deal, the hardcover publisher usually takes $50,000, the agent $5,000, and the writer's share on paper is $45,000, except that she got a $15,000 advance to finish the book, so that $15,000 is taken out of her share. That gives her $30,000 minus taxes. Let's say it takes her three years to write a novel, I would think a decent average of what people need. My shortest book took two years; the others, all longer. That gives her about $8,000 a year income for the next three years. Happy $100,000 deal!

For a writer, having some fame is surely better than having none, since if people have heard of you they are likelier to buy your books than if they have not; but it doesn't mean you're drinking champagne out of crystal goblets while you count your oil revenue shares, and it doesn't mean you have any choice about how the world is run and what happens in the society you're part of. Similarly the writer above with the $8,000 coming in for the next three years is immensely better off than she was when she wrote for an occasional $5 or $50 fee from the quarterlies, or when she did a reading a week for twenty weeks at one hundred bucks per reading, ending up sick in bed and worn out with no writing done and having earned a total of $2,000 after her expenses on the road are deducted.

Make no mistake: I like applause. I adore being admired. I even like signing books, which I understand some writers don't. I'm tickled somebody is buying them. I work hard when I give workshops and try to make intelligent political points when students question me. I like having my books discussed; I passionately care to have them read.

But I resent jealousy, especially when beamed at me by people who have made as clear choices in their lives as I have. I know how invisible I was to the kind of people I meet around universities and

other institutions in my nonfamous life, when I was poor and sub-
sisting on various underpaid part-time positions. I know how they
treat their secretaries, waitresses, telephone operators, cleaning
women, store clerks. I was living in a slum, eating macaroni and
wearing second-hand clothes (not then fashionable) and chewing
aspirins because I couldn't pay a dentist while I wrote the first six
novels before the one that got published.

If I could possibly forget how little respect or understanding I
received from other people when I was a serious but largely unpub-
lished writer, I'd get a refresher course every day. I live with a
young writer, Ira Wood, and I see how little respect he gets because
he has not yet been sanctified by the fame machine. It's hard get-
ting started in the arts, and one of the things that is hardest, is that
nobody regards you as doing real work until somebody certifies
you by buying what you do. "For the young who want to" was
written for him, to cheer him on a few years before we were actu-
ally living together.

Another kind of irritation I provoke in resident or visiting male
writers is drawing larger audiences or selling more books than they
do, whereupon they are careful to inform me it's because I
"jumped on this women's lib bandwagon." I'm fashionable, but
they're universal. Universal includes only white men with university
degrees who identify with patriarchal values, but never mind even
that. If they imagine it helps me to be known as a feminist, they
have never read my reviews. The overwhelming majority judge my
work solely in terms of its content by a reviewer who hates the
politics and feels none of the obligations I do when I review works
to identify my bias and try to deal with the writer's intentions.
Jealous males also seem to have failed to notice that the women's
movement while touching the lives of a great many women no
longer has access to the media, and enjoys little money and no
political clout. To try to bring about social change in this country is
always to bring down punishment on your head. My grandfather, a
union organizer, was murdered. At various times in my life I have
had my phone tapped, been tailed, been beaten very, very thor-
oughly with a rich medley of results to this day, gassed, had my mail
opened, lost jobs, been vetoed as a speaker by boards of trustees as
in Utah, been heckled, insulted, dismissed, refused grants and posi-
tions that have consistently gone to lesser writers, and they imagine
there is some bandwagon I am riding on. A tumbril, perhaps.

Then there are local politicos. A phenomenon I have noticed
since my antiwar days is how rank and file in American movements
for social change treat those who have assumed, perhaps fought for
or perhaps had thrust upon them, some kind of leadership. Fre-
quently the mistrust with which your own treat you is sufficient to

send people into paranoia or early burn out, away from political activity damned fast; it certainly contributes to crossing over to the Establishment where at least you can expect that people will be polite to you.

If you are effective at anything, you will be sharply criticized. The real heroes of many people on the Left and in the women's community are failures who remain very pure according to a scriptural line and speak only to each other. Also many harbor fantasies that you are rich. The creeping desire I suppose is to believe that if you sacrificed a principle or two and perhaps actually spoke in American rather than jargon, you would instantly be pelted by hard money. At every college where I go a feminist will demand to know how I dare publish with New York houses rather than the local Three Queer Sisters press—as if the point of feminism isn't to try to reach women who don't agree already, rather than cozily assuming we are a "community" of pure souls and need only address each other. Often women who have some other source of support (husband, family, trust fund, academic job) will accuse you of selling out if you get paid for your writing or for speaking.

Feminist presses have an important function, as do all small presses. With the New York publishers almost to a house owned by large conglomerates, they are the one hope for freedom of expression and opinion. The all-pervasive electronic media are not open to those of us who do not share the opinions of the board of directors of Mobil Oil Corporation and Exxon, of I.T.T. and Anaconda Copper. What was true in the days of Thomas Paine and what is true today is that you can print your own pamphlet or book. The printed word is far more democratic than television or radio. You do not need to be a millionaire to acquire and run a printing press.

Just as a small press does not take much capital to set up and run, owners whether collective or individual of small presses can and do take chances on books that will make little money, that appeal to a small group. Most of the important writers of our day were first published by small presses and some such as James Joyce were published by small presses for their whole professional lives.

Conglomerate publishers may not be interested in a book because it is too original. They may be offended by its politics. I found out with *The High Cost of Living* it is still impossible to write a novel with a lesbian as a protagonist and have it reviewed as anything but a novel with a lesbian as the protagonist—nothing else is visible behind that glaring and overbearing fact. A book in fact may appeal to only a small audience, quite honestly, but appeal strongly to that audience and thus remain a good backlist item for a small publisher who can keep that book in print.

You can print a book as fine and beautiful and much more

attractive in fact than the big publishers. The nub is distribution. The women I most want to reach do not come into feminist bookstores and may not walk into bookstores at all. They buy books at the supermarket, the drugstore, the bus station, the airport. I cannot reach those women if I publish with small presses, because small presses do not get their books into such places.

At a certain point I may be forced out of the mass paperbacks. I am always aware of that political and economic squeeze. But as long as I can get into mass paperback, I will. And I will resent the attempt to make me feel guilty for (1) lacking inherited money, the security of any other profession, or a husband to support me; and thus needing to make my living by the work I do; (2) trying to reach as many women as I can through the system I am trying to change, until it is changed enough to bypass it.

Fame has a two-edged effect on the character. On the one hand, if you suffer from early schooled self-hatred, then fame can mellow you. If you like yourself, you may be able to like others better. Naturally I apply this to myself, believing myself easier-going since the world has done something besides kick me repeatedly in the bread basket. However, I would also say that fame—like money and probably like power—is habituating. You become so easily accustomed to being admired, that you begin to assume there is something inherently admirable in your character and person, a halo of special soul stuff that everybody ought to recognize at first glance.

Fame can easily oil the way to arrogance. It can as easily soften you to cozy mental flab, so you begin to believe every word you utter is equally sterling and every word you write is golden. There is a sort of balloon quality to some famous men—including famous writers—and you know they may never actually sit alone in a room agonizing and working as hard as it takes to do good work, ever again. You may even come to regard yourself as inherently lovable, which is peculiar given how writers actually spend a lot of time recording the bitter side of the human psyche and our utter foolishness. Having a fuss made over one leads to the desire to have more of a fuss made over one, and even to feel that nobody else quite so much deserves being fussed over.

We can easily confuse the luck of the dice and the peculiarities of remuneration in this society with inner worth. I recently overheard an engineer who writes occasional poetry berating the organizer of a reading because he felt he wasn't being given a prominent enough spot in the line-up. "My time is worth something," I heard him announce, and he meant it: he considered what he was paid by the hour and day as an engineering consultant somehow carried over to his poetry and meant that his poetry was more to be valued, since the time he spent writing it was worth more an hour than the time of other poets. A fascinating assumption, it launched this particular observation about the confusion between what the pinball machine of financial rewards and public attention spews out at any given moment, and the assumption that the subsequent money or attention reflects some inherent superiority over the less lucky.

Once in a women's workshop at a writer's conference, several of the mothers were talking about feeling guilty about the time they took to write, time taken from spending with their children. I asked one woman who had been published a goodly amount by now if being paid for her work didn't lessen her guilt, and she agreed. Finally the group decided that if enough people seemed to value your work, whether by paying for it or just by paying attention to it, showing that they read or listened to your work and got pleasure and/or enlightenment, something real, out of what you wrote, then you felt less guilty for demanding from the others in your life the time and space to write. Certainly attention paid to your work and even to you seems to validate that work and make it easier to protect the time necessary to accomplish it.

I suppose the ultimate problem with the weirdness I encounter on the road is that it makes me wary. It's hard to respond to people I meet sometimes, when I am not at all sure what monsters are about to bulge up from under the floorboards of the suburban split level where the reception is being held. I also find demands that I provide instant intimacy, or the idea that I should walk in to rooms ready to answer probing questions about my life and my loves patently absurd. The books are public. They are written for others. They are written to be of use. But I am not my books.

I never doubt that:

> the best part of me (is)
> locked in those
> strange paper boxes.

But I don't believe that people who have bought or read the books have a right therefore to sink their teeth in my arm. I had an unpleasant experience at a fancy Catholic school recently where a group of women made demands on me I found silly. I gave a good reading, worked hard to make the workshop useful, went over their work. Then I was attacked because I was not "open emotionally." One of them quoted to me a phrase of mine from "Living in the open" which apparently meant to her that you must "love" everybody you meet and gush and slop on command.

For some people admiration of something you have done easily converts into resentment of you—disappointment you are not Superwoman with a Madonna smile, or resentment if you do not bear obvious scars. They can forgive accomplishment if the woman who arrives is an alcoholic, suicidal, miserable in some overt way. To be an ordinary person with an ordinary life of ups and downs and ins and outs is not acceptable.

That admiration that can sour into hatred, sometimes off by itself, is frightening. Bigger celebrities inspire it far more than small fry, for which I am merciful, but I would rather not inspire it at all. It is sometimes as if when people meet you if you do not work a miracle—light up their life, change things, take one look at them and say, Yes, you are the one, then they have been failed in some way.

If what people want in a place is a good energizing reading, a useful workshop, an honest lecture, answering questions as carefully and fully as I can, then they are satisfied. If what they want is a love affair with a visiting Mother Goddess, a laying on of hands to make them real, a feeding of soul hungers from a mystical breast milk fountain, then they are doomed to disappointment. For that act, I charge a lot more.

IV. Knots of Wild Energy
Poets on Politics and Poetry

ROBERT BLY

From Knots of Wild Energy
An Interview with Wayne Dodd

Athens, Ohio, May, 1978

I see a curious contradiction in contemporary poetry. On the one hand, there is the most incredible amount of poetic activity going on. On the other hand, there is evidence of a real absence of sureness of direction and even purpose. This uncertainty is reflected even in such things as a call recently by a literary magazine for people to comment on what is to be the role of, say, form, or content, in poetry. It seemed to be symptomatic of a deep uncertainty. I wonder what would be a way of trying to make sense of that. Maybe you could talk about, for example, what the generation of poets under thirty-five show us, in their work, that would comment on this.

I think I feel the same disquiet as you do. Twenty years ago there may have been fifteen books of poetry published every year. Now, there may be sixty or seventy. They are published by the commercial presses, by the university presses like Pitt, and maybe another hundred or two hundred by small presses. I think the directory of poets includes four or five hundred poets now. It's an extremely new situation, because poetry in this country has always been associated with what could be called knots of wild energy, scattered at different places throughout the country. In the fifties there were only a few visible: William Carlos Williams, E. E. Cummings, Richard Eberhart, Kenneth Rexroth, Robinson Jeffers, Wallace Stevens, and Marianne Moore. They were geographically separate, and none were connected to universities. Ezra Pound and T. S. Eliot were in Europe. They represented self-creating and self-regulating knots of psychic energy. In fact they resembled wild animals. Even though Wallace Stevens was working for an insurance agency, the part of him that wrote poetry was a wild animal.

It seems to me that what has taken place is the domestication of poetry. If you're going to follow that through, you're going to have to imagine the mink or the otter being brought into cages and bred there. Oftentimes, animals reproduce more in captivity because the young are not killed off. If you bring a species to optimum conditions, you have a vast supply of them in the next generation. But the new otters don't know the same things that their parents did.

The original otter knew what cold water was like or knew how to live in the snow. That's one metaphor to explain the amazing tameness of the sixty to eighty volumes of poetry published each year, compared with the compacted energy of a book by Robinson Jeffers that appeared the same year as a book by Wallace Stevens, and those appearing the same year as one of Eliot's extremely kooky books.

Not only tameness, but sameness.

Sameness! It would follow somehow that someone is controlling the genetic breeding, and no new blood is coming in from the outside. So you have that sameness of the workshop. The workshop would be the breeding stations, I suppose.

I feel that the domestication is being done by two entities now: the universities, and the National Endowment for the Arts. When the government gives money, it results in domestication of the poet. I think that the National Endowment is an even worse catastrophe, in the long run, to the ecology of poetry than the universities. Talking yesterday to your class, I said, "Wayne understands the whole issue of the wildness that's involved with poetry, and how slowly animals in the wild learn to do things." You have grown slowly in poetry. So you're in a spot, actually, when you teach a workshop, because as you know, the funny thing about a workshop is that we want people to write fast, to write in their early twenties. That's impossible! They even want to get a job with it.

*   *   *   *   *

I can hear a typical workshop poet say to you: "What do you mean? I wrote a poem on my grandfather last year and I made it very clear he went through certain experiences cutting wood or farming that I haven't. Now my admission is tension and it is anguish, it is a navel." What do you say to that?

I think that the poem that we're talking about at the moment is the poem that, finally, lacks content. I think the only content of a poem is the positive or true emotional life of the individual.

Then he or she might say, "You're being insulting to me. I am twenty-three years old. I have a true emotional life. What right do you have to say that I don't have one?"

Who can answer that? But I know talking to you that I am not talking with a twenty-four year old. You have been working in poetry for fifteen to twenty years, and your poetry has grown slowly stronger and stronger. You know how long it took you to arrive at the place where you are. Don't you find a contradiction between your experience and the expectation of the workshop student, who expects that within two years, if he studies with you, he will have a manuscript acceptable enough to get an MFA, and possibly get published? How do you deal with that contradiction?

I deal with it by agreeing with you and saying I accept it. I try to tell students about it. Anyone who comes into a program thinking he's going to learn shortcuts is doomed to failure. There is no such thing as a shortcut. I think that one can learn certain skills, certain devices, and maybe indeed speed up the process of learning poetry somewhat. But there are no real shortcuts.

But they're still winning. They're winning because they're receiving the knowledge that you have received in fifteen years of writing poetry, and you are giving it to them and they are accepting it. Both of you have the tacit understanding that out of it will come a manuscript acceptable for an MFA, and possibly for a published book. So actually, even though you are warning the students about it, they are still winning and taking what they want and you are giving it to them.

I certainly think that that is the case with many writing schools in this country.

I'm in the same situation. If I come into a college, even for one day, I can find no reason for not teaching what I know. But I'm still going along with the unreality of the student, who imagines that by listening to an older poet for a while, he or she will be able to substantially improve the manuscript, so it will be more likely to be published. This ignores everything that the Tao Te Ching talks about, in terms of the slow flow of human life, the slow growth of oak trees, and all of that. There's some kind of lie that the workshops, and visiting poets, are involved in. I'm involved in it.

Don't you think that the real problem lies somehow outside the expectations of the student? I think their expectations *are a problem, but perhaps there is a real problem also in the response of—I don't know what we're going to call it—the keepers of the system and the tradition, in their accepting and reinforcing that expectation.*

Who are the keepers of the system?

Well, I suppose book publishers and editors.

It is a responsibility of publishers not to publish so many books of poetry. But you know what's happened. With the National Endowment supporting presses, a young man or woman can start a press. The National Endowment does not pay him a salary, but he can use some of the money given him to pay at least for the secretarial work, which the wife or husband or friend may do in connection with a book. There's a lot of genial corruption going on in that area. Books get published without risk or sacrifice—that's a book that shouldn't be published. That may sound stupid. I hear people say that the more books of poetry published the better. I don't agree. First of all, one often notices that poets who publish a book early often end up repeating themselves later on. Readers want to be amused. If you do something well—and we all know poets who have done that early on—the readers constantly urge the poet to do the same thing over again. By thirty-five he hasn't grown a bit. If he hadn't published early, but waited till his thirties, then, like Wallace Stevens or Walt Whitman, both of whom didn't publish until their late thirties and early forties, more growth would have taken place before *and* after that time. It seems to me that workshops are extremely destructive in the way they prepare students for publishing ten years too early.

You would agree, then, that that system is a system of avoidance of pain? It seems to me that's the exact opposite way of going about discovering how to write profound poetry.

That's very interesting, because the best part of workshops, probably, is the pain that a writer feels when someone criticizes his poem in public. But it hadn't occurred to me that this may be a substitute for the long-range pain which a person working alone feels, when he feels despair looking at his manuscript, knowing it is inadequate.

I've had that experience so many times. I'd prepare a group of two dozen poems, in my twenties, type them up excitedly, and then discover I had only two or three poems. Then I would fall into a depression for several weeks. After a few months I would put together another group of twenty, and this time find again in despair that maybe five were genuine. This solitary pain, with no one to relieve it, is a typical situation of the wild animal writer. The workshops take away some of that pain by having someone there to encourage you. Your friends in the workshop encourage you; "This is better than your last poem. I'd publish it." And I guess that amounts to an avoidance of pain.

I found out recently that one of the stronger labors in my life has been the labor to avoid unpleasant emotions. Pain is probably one of those.

I worry too about the writer's perception of what a poem is. I worry that the person will come genuinely to believe, as he's working on and living with a poem, that doing certain things is equivalent to the poem itself and to the basic instinct or impulse to poetry. I worry about the possible insinuation of a kind of "imitation" as the essential gesture of poetry. What do you think?

Let's go back to the image of domestication. In the wild state males fight each other. One of the things that has disappeared in the last twenty years in poetry has been the conflict between the young man and the old one. And the progress of the generations does not move well in any field unless the younger scientists or poets are willing to attack the older ones. Ortega y Gasset describes the process clearly in *Meditations on Quixote*. He begins four or five generations before Galileo. Astronomers then loved their teachers. But the young astronomers worked hard to find the flaw in their teacher's work. Each generation by that labor overturned the one before. This constant thought movement finally led to the astounding achievements of Galileo. Ortega makes it clear that in a healthy situation that is how males behave.

I participated in that a little when I started *The Fifties*. I started the magazine precisely to attack Allen Tate's and Robert Penn Warren's view of poetry. The reason for that is not because I hated Allen Tate. As you remember, in the fifties the shade from Eliot and Pound and Tate and William Carlos Williams was a heavy shade. It was necessary to clear some ground, so there'd be a place for new pine trees to grow. That clearing is not being done now. Perhaps my generation is casting shade now. The younger poets are not attacking Galway enough, or Merwin, or Wright, or Creeley, or Ginsberg. They're a little slow in attacking me too. The women don't attack Levertov or Rich. The younger poets are being nice boys and girls. Partly it is cultural, the sixties' obsession with good feeling. But the normal process of human growth from generation to generation involves, as Ortega details, the new generation attacking the older one. And attacking them strongly, wiping them out as far as possible.

*   *   *   *   *

You mean, of course, they are not attacking them in criticism and reviews. But you mean in their work too? That they're not attacking them there also?

I think it's mainly the absence of public criticism that's a disaster: the disappearance of criticism. Private criticism doesn't count. We notice magazines with nothing but poems in them, not a single review or "idea" article. The cliché of the last ten years is, "I want to say something positive. If I can't say something positive I don't want to say anything at all." There is a fear of having and using power. Imagine a stag in the north woods saying, "Well, I want to like all the other stags. I don't want any power. So I'll just take my horns off." To me one of the disasters that's happened is that so many poets have gotten the habit of emphasizing their own work, and have been unwilling to face head-on the poetry of others, older or even their own age. Ashbery is an example, Berrigan, Wakowski, Dubie, Gluck, Ginsberg. Many poets at poetry readings read nothing but their own work.

The point is not that Eliot disliked Browning; he never met Browning. It was an attack of psychic energy only. But think of this situation by contrast: the medium generation of poets, Donald

Justice, Marvin Bell, Dick Hugo, etc., are teaching in a college. The younger poets are grateful to poets like Justice and Bell for teaching them. This gratefulness to the older poet prevents them from doing the natural thing, which is to take the work seriously, turn on poets in the older generation, and attack them. Justice and Bell and Hugo don't want to be attacked, and they encourage the good feeling.

I was thinking of this only yesterday: that the university system, which seems in the beginning so sweet, where one can go in as a younger poet and find an older poet whom you admire to work with, causes everything to break down. We're living in a swamp of mediocrity, poetry of the Okefenokee, in which a hundred and fifty mediocre books—and they're mediocre partly because the men writing them are somehow not completely males, because they haven't broken through to their own psychic ground—are published every year. When a man or woman succeeds in grasping what his or her master has done, and breaking through it, he doesn't create something artificial. He enters through his belly button into the interior space inside himself. And there, to everyone's surprise, are new kinds of grass, and new kinds of trees, and all of that!

So that suddenly makes the term "tame" a real, living metaphor.

*   *   *   *   *

When my own generation began to write, around 1954–58 or so, poetry and the persona were considered linked, and both were considered a child of the iambic rhythm. Allen Ginsberg, following Whitman, attacked those linkages by talking about his own life in *Howl*. And Jim Wright altered the relation of the iambic line to English poetry by bringing in whole areas of things that Keats had never thought about in relation to grief among the coal miners. And when he brought the slag heaps in, he found, following Trakl, that some new kind of consciousness in the twentieth century passes to the reader through the precise image, conscious and unconscious. Ginsberg uses mainly the mental or general image. I studied the precise image a great deal too. But we must see that the image is not a final solution. Many young poets are still writing calmly, almost smugly, in the image, without looking around. Obsession with image can become a psychic habit as much as obsession with persona, and we need new ways of bringing forward consciousness. Some hints have appeared, but few younger poets have cleared ground for themselves in that area. They have simply accepted the whole discovery of the image as it comes through, through Neruda, through Trakl, and the Americans.

And you could also say that this shows that the American male is solving his father problem less and less. It's quite possible that a hundred years ago there was much more resentment of the son against the father. The father after all controlled the keys to the economy, particularly if he were a master and you were the apprentice. Now the son can avoid living the whole father problem by going into a completely different field, say, computers. Maybe he doesn't realize that he still has to confront the father in some way. I think this failure in the artistic world is a reflection of a desire of the young males to live in a state of comfort, as opposed to the terrific state of tension and anger with your father which was more the situation a few generations ago.

*   *   *   *   *

We have never before faced what it's like in the culture when hundreds of people want to write poetry and want to be instructed in it. In the Middle Ages, in the Renaissance, there weren't that many people who wanted to be painters; but if they did they went to a studio and entered into a deep father-son relationship with a painter, privately, one-to-one in his workshop. Now we are trying to instruct hundreds of beginning poets in the universities. We don't know how to instruct in that area. We know how to instruct a hundred engineers, or a thousand computer technicians, but that knowledge doesn't help. If you read a history of Ch'an Buddhism, you'll notice that Buddhism faced the same problem. It began with just a few people, and later huge numbers of people wanted Buddhist instruction. Ch'an Buddhism does not involve doctrine; it involves the same kind of thing we're talking about, breaking through the ego and getting down to the unconscious, breaking through conventional attitudes and getting down to the real ones, breaking through your society face and getting down to your genuine face.

They learned how to do that. Their method doesn't resemble a workshop. They didn't teach politeness or the smooth surface. They didn't teach "the poetry of fans" as Neruda would say. The teacher wouldn't assign an exercise to be done at the desk for the following week, but his plan would involve something entirely outside the building. Perhaps a man might come in and say, "I want to learn something about Buddhism. I want to get my degree in Buddhism in a year and a half. What books shall I read? You want me to do meditation exercises now?" The monk would say, "No, I don't think so. You go out in the woods there, and build yourself a little house, and live there six months, and then come back and see me."

"What shall I do?"

"Oh, that's your business. I don't know; you do what you want to. Don't have any servants or anything like that. Get your own water and bake your own bread."

So the man is out there for six months all by himself, and he is in charge of his own body. Finally he comes back and says, "OK, I've done it. I've built my house and I'm ready now. Will you give me instruction?"

"Oh no, I don't think so. Actually we need a meditation hut out there very bad. I think you had better build that."

"What do I build it out of?"

"Oh, stones. There're a lot of stones on that hill there. You can use those stones and build a house up there."

"How long will it take me?"

"Oh, six or eight months. When you're done come see me."

He comes back and says, "Well, OK. I'm done now. I want my instruction in meditation."

"Well, you haven't been moving around very much. Probably a good thing you see a little land. Why don't you take a trip around China? Make about a six-month trip. I'm busy. You come back, see me in six months."

And if he's willing to go through all that—actually during all that he is *doing* something and getting away from his mental attitude— he has received instruction. The instruction throws him back on his own body. By making him do things he understands that art is not a matter of getting something from a teacher. Art is a matter of going into your own resources and building. You may even have shown the student that it's necessary to build a house out of stone.

We're doing the opposite. We allow people to come to a workshop and receive immediately what you, for example, have worked ten to fifteen years to learn yourself. A nineteen-year-old student comes to your office, and because our teaching is structured so, we offer him that material right away. We can't say that plan is wrong or right. We can only say the Buddhists learned not to teach that way.

I must say that if I were going to teach a workshop on a long-range basis I would try to introduce some method of that sort. I would refuse to meet with the students regularly; but they would have to live away from the campus, in the woods or desert. They wouldn't be able to get any instruction until they had earned it, by breaking dependencies, doing things for themselves. One might say to a student, "After you have your hut, translate twenty-five poems from a Rumanian poet."

"But I don't know Rumanian."

"Well then, that's your first job. You learn Rumanian, translate the twenty-five poems, and then come back to see me, and I'll tell you what I think about 'the deep image.' "

One learns a lot by translating a great poet. By that method, we get closer to the actual way that art was taught in the Renaissance.

You might go to Rubens, for example, and say: "I would like to be your student. Would you teach me your philosophy of painting?" And he might say, "Well, there's a shoe missing down in the left hand corner. Please paint it so it looks exactly like the other shoe. Don't talk, paint."

*   *   *   *   *

What is the effect on poets of all the "sameness" you spoke of earlier?

Perhaps poetry is developing a protective camouflage of brown and gray feathers. A poetry shelf has fewer and fewer peacocks with long tails, like Robinson Jeffers. Probably this heavy breeding is nice. And it's possible that hawks don't see some gray birds and don't attack them, you know.

But if a person just beginning to read poetry walks into a bookstore and starts paging through all the boring gray and brown books of poetry, what does that do for the readership of poetry? When too much boring poetry is published, poets themselves begin to lose morale. I'm wondering how that could change.

I assume that the number of workshops will continue to increase. Then as the job offers go down, the new poets' wills becomes more and more tame, and more and more like the last generation. Suppose a number of poets would like a new position at Wisconsin, but Wisconsin wants to hire Galway Kinnell. That means that unconsciously, even consciously, the young poets will try to be more like Galway Kinnell. William Carlos Williams did not want to be like Galway Kinnell. Cummings or Marianne Moore did not have bureaucracy mentality. Each wanted to be wild separately! I don't see any possibility but it's getting worse.

It may also be that poets will be afraid to risk doing the really different thing, that might seem to be profoundly true to them nonetheless, for fear of being accused of peeing on the floor.

Oh, indeed! That's right! I'm sure that the reviewers of Pound's early work, which had a lot of freaky originality, accused him constantly of being poorly housetrained. What would originality look like today? Perhaps it would involve intimate revelations not confessional, such as Akhmatova writes.

I don't believe originality will increase if the poetry becomes more primitive. Jerry Rothenberg to the contrary, most primitive poetry is probably boring. After you've said, "Here comes the otter, here comes the otter, here comes the otter. A woka-woka-woka! The bird flew down from the sky. Dawn is coming, Wok-i-way, I'm alive." You say that about ninety-eight times. . . . We live in an industrial society. I love the oral quality of primitive poetry, but how can a university be oral?

The problem is, how does poetry maintain itself as a vivid, highly colored, living thing? It's possible that originality comes when the man or woman disobeys the collective. The cause of tameness is fear. The collective says: "If you do your training well and become a nice boy or girl, we will love you." We want that. So a terrible fear comes. It is a fear that we will lose the love of the collective. I have felt it intensely. What the collective offers is not even love, that is what is so horrible, but a kind of absence of loneliness. Its companionship is ambiguous, like mother love.

ROBERT HAYDEN

"How It Strikes a Contemporary"
Reflections on Poetry and the Role of the Poet

I call him the Inquisitor, though he is more like Chekhov's Black Monk than anything else. He has appeared in my study on several occasions—once or twice during the sixties and most recently a few weeks ago.

Each of his visits has been unannounced, if not entirely unexpected.

I cannot say that I wholly dislike the Inquisitor, though neither can I say that I enjoy his company. But his attitudes toward me and my work do have a stimulating effect, and, I have come to believe, an ultimately salutary influence. Nevertheless, I wonder sometimes if the remedy isn't worse than the disease. I can value him at certain moments as a sort of Reader over your Shoulder—to use Robert Graves's term. He often reminds me of the tough old woman I once knew who said to me, "Boy, what you messin' round with all that poetry stuff for? Ain't no percentage in *that*."

Quite often this Devil's Advocate looks and sounds like certain acquaintances of mine who feel it is their duty to see that I keep both feet on the ground. Or like certain professors I have endured who have tried in vain to convince me that Shakespeare said it all and therefore I should accept the fact that I was born with too little too late. Yes, he is very similar at times to these self-appointed guardians of poetry. Not to mention his resemblance to certain "criticasters" for whom my blackness is so dense they can never see their way through or beyond it to me as a poet.

On his most recent visit, the Inquisitor seemed, I thought, more cynical and querulous than ever. But far less original. What he said then I have heard him say before. Most of his comments were simply repetitions of the misconceptions about poets and poetry current nowadays. And they brought out the unwilling didact in me.

I was writing when the Inquisitor entered the room. He seated himself on my worktable and began talking in his usual, peremptory fashion:

> INQ.: Long time no see. How's the poetry business these days?
> POET: You know how it irritates me to have you ask about "the poetry business."

INQ.: *But it's such fun to needle you. All you poets take yourselves much too seriously. What're you writing?*

POET: A talk I'm to give as my final performance at the Library of Congress. I'm having a hard time getting it into shape. I don't like lecturing anyway. I'm not good at it.

INQ.: *Yes, I know. I've heard you.*

POET: I'm not *that* bad.

INQ.: *I've heard worse.*

POET: Look here—I've more interesting things to do than listen to your snide remarks. Anyhow, we've been through something like this before.

INQ.: *When did we last meet, by the way?*

POET: During the late sixties. A couple of midnight sessions, as I recall.

INQ.: *It was when you were trying to define the role of the poet in twentieth-century America—your own in particular; or some such nonsense. Did you succeed?*

POET: I thought I had. But I've changed my mind since then, several times. I see the question differently now and rather feel that . . .

INQ.: *Later, later. We'll get to your diatribe later, if you'll be so kind. Now this talk of yours . . .*

POET: Just some of my own thoughts about poets and poetry.

INQ.: *Well, you've always been one to take foolish risks. Got a title yet?*

POET: Sure. "How It Strikes a Contemporary."

INQ.: *Hey, ain't that from old Bob Browning?*

POET: From *Robert* Browning, yes. One of my favorite poets, if you remember. I'm using the title of one of his poems. It's the one where he sees the poet as God's confidant:

> We had among us, not so much a spy,
> As a recording chief-inquisitor,
> The town's true master if the town but knew!
> We merely kept a governor for form,
> While this man walked about and took account
> Of all thought, said and acted, then went home,
> And wrote it fully to our Lord the King. . . .

INQ.: *Spare me. I've told you before I can't stand that old pious fraud. I consider him the Billy Sunday of English poetry—always grandstanding, always kidding himself that he's hitting home runs for Jesus or something.*

POET: Oh, come off it. That's pretty silly, even for you. Anachronistic besides.

INQ.: *You know what I mean. So now you're cribbing from Browning.*

POET: Call it what you will. Twenty years ago you might have hurt me by saying that. But not now.

INQ.: *I'm just getting warmed up. I guess you're feeling pretty feisty now because you've been Consultant in Poetry in Washington for a couple of years. Yes, I guess that would go to your head, wouldn't it? But tell me, what is it you do as Consultant—just prop your feet up on a desk and write deathless verse every day, or what?*

POET: You *know* I never write with my feet propped up on a desk.

INQ.: *You're not answering my question.*

POET: I've heard it so many times that I'm sick and tired of answering it. I *consult,* what else?

INQ.: *You've really got it made, if that's all you do.*

POET: And that's plenty for a working poet, if you do it right. But to get on with this tedious discussion: I write letters, talk with visiting poets, take part in Library programs, give readings, talk to schoolchildren, and so on and so on. And in the time that's left, I sometimes have enough energy to work on my poems.

INQ.: *You've won some awards and stuff, haven't you?*

POET: Yes, as if you didn't know.

INQ.: *Think you deserved them?*

POET: Yes and no.

INQ.: *What do you mean, yes and no? Explain yourself.*

POET: Never. You want me to have to give the money back—have the citations canceled?

INQ.: *You're forgetting something.*

POET: And what's that?

INQ.: *You're black. A black poet. They wouldn't dare ask for their money back. That's why you got it in the first place.*

POET: You just had to get that in, didn't you? You really are contemptible.

INQ.: *I'm a realist.*

POET: You're a philistine, a bigot, a schlemiel.

INQ.: *You know I'm right. You're a token.*

POET: Of what?

INQ.: *Somebody's bad conscience.*

POET: Now listen, Buster, why don't you just get out of here?

INQ.: *You can't make me. You know you can't get rid of me until I choose to leave. Remember last time when I made you so mad? Now that I've hit a nerve I'm going to stay here and enjoy seeing you squirm.*

POET: Don't count on it. I've heard this kind of blather a good many times by now, and I shouldn't react to it, but I guess I always do. I'm old enough to know there's no defense against mean-spirited ignorance except to keep away from it. I know that but still react. You're implying that standards are different for me from what they are for other American poets. You're saying I must be granted considerations not on the basis of my work, but purely in terms of racial quotas, politics, and sociology.

INQ.: Well, not entirely, maybe. But you will admit, won't you, that people are less interested in you as a poet than as a black *poet?*

POET: Yes, I have reason to believe that's partly true—and true on *both* sides of the American color line today. But it's not *my* problem—my problem is to go on trying to be the poet I think I may some day become.

INQ.: But, look, you can't just ignore the social context—the, er, social situation your people are in. Don't you feel any responsibility toward them?

POET: You know very well, if you know anything about me at all, that I do, that I'm fully conscious, and sometimes painfully conscious, of their and my situation. But I assert my right to approach it in my own way as a poet. I deal with it as I feel it, and not as people like you think I should. After all, as a poet I am trying to come to grips with reality, yes, to define reality, as I can perceive it. Isn't that what every poet worthy of the name is attempting to do? Why does a particular racial identity make me any the less aware of life, life as human beings live it? What is a poet but a human being speaking to other human beings about things that matter to all of us? And of course some of these concerns are social and political— racial or ethnic, to use a currently fashionable word. But there are other matters that are also important. Sermons in stones—that sort of thing. To put it succinctly, I feel that Afro-American poets ought to be looked at as poets first, if that's what they truly are. And as one of them I dare to hope that if my work means anything, if it's any good at all, it's going to have a human impact, not a narrowly racial or ethnic or political and overspecialized impact. But, as Fats Waller said for all time, "One never *know, do* one?"

INQ.: You always put too much importance on poetry. All you verse-makers do. Wasn't it Oscar Wilde who said that all art is quite useless?

POET: I think it was. And then W. H. Auden wrote in his elegy on Yeats that poetry makes nothing happen. I disagree with both points of view.

INQ.: So what else is new? I recall your having some inflated notions about poetry being a spiritual act. And you once argued that a poet was a kind of priest—was at least the conscience of his culture. To all of which I say nonsense. Poets are just guys or dames who sit around playing with words like kids with brightly colored building blocks. They fool around long enough, they make something that looks like a poem. And poems are nothing but artifacts like blocks or chairs.

POET: And for the sake of argument, let us say that chairs are useful, aren't they? And necessary and sometimes beautiful.

INQ.: This is taking a funny turn. But, touché, touché.

POET: You're giving in? That's not like you.

INQ.: Twinges. I'm not myself tonight. I'm getting old. And so are you, incidentally.

POET: You recall Browning's lines: "Grow old along with me; / The best is yet to be. . . ."

INQ.: Oh, please, no more, no more. Sententious doggerel of a pompous old burgher. Let's get back to the subject. I was saying poetry is . . .

POET: You can't define it any better than I can. But I would make so bold as to say it's probably best defined by the poems a poet writes. For me that's the most fruitful attempt at a definition. Actually, I'd much rather spend my time writing poetry than worrying over what it is or isn't. A matter of feeling anyway, a matter of sensibility. I haven't much patience, hardly any in fact, with theories of poetry. They're all *after* the fact. It's the practice that gives rise to theory anyway, wouldn't you agree, however grudgingly?

INQ.: I'm sure I wouldn't. Does it matter whether I do or not?

POET: No.

At this point, the Inquisitor left abruptly. I was glad to be rid of him. Still, though he angered and disconcerted me, as he usually does, he has also left me with some ideas that might be developed for my talk, even if only in a negative way. I took some scratch paper and scrawled several pages of notes:

1. *The nature and function of poetry:* Poetry as the illumination of experience through language. (The Inquisitor would surely accuse me of cribbing again; this time from Virginia Woolf, etc.) Poetry has always dealt with fundamental human concerns. Could we think of it as a species of Primal Scream? Did it not grow out of primitive mysteries? And does it not remain, despite all we know about it, rather mysterious?

2. *Poetry as a medium, an instrument for social and political change:* Poetry *does* make something happen, for it changes sensibility. In the early stages of a culture it helps to crystallize language and is a repository for value, belief, ideals. The *Griot* in African tribes keeps names and legends and pride alive. Among the Eskimos the shaman or medicine man is a poet. In ancient Ireland and Wales the bard was a preserver of the culture. Academicians and purists to

the contrary notwithstanding, great poets of the past as well as the present have often been spokesmen for a cause, have been politically involved. A point to consider: What would I as a poet do if my people were rounded up like the Jewish people in Germany under the Nazis? Claude McKay's sonnet "If We Must Die"; the poems of the Greek poet Yannis Ritsos that were recited and sung by men and women fighting in the streets for the freedom of their country; Pablo Neruda, William Butler Yeats, Emily Sachs, Muriel Rukeyser, Gwendolyn Brooks, Walt Whitman; they stand out as poets even if you dislike their politics. To be a poet, it seems to me, is to care passionately about justice and one's fellow beings. Sometimes this is not true. Ezra Pound, for instance. Also note that much political or protest or socially conscious poetry is bad, not because of the poet's loyalties or affiliations but owing to lack of talent; sometimes to a pragmatist's contempt for art as a means of understanding and grace.

3. *Poetry as therapy:* A great many people are writing poetry today—I do not call them poets—who are not so much concerned with art or craft as they are with achieving some kind of emotional or psychic release. I'm sure this is good for them, and there is no questioning the therapeutic value of poetry, of the arts in general. But if therapy is all one is after I hardly consider it justifies one considering himself a poet. But of course they do. They are, I am well aware, often seeking escape from the anonymity that threatens us all. They are seeking affirmation of their being, their uniqueness, through poetry or other forms of art. But self-expression becomes an end in itself; questions of craftsmanship, form, style are likely to be dismissed as "elitist" and therefore irrelevant. I would not object to the self-expressionists but for the fact that their efforts result in delusions of poetic grandeur. When I discussed Mr. X's poetry with him in the Poetry Office one day, I soon recognized him as the counterpart of Miss Y, who invaded my office at the University of Michigan with a sheaf of mediocre verses—all terribly *fraught,* as an old friend used to say of such efforts. Both would-be poets were visibly annoyed when I pointed out weaknesses in diction, imagery, *and* grammar, because they thought these things of minor consequence, since the poems expressed their feelings. And, oh, the sine qua non of all sine qua nons: their poems were *spontaneous* (not labored over like yours, sir). "No, I never rewrite my poems; I let them come out as they will and do not revise. I've been writing for about a year, and all my friends are after me to publish a book. Tell me how to get my work published."

Well, you do what you can with these hopeless cases. You send up a silent prayer that time and hard-nosed poetry editors will show these people the error of their ways.

4. *Poetry as the art of saying what cannot be said or at least not said quite so effectively in any other form:* Maybe I've worn this statement out, I've used it so many times, and should give it a long rest. But somehow I can't resist repeating it. What I have said in my poems I am sure I could not otherwise have said. Indeed, I might have said too much. A poem is built on silences as well as sounds. And it imposes a silence audible as a laugh, a sigh, a groan.

A few nights ago, I was looking over these notes and wondering how on earth I'd work them into the talk when the Inquisitor arrived. Shall I pretend I was not glad for the interruption?

INQ.: *I know why I've been so groggy lately that I let you get the better of the argument sometimes. I know what's wrong, yesiree.*

POET: Then tell me. The suspense is unbearable.

INQ.: *I'm tired of poets and poetry, worn out by all the rapping I've had to endure regarding the role of the poet, the function of poetry in this society.*

POET: You're one of the chief instigators. And you've never been exactly our friend. You've always . . .

INQ.: *Don't interrupt. All this palavering about the American poet's role. What else is it but to be a poet and write verses? A useless function at best, but never mind. You don't hear electricians and plumbers bellyaching the way you versifiers do.*

POET: They've got unions.

INQ.: *Well, your crowd has too, in a manner of speaking; you're all professors nowadays, most of you at any rate. You're all safely inside the ivy-covered walls of Academe, grousing, or as you say when you're being cute,* kvetching. *No two ways about it, you're a sorry bunch. All you characters calling yourselves poets, oh, but playing it safe, observing the rules, conforming to what is expected of you as responsible citizens. Baudelaire and Rimbaud would laugh their heads off if they could see you. You and your faculty club teas, your polite conversation and mildly vicious gossip. No passion, no wildness, no risking anything. What a bunch of phonies you are. And, oh, those carefully contrived little poems you write about life in outer suburbia.*

POET: Stop it already. Why don't you say anything original for a change, even if you can't distinguish between truth and appearances. You're stereotyping us because you're intellectually too lazy to be discriminating. I grant you that the university is not necessarily the best environment for poets, because energies that should go into creative work too often are dissipated by routine and academic drudgery of one kind or another. Still, it's less enervating than picking cotton or working in a factory. And I guess as teachers we must be making some contribution to students, giving them what they couldn't get from anyone else. Few of us, and it's a very small few, earn enough from our books and our poetry readings to live on. So we have to do the impossible and somehow manage as best we can to pursue what are really two full-time jobs, two demanding careers.

INQ.: Careers, careers! You poets today think too much about your careers. You're so busy being seen by the right people at the right time in the right place, you're so greedy for publicity and fame, you're so busy promoting yourselves I wonder that you ever find time to do what poets are supposed to do—write poems. I'm fed up with the whole flipping lot of you. Nothing but hustlers.

POET: If we are, it's because of you and your crowd.

INQ.: Let your poems do the hustling.

POET: And let your fingers do the walking, I suppose.

INQ.: That's clever, that is. I'll die laughing.

POET: Let your poems do the hustling, indeed!

INQ.: That's what I said. Worry about writing well. That's all that's important.

POET: As if you give a tinker's dam about poetry. You're only saying it because you know it gets me worked up. And you'll be telling me next to live in a garret and go hungry so's to produce a masterpiece.

INQ.: Why don't some of you birds give it a try?

POET: Because we're none of us characters in *La Bohème*. And because some of us know what real poverty is. Food and shelter and a few amenities have never prevented a real poet from writing real poetry.

INQ.: Enough of this blather. I told you I'm tired of talking about poetry.

POET: Well, you started it, Buster, and I'm not going to let you have the last word. You flout the value, the importance of poetry and you heap ridicule on poets. But there are thousands tonight who except for us would have no one to speak in a human voice for them. Who more earnestly than poets have warned of the dangers of abstraction and anonymity to the human spirit?

INQ.: He's off and running.

POET: Let there be poets and more poets—just as long as they are poets. For poets too are the keepers of a nation's conscience, the partisans of freedom and justice, even when they eschew political involvement. By the very act of continuing to function as poets they are affirming what is human and eternal. And as I have contemplated the almost bewildering diversity of American poetry, I have come to see a vital relationship between the poetic endeavor and freedom of speech in this country. In the monolithic dictatorships poets are silenced unless they repeat the clichés of the state. The dangers of censorship in our own country are certainly present, and although I would not overstate the case by saying it is poets who are chiefly keeping the lines of verbal communication open, I will say that we know the dangers of censorship and we are therefore part of the advance guard in the struggle. When poets are silenced then tyranny has won.

Well, maybe the Inquisitor did have the last word, for he disappeared while I was still talking. It was quite late, way past midnight, and I was exhausted, but I stayed up to make a few notes. I wouldn't have slept even if I had gone to bed, because I was thinking of all the things I should have said to that old curmudgeon but had not had the presence of mind or sufficient wit to say. I reached for a notebook and scribbled some of them down. Perhaps I could use them in my talk.

CHARLES SIMIC

Negative Capability and Its Children

... that is, when a man is capable of being in uncertainties, mysteries, doubts, without any irritable reaching after fact and reason.

—John Keats

Today what Keats said could be made even more specific. In place of "uncertainties," "mysteries" and "doubts," we could substitute a long list of intellectual and aesthetic events which question, revise and contradict one another on all fundamental issues. We could also bring in recent political history: all the wars, all the concentration camps and other assorted modern sufferings, and then return to Keats and ask how, in this context, are we capable of being in anything *but* uncertainties? Or, since we are thinking of poetry, ask how do we render this now overwhelming consciousness of uncertainty, mystery and doubt in our poems?

To be "capable of being in uncertainties" is to be literally in the midst. The poet is in the midst. The poem, too, is in the midst, a kind of magnet for complex historical, literary and psychological forces, as well as a way of maintaining oneself in the face of that multiplicity.

There are serious consequences to being in the midst. For instance, one is subject to influences. One experiences crises of identity. One suffers from self-consciousness. One longs for self-knowledge while realizing at the same time that under the circumstances self-knowledge can never be complete. When it comes to poetry, one has to confront the difficult question: Who or what vouches for the authenticity of the act? After more than a century of increasing and finally all-embracing suspicions regarding traditional descriptions of reality and self, the question of authenticity ceases to be merely an intellectual problem and becomes a practical one which confronts the poet daily as he or she sits down to write a poem. What words can I trust? How can *I know* that I trust them?

There are a number of replies, as we'll see, but in an age of uncertainties there has to be a particular kind of answer. It includes, for example, the notion of experiment, that concept borrowed from science and which already appears in Wordsworth's *Advertisement to Lyrical Ballads* (1798) and implies a test, a trial, any action or process undertaken to demonstrate something not yet known, or (and this is important) to demonstrate something known and forgotten. I was simply quoting Webster's definition and he reminded me that "experimental" means based on experience rather than on theory or authority. Empiricism, yes, but with a difference. In experimental poetry it will have to be an empiricism of imagination and consciousness.

Back to the notion of being in the midst. "Given the imperfect correspondence between mind and objective reality" (Hegel), given the fact that this "imperfect correspondence" is the product of a critique of language which since the Romantics has undermined the old unity of word and object, of concept and image, then modern poetics is nothing more than the dramatization of the epistemological consequences of that disruption. Certainly, to call it "dramatic" is to suggest contending voices. My purpose here is to identify some of them and establish, as it were, their order of appearance.

We can proceed with our "translation" of Keats. We can speak of Chance in place of his "uncertainty." Is it with Keats that Chance, that major preoccupation of modern experimental poetics, enters aesthetics?

One aspect of that history is clear. Dada and then surrealism made Chance famous, made it ontological. They turned it into a weapon. Cause and effect as the archenemies. Nietzsche had already claimed that "the alleged instinct for causality is nothing more than the fear of the unusual." Fear, of course, and its offspring, habit, which is there, presumably, to minimize that fear. But isn't poetry too a habit, a convention with specific expectations of content and form which have their own causal relationship? Certainly—and this I believe was understood by these poets. So the project became one of using Chance to break the spell of our habitual literary expectations and to approach the condition of what has been called "free imagination."

There's more to it, however. There's a story, almost a parable, of how Marcel Duchamp suspended a book of Euclidian geometry by a string outside his window for several months and in all kinds of weather, and then presented the result to his sister as a birthday present, and of course as an art object. A lovely idea. Almost a philosophical gesture, a kind of ironic critique of Euclid by the elements. Even more, this example and others like it offer a fundamental revision of what we mean by creativity. In that view, the poet is not a *maker,* but someone able to detect the presence of poetry in the accidental.

This is a curious discovery, that there should be poetry at all in the accidental, that there should even be lyricism. The implications are troubling. If we say "lyricism," we imply an assertion of a human presence and will, but how do we locate even a hint of human presence in operations that have no conscious intent and are left to Chance? Is it because there's a kind of significance (meaning) which is not the function of causality? In any case, you don't achieve anonymity when you submit yourself to the law of accident. "Chance," as Antonin Artaud said, "is myself." This is a magnificent insight. It humanizes the abstraction (Chance) and shifts the problem into an entirely different area.

Pound, Olson, and that whole other tradition we are heirs to, with its theory of "Energy," perhaps provides the next step. That theory, it seems to me, accounts for this astonishing discovery that the text is always here, that the content precedes us, that the labor of the poet is to become an instrument of discovery of what has always been with us, inconspicuous in its familiarity.

Olson says "a poem is energy transferred from where the poet got it . . . by the way of the poem itself to, all the way over to, the reader." Pound called it "Vortex." Both of them were pointing to the experience of one's own existence and its dynamics as the original condition which the poet aims to repossess. And for Olson, "there's only one thing you can do about kinetic, re-enact it."

That's the key term: re-enactment. Their definitions are concerned with locating the agent that fuels the poetic act. Their hope, above all, is to give us a taste of that original preconscious complexity and unselected-ness. The problem next is how to accomplish it? And the question remains: What does Chance re-enact? Suppose what we call Chance is simply a submission to a message from the unconscious. The random then becomes a matter of obedience to inwardness and calls for an appropriate technique. The surrealists, as we know, took it over from professional mediums and renamed it "automatic writing." In any case, it's still an interior dictation they are after, a trance, an altered state of consciousness. Breton gives the prescription: "A monologue that flows as rapidly as possible, on which critical spirit of the subject brings no judgement to bear, which is therefore unmarred by any reticence, and which will reproduce as exactly as possible spoken thought."

Now anyone can cut up words from a newspaper and arrange them at random, while only a few have a gift of speaking in tongues, so the technique of automatic writing is problematic and in practice obviously less "automatic" than one would like. The hope that runs through Breton's writings is visionary. He was after the angelic orders. In his pronouncements there's an element of faith which in turn simplifies the actual experience.

On the surface of it, what the other modern tradition proposes has some similarity. Creeley, for example, quotes William Burroughs to describe his own technique: "There is only one thing a writer can write about: *What is in front of his senses in the moment of writing.*" Olson is even more categorical: "The objects which occur at every given moment of composition (of recognition, we can call it) are, can be, must be treated exactly as they occur therein, and not by any ideas or preconceptions from outside the poem." There's a difference, of course. The faculty implied and cultivated here, and conspicuously missing from automatic writing, is attention. Consequently, the emphasis in this kind of poetry is on clarity, precision, conciseness, although still without any attempt at interpretation. The object of attention is set down without a further comment. The aim is that "precise instant when a thing outward and objective transforms itself, or darts into the inward, the subjective." The cutting edge.

In both cases, however, the emphasis is on immediacy, and the purpose is an exchange of a particular kind of energy. In both instances, the ambition is identical: to discover an authentic ground where poetry has its being and on that spot build a new ontology.

Unfortunately, there's always the problem of language, the problem of conveying experience. It's in their respective views of language and what it does, that surrealism and imagism part company.

Surrealism suspects language and its representational powers. In its view, there's no intimacy between language and the world; the old equation, word equals object, is simply a function of habit. In addition, there's the problem of simultaneity of experience versus the linear requirements of grammar. Grammar moves in time. Only figurative language can hope to grasp the simultaneity of experience. Therefore, it's the connotative and not the denotative aspect of language that is of interest, the spark that sets off the figurative chain reaction and transcends the tyranny of the particular.

But Pound, Williams, Olson, and Creeley are in turn suspicious of figures of speech. The figurative draws attention. It tends to take us elsewhere, to absent us from what is at hand. Furthermore, there's a strong commitment in their poetry to living speech. "Nothing," as Ford Madox Ford advised Pound, "that you couldn't in some circumstances, in the stress of some emotion *actually* say." As for grammar, we have their related ideas of prosody, form, and poetic line, which are nothing more than attempts to create a grammar of poetic utterance which would pay heed to the simultaneity of experience.

I think what emerges out of these apposite views is a new definition of content. The content of the poem is determined by the attitude we have toward language. Both the attentive act and the figurative act are profoundly prejudiced by the poet's subjectivity. (Heisenberg's discovery that observation alters the phenomena observed applies here.) The content is that *prejudice,* at the expense of the full range of language. This is a constant in modern poetics regardless of whether we conceive of language as the expression of a moment of attention or, as in the case of surrealism, as the imaginative flight out of that privileged moment.

Nevertheless, we find both traditions speaking of *the image,* and insisting on its importance. And yet, the contexts are very different and carry incompatible views of the nature of our common reality.

For surrealism, the characteristic of a strong image is that it derives from the spontaneous association of two very distinct realities whose relationship is grasped solely by the mind. Breton says, "the most effective image is the one that has the highest degree of arbitrariness." For the imagists, an image is "an intellectual and emotional complex in an instant of time," but a complex (we might add) derived from a perception of an existing thing. Imagism names what is there. Surrealism, on the other hand, endlessly re-names what is there, as if by renaming it it could get closer to the thing itself. The goal in surrealism as in symbolism is a texture of greatest possible suggestiveness, a profusion of images whose meaning is unknown and unparaphrasable through a prior system of signification. The surrealist poet offers the imaginary as the new definition of reality, or more accurately, he equates the imaginary with a truth of psychological order. Here, the separation between intuition and what is real is abolished. Everything is arbitrary except metaphor, which detects the essential kinship of all things.

For imagism, that "necessary angel" of Stevens's, that reality out there with its pressures and complexities is unavoidable. Imagism accepts our usual description of that reality. The image for Pound is a moment of lucidity when the world and its presence is re-enacted by consciousness in language. He calls for sincerity, care for detail, wonder, faith to the actual. Zukofsky compared what was attempted to a photo lens "free or independent of personal feelings, opinions . . . detached, unbiased." In this context, attention and imagination mean almost the same thing, a power which brings the world into focus.

The surprising outcome of many surrealist operations is that they uncover the archetypal—those great images that have mythical resonance. Perhaps we can say that the imagination (surrealist) could be best described as "mythical," providing we understand what that implies. The characteristic of that mode is that it doesn't admit dualism. It is decidedly anthropomorphic. It intuits a link between the freedom of the imagination and the world. Owen Barfield has observed that already "the Romantic image was an idol-smashing weapon meant to return men to their original participation in the phenomena." Rimbaud, too, as we know, wanted to bridge that gap. However, the vision of the romantics and symbolists was essentially tragic, while that of the surrealists is comic. The surrealist mythmaker is a comic persona in a world which is the product of a language-act, and an age in which these language-acts have proliferated.

When Arp writes of a "bladeless knife from which a handle is missing," when Norge speaks of a "time when the onion used to make people laugh," we have images, configurations, which employ archetypal elements but are not properly speaking archetypes. Instead, we have the emergence of entities which only by the force of utterance and the upheaval they cause in the imagination and thought acquire existence and even reality. These "useless objects" have a strange authority. Even as visionary acts, they consist of particulars and thus curiously provide us with a semblance of an actual experience.

For as the imagists would say, "knowledge is in particulars." Nothing is in the intellect that was not before in the senses, or Williams's well-known "no ideas but in things." At issue here is an attempt to re-create experience which preceded thought and to uncover its phenomenological ground. To allow phenomena to speak for itself. "To let that which shows itself be seen from itself in the very way in which it shows itself from itself" (Heidegger). There's a kind of responsibility here, care toward the actual, the sheer wonder of dailiness, the manner of our *being* in the world. Authenticity in imagism is primarily this confrontation with the sensuous for the sake of recreating its intensities.

The great ambition in each case is *thought*. How to think without recourse to abstractions, logic and categorical postulates? How to sensitize thought and involve it with the ambiguity of existence? Poems, in the words of the Russian formalistic critic Potebnia, are a "method of simplifying the thinking process." The surrealist Benjamin Péret goes further. He says simply that "thought is one and indivisible." Eluard says somewhere that "images think for him." Breton, as we have seen, defines psychic automatism as "the actual functioning of thought." Not far is Pound with his poetry as "inspired mathematics," or Duncan's saying that a poem is "the drama of truth." These are outrageous claims, but only so if we equate thought with "reason" and its prerogatives. To say that Chance thinks wouldn't make much sense, but to admit that Chance causes thought would be closer to what these statements intend. Again Olson raises an interesting question: "The degree to which projective (that is, the kind of poem I've been calling here imagist) involves a stance toward reality outside a poem as well as a new stance towards the reality of the poem itself." This is the whole point. Obviously, the rigorous phenomenological analysis of imagination and perception that surrealists and imagists have done has opened a whole new range of unknowns which address themselves to thought, and in the process alter the premises of the poems being written and the way they conceive of meaning.

Current criticism has unfortunately tended to simplify that historical predicament. It has seen the developments in recent poetry only within one or another literary movement, even when the strategies of these poetries have partaken of multiple sources. One can say with some confidence that the poet writing today can no longer be bound to any one standpoint, that he no longer has the option of being a surrealist or an imagist fifty years after and to the exclusion of everything else that has been understood since. Their questioning has involved us with large and fundamental issues. Their poetics have to do with the nature of perception, with being, with psyche, with time and consciousness. Not to subject oneself to their dialectics and uncertainties is truly not to experience the age we have inherited.

The aim of every new poetics is to evolve its own concept of meaning, its own idea of what is authentic. In our case, it is the principle of uncertainty. Uncertainty is the description of that gap which consciousness proclaims: actuality versus contingency. A new and unofficial view of our human condition. The best poetry being written today is the utterance and record of that condition and its contradictions.

1978

PHILIP LEVINE

From an Interview with Calvin Bedient

Los Angeles, California, Winter, 1977

On the Murder of Lieutenant José del Castillo by the Falangist Bravo Martinez, July 12, 1936

When the Lieutenant of the Guardia de Asalto
heard the automatic go off, he turned
and took the second shot just above
the sternum, the third tore away
the right shoulder of his uniform,
the fourth perforated his cheek. As he
slid out of his comrade's hold
toward the gray cement of the Ramblas
he lost count and knew only
that he would not die and that the blue sky
smudged with clouds was not heaven
for heaven was nowhere and in his eyes
slowly filling with their own light.
The pigeons that spotted the cold floor
of Barcelona rose as he sank below
the waves of silence crashing
on the far shores of his legs, growing
faint and watery. His hands opened
a last time to receive the benedictions
of automobile exhaust and rain
and the rain of soot. His mouth,
that would never again say, "I am afraid,"
closed on nothing. The old grandfather
hawking daisies at his stand pressed
a handkerchief against his lips
and turned his eyes away before they held
the eyes of a gunman. The shepherd dogs
on sale howled in their cages
and turned in circles. There is more
to be said, but by someone who has suffered
and died for his sister the earth
and his brothers the beasts and the trees.

The Lieutenant can hear it, the prayer
that comes on the voices of water, today
or yesterday, from Chicago or Valladolid,
and hangs like smoke above this street
he won't walk as a man ever again.

* * * * *

*How did the subject of "On the Murder of Lieutenant José del
Castillo by the Falangist Bravo Martinez, July 12, 1936" come to you?*

It came to me mistakenly. It's an interesting story. José del
Castillo's death, I believed, was one in a series of deaths that led to the
death of García Lorca. That's what I read in one of the older his-
tories of the Spanish Civil War . . . he was killed because there
was a large building strike in Madrid—construction workers were
striking—and right-wing newspapers were urging action against
these strikers, saying it was outrageous that they were slowing down
this building, etc. And what in Spain is called a señorito, which
means a rich young man—these señoritos were riding around in
their cars and stopping at building sites and shooting these guys that
were striking, and killing them. And del Castillo got involved in one
of these incidents, and he killed a couple of señoritos. A note was
thrown into his barracks saying that he was going to be killed. And
on a particular Sunday, which was I think one week before the begin-
ning of the Spanish Civil War, he was murdered right out in the open
in a park in Madrid. I put him in Barcelona. I take the liberty that
painters have always taken: to move the scene to a congenial one. I
don't know Madrid. I never saw it as an energetic and lively and
beautiful city. I saw it only under Franco. Just the way a Dutch
painter puts the crucifixion in Holland, I said, "Hell, I'll move it, to a
street of enormous energy and beauty, the Ramblas," which is my
favorite street in the world. At any rate, to get back to the other
thing, his fellow soldiers, policemen in the Guardia de Asalto wanted
to revenge his death, so they went out and grabbed . . . a right-wing
journalist of enormous importance, Calvo Sotelo. . . . And the story
was, then, that that murder brought about the uprising, the civil war.
And the story in the early history of the Spanish Civil War that I read
was that García Lorca was then murdered . . . that his life was taken
away, a writer for a writer. And I wrote the poem believing that.

Then along came Ian Gibson's book *The Death of Lorca* and it
became perfectly clear that those guys would have killed him if he
had turned into an angel. I mean they didn't give a shit about the
journalist, Sotelo. They killed him . . . out of envy; they killed him
the way people with no talent want to kill the person who's just
extraordinary. . . . His bisexuality probably had something to do
with it too. . . . Then when I saw what I had done, when I read the

Gibson book, I was kind of glad. A great many poets have mourned the death of García Lorca, but nobody had mourned the death of José del Castillo in a poem; and so I'm sort of happy that I mourned him for the wrong reasons. They turned out to be the right reasons, in a way.

One of your poems speaks of the laborers in Detroit as entering the fires, as if they were martyrs. Do you feel about laborers in the California fields the way you felt about the workers in the auto industry in Detroit? And what is it that you feel? Is it simply the sense that they're being insulted and injured?

Yes, and it's also the sense (because I participated in it) of the extraordinary physical agony of that kind of brutal work. I mean, just so I could see what it was like I went out and spent a day . . . two days as an agricultural worker in California. The days were separated by years. But I wanted to see what one of those long, endless days was like. And it seemed to me just as agonizing a kind of work as the heaviest work I'd done . . . I used the word *fire*, I suppose, because I worked in a forge room for a long time, and you were dealing with metals that had been heated white hot. In a way you almost *were* entering fire, you see.

Do you have any thoughts on why there seems to be so little political commitment in American poetry—at least in the poetry that lasts?

There's some. I think there's too little, sure . . . I see it, of course, in Whitman. And I see it very powerfully in a lot of novelists: in Dreiser, Sherwood Anderson, Dos Passos at his best in *USA;* I see it in Anderson's and Dreiser's poetry, too—it's terrible poetry but it has political commitment. I see it in Patchen very much. I see it in some of Rexroth, some of his best poems. And then there was some during the Vietnam war. A lot of poets got political for a short time.

Is there something defused, or diffuse, about the American political situation that discourages poets from taking a strong political stand in their poetry?

I think that's part of it. I think also that when you think about who's formed American poetry as it is now, you go back to, say, the Fugitives, you go back to Eliot, to Pound. The only politics they have are very conservative. Most of the poets are coming out of the universities too, and God knows they don't fool around with politics; I mean when they teach books they talk about structure and irony and things like that. And so I don't think people are encouraged to . . . and then we don't have to endure the kind of hell that a Latin American writer has to endure. We don't have to cope with censorship. The government here is much more efficient about the way it takes our money and takes our lives and our land and our water and our air. The Latin Americans are clumsy by comparison. They throw the poets in prison, they torture them, they break their hands, they shoot them. Here, they can write whatever they want. And all five thousand writers can read it and memorize it and it won't do a goddamn thing. They're not the kind of people who are going to go out and buy guns and shoot anybody. . . . We are so efficient that a poet can forget what poetry can do, it seems to me. I forgot what it can do for a long time.

Are you writing political poetry now?

Yes. I have been for many years. I think there came a point where I came back to my original reasons for wanting to write. Probably around 1964. Although when I look at even my first book I see—I don't know if you know the poem "The Negatives" in my first book. It's about French deserters from the French Algerian army, and there's a guy in there, an American, who has come back to the United States from Algeria, and he feels "caught in a strange country for which no man should die." And I must have written that when I was thirty. So I was aware of why I started to write . . . but without readers it seems pointless to keep raging about politics. If you don't have readers you're not going to change anything. . . . I began writing poetry to do something with it, to effect some kind of moral change; but without readers I knew I couldn't do that. Meanwhile I was writing it and I enjoyed writing it, and I got better. And the most wonderful times in my life were when I was inspired writing poetry.

Do you feel a strong kinship with certain other poets in your generation? Do you feel closer, perhaps, to some dead poets?

Yes, I think I feel closer to some dead poets. There are a couple of poets in my generation . . . I like a lot of them personally and I know them, some I like a great deal. And I like the work of many even though it isn't anything like mine . . . I'm glad they don't write like me; it would be very boring if everybody wrote like me. . . . There are certain poets who write poems that I wish I had written, because they're so beautiful. And they are about things that I'm concerned with. A few of Gary Snyder's poems strike me that way; a couple of Ginsberg's poems, a lot of Galway Kinnell's poems, of Jim Wright's, a lot of Denise Levertov's poems. . . . Some of the younger poets that I read—Laura Jensen, Louise Glück, Larry Levis, Michael Harper, Charles Wright: they don't write poems that I want to write, but I'm awfully glad they're writing, because they write so goddamn well. But the poets that I derive from, none of them are my contemporaries, it seems to me.

Would you name some names?

In an article I wrote for an anthology I was in, I talked about the influence of Bly and Rexroth, and I've always regretted it. At the time I thought it was true, but as the years have gone on I think that it's not true and I should have kept my mouth shut and waited to see. . . . I think a poet who has had an enormous influence on me is Robert Penn Warren, because I'm a narrative poet almost always, and he was a narrative poet; and I love the way he put narrative into his poetry. . . . Patchen was another, in his better poems. . . . They too were narrative, like "The Orange Bears." And there are poets of other countries that I feel great kinship with: Zbigniew Herbert and Czeslaw Milosz, the Polish poets. Some of the Spanish poets. . . . But there are other poets I learned a great deal from, because they just wrote so goddamn well that I studied the way they did it. Hardy was a poet like that. I love Hardy; I think he's a great poet. I love the way he puts a poem together when he's hitting it. Yeats—I don't think I could sit in a room with Yeats for five minutes without hitting him, but my God the poems are just extraordinary. . . . And Stevens is such a snob. Williams and Whitman I feel great kinship with.

Whitman I expected you to name.

I forgot. He's my favorite poet.

I hear an occasional line in your poetry that reminds me of Dylan Thomas.

I'm afraid I do too.

And there's a launched quality to some of your lines that is like Thomas's—like those in "A Refusal to Mourn" . . . But there's less vibrato, less blur. . . . One thing you may have in common with Merwin and Kinnell is a certain orphic drive—though "orphic" doesn't really tell one much. Paul Zweig, in a review of They Feed They Lion *in* Parnassus *(Fall/Winter, 1972), said that American poets have begun to create a language of revelation. And he sees you as engaged in this—what Rilke called building God through the labor of seeing. . . . Is revelation a term that. . . .*

It doesn't distress me. I don't know if I'm trying to create a language. I've never really thought about that. In a curious way, I'm not much interested in language. In my ideal poem, no words are noticed. You look through them to a vision of . . . just see the people, the place. . . . Now obviously I'm never going to write my ideal poem, and maybe I'm talking about creating a language.

You said in correspondence that you believe in romanticism—in all that bullshit. Are there aspects of romanticism that make you uneasy?

I don't think that there are aspects of romanticism that make me uneasy. I grew up in a time when the word *romantic* was a dirty word, when the romantic poets were being thrown out of the window, so that we could all worship John Donne, John Crowe Ransom, and poets of ahrny [irony], as Ransom used to say. But my favorite poet at that time was Keats, and I wasn't going to throw him out of the window for anybody.

I had the misfortune to spend one year of my life with Yvor

Winters; and of course he wanted to heave all those guys out of the window in the worst goddamn way. For some dumb reason he picked me to come to Stanford on a writing grant; and when I got there he liked me personally, we got along pretty well; but he loathed my poetry. And that was a source of some satisfaction to me, because although I liked some of his poetry and I like the way he had illuminated some Renaissance poetry, I wasn't really interested in the way he treated his contemporaries. And I wasn't interested in the poets he thought were gigantic in the twentieth century. I thought they were pretty puny, really. I remember once saying to him about Robert Frost, "You don't talk about a single one of his greatest poems. . . . You pick out his worst poems so that you can dismiss him. Is that fair?" And he said: "I wasn't trying to make him look good." Which was honest, but it told me where he was. He wasn't in the house of criticism that I felt was going to be useful to anybody. . . . He just scored a touchdown for neoclassicism or something. . . . So when I say "all that bullshit," I guess I'm sensitive to the fact that it has been written off as dreck. . . .

Do you see yourself as a poet who uses romanticism as a criticism of what we do to each other and what life does to us?

Yeah. The Keats for example that I loved was the Keats of the letters, not the poems, as much as I admire the odes. Because I think that he inherited a poetic tradition that was so puny that he could say, I would jump down Etna for any public good but I want to write beautiful poems. As though you couldn't perform a public good with poetry. And I think you can. . . . I mean, you think of all the misery that he saw and you read about it in his letters, and how little of it ever gets into his poetry. . . . He sits there for months while his brother Tom dies day by day of tuberculosis in what must have been one of the most polluted shitholes in the world, the London of the nineteenth century. And what does he get: "Here where men sit and hear each other groan, . . . Where youth grows pale, and spectre-thin, and dies." Tom gets two lines. And that's it. Bingo. I mean, I couldn't let America take my brother and kill him at seventeen or eighteen, and just sit there and say, "Well, I have to write poems about Grecian urns." Shit. I mean I don't think I'd ever get over it. And I don't think Keats wanted to get over it. I don't think that he inherited as strong a tradition as I did. He didn't *have* Whitman.

When I say I'm a romantic poet, it seems to me that I feel the human is boundless, and that seems to me the essential fact of romanticism.

In "On the Murder of José del Castillo" you refer at the end to a kind of romantic hold-all that is beyond mortality altogether, transcendental. And this seemed to me rare in your work, where the romanticism is mostly immanent. Did you feel, "This is a departure for me, I'm walking out on a plank"?

The poem originated in the ending. It just so happened that I was reading this book about José del Castillo and at the same time I was reading I had a very odd experience, which was a repetition of a youthful experience. I was driving on a Sunday morning and I turned on the radio and I heard a black preacher that I heard often when I was a kid. And this black preacher was talking in a way that was very familiar to me. And I got into the rhythm of what he was saying. . . . He was talking to people out there in the radio audience who couldn't be in the church because they were in one way or another hurt, sick, suffering. . . . And he was saying like, 'Sally Benson, I know you're sick, I know you've had an operation. Hang on. We're praying for you." And then suddenly he said, "And you, Charles Something, old soldier, I know your wound. . . ." And then the problem became, How can I build a poem that will use this ending that I have in my head? . . . What I think I did was sit down and try to build a poem in which a man's death flows out from him. He dies, and his dying sort of goes out out out. And then what comes back is this prayer for him, back back back from the world. . . . That's what I saw as the structure that I had to create. I felt it was very different from anything I'd ever done. I felt very excited about it. I mean, I went home and, man, I mean I was just, you know, flying, I knew I was going to get this son of a bitch.

It's an exciting poem. It shares a quality that some of Robert Penn Warren's poems have: a kind of scattered sublimity, the scatteredness of sublimity. . . . Do you have any particular don'ts as a poet? What do you tell your students that they should try to avoid?

One don't is never to defend your poetry against anybody. . . . A lot of what you hear is stupid, but you should keep your mouth shut and listen; you might learn something . . . And I tell my students that. Defend your right to be a poet . . . but not your poetry, because you'll stop people from trying to tell the truth. That's one. The other is never to follow the idea that got you to sit down and write the poem if the poem seems to be going someplace else. It knows better than you do. I don't see myself as the captain of the ship, if you can say that writing a poem is like taking a voyage or something . . . I don't think I'm the captain; I think I'm down in the hold throwing coal into the thing, trying to stoke it. . . . But I'm not a cabbage, I have a mind, and when I see suddenly that I'm writing something that William Carlos Williams writes, or something that I've already written, I say, "Hey, come on." My biggest danger is that I'll imitate myself. And that's the thing I—my wife is very good on that. She's very quick to point that out. And she's very precise in telling, in the way she does it . . .

Your poetry contains few abstract statements. Is this because you agree with Edmund Burke that a clear idea is a little idea?

I think part of it is that in a lot of poems (not my own) I'm aware of the fact that people create characters so that they can kill them and then make a point. And it seems to me that the people are more interesting than the point. And I don't want the characters in my poems giving up their lives so that a point can be made. . . . You know, abstract ideas are so monumental all the way from Plato to the present. They bore me. Philosophers bore me. I find them the most boring people I've ever come across in my life. I would much prefer spending, you know, an afternoon with a bunch of jockeys or car mechanics than with philosophers. I remember renting my house to a philosopher who let all the trees die. And when I got angry with him, because my wife planted those trees and loved them—seven trees he let die—he said, "I didn't think you were the kind of man who would care about something like that." And to me that was the voice of the philosopher—"something like that": a living thing.

ANNE SEXTON

The Freak Show

One way poets make a living, make it by their own wits, [. . .] is by giving readings. On January 4, 1973, I stopped giving readings, and believe me, I needed the money. Furthermore, I asked such preposterous sums that I gave fewer readings than most poets do.

What's in it for the poet? Money, applause, adulation, someone to hear how the poems sound coming out of the poet's mouth, an audience. Don't kid yourself. You write for an audience (I think of myself as writing for one person, that one perfect writer who understand and loves). If the audiences were this one person multiplied by a hundred or a thousand, everything would be okeydokey.

From my limited experience, it does not go that way. You are the freak. You are the actor, the clown, the oddball. Some people come to see what you look like, what you have on, what your voice sounds like. Some people secretly hope your voice will tremble (that gives an extra kick). Some people hope you will do something audacious, in other words (and I admit to my greatest fears) that you vomit on the stage or go blind, hysterically blind or actually blind.

Once at a college in New Hampshire, I cried after I read a poem. I had never read this poem before an audience, and I had no idea it would move me so. I was embarrassed to cry. I had to go offstage and get my pocketbook, which had a Kleenex in it, so that I might blow my nose. The audience cheered. Maybe they didn't cheer because it was more of a show to see me cry. Maybe they only meant, "Anne, we're with you."

However, it was reported to me that my lecture bureau (one of their agents happened to be in my audience that night when I cried) speaks proudly of my presentation to their clients thusly: "It's a great show! Really a pow! She cries every time right on stage!"

Watch out for those lecture bureaus. They may get you bookings, they may get you more money, but they exploit your soul in ways such as these.

At the last reading I gave, at a luncheon before the reading with many professors (at universities all over the United States you can meet some of the kindest, most soulful, dearest people—once in a while some of the most cruel) who ate and drank with me and did their best to hold me up, for I drink like a drunkard before a reading because I am so scared.

I was so sure I was to die flying out there to the Midwest, that the plane would crash, fall like the *Hindenburg* from the sky, but it was a different death that came about—the death of Anne as a performer. I was met (alive) by a very sweet and understanding English professor, who also happened to like poetry. We had a beer at the airport, and I vented my feelings about readings and how poets shouldn't give them, and he listened with compassion, but without comprehension.

Then the drive into the city and the luncheon at the student bistro, a barnlike place, our table on top of a hot but fake fireplace, four men and one token woman professor, Janet Beeler. She was seated as far from me as possible, so that we kind of had to yell out our sisterhood, our commonwealth of similar sensibilities. I could feel her compassion as I guzzled down the double vodkas, once even with vomit rising in my throat and me swallowing it—not vomit because I was drunk, but because I was drinking too fast and I was scared.

At that point all immediately said, "Let's go out and get you some air." I replied very softly, "I don't need air. If you'd only just be quiet for a moment, I'll get hold of myself." The men immediately started talking as fast as possible (not comprehending my request), and Janet Beeler hushed them and reminded them of my request.

Later the man who had arranged the reading, a vibrant, attractive, understanding type, although one felt he had never read any poetry, walked out to the chef and got me a western sandwich, because previously I had only picked at a badly burned hamburger and said wistfully, "The luckiest thing for me to eat before a reading is a western sandwich." Three good omens: I was alive, there was an understanding sister, and a western sandwich. I would indeed be able to give the reading.

One professor who was, as I recall, in business law, told me he was forcing fifty of his business students to come to my reading, although they knew nothing about poetry. I said, "Thanks a lot," meaning thanks for sticking fifty bodies in the audience who do not like poetry and will see *nothing* but the freak.

Poetry is for us poets the handwriting on the tablet of the soul. It is the most private, deepest, most precious part of us. Yet somehow in this poetry biz, as one of my students calls it, we are asked to make a show of it. [. . .]

I don't feel this way about New York audiences. I'll tell you why. For some reason unexplainable to me, the audiences I have had at the Y or the Guggenheim seem to have read my poetry from the very beginning and want to hear the new stuff or the old stuff just because they want to know what it sounds like when I say it. The last time I read at the Y and I had a temperature of 104 and bad bronchitis, a man yelled up from the audience as I was speaking (forgive me; I can never remember quotes or dialogue correctly—I can only approximate), "Whatever you do, Annie, baby, we're with you."

Once at the Hatch Shell in Boston, after I was introduced by the huckster (wine company PR man) who was paying for the reading, someone screamed out, "Long live Anne Sexton." Those two voices will remain in my head forever. I do know there are many who do not yell, all over the country, but feel that way. I can only say to them, "God bless you."

I remember being a fledgling poet and going to hear the famous poets read. I wanted to hear what they had to say, but there was a sneaky, unconscious, underground part of me that wanted the poet to be a little weird. Why? I think all of us poets feel so alien inside, so alien from the world, that we want the big names to act a little alien, a little crazy, just to confirm what is in the deepest soul of the young poet.

I have been told often what a thrill it was to see if poor but wonderful Dylan Thomas would last through the reading on all that booze. I have also been told of W. H. Auden coming on stage absentmindedly in his carpet slippers, and how delighted the poets and others were to observe such a unique characteristic in one of the world's great poets, etc. etc.

I find that a poetry reading takes a month from my writing—the trauma. I spoke to a dear friend, a very famous poet—you would all know him—and he said after a certain reading, he came home and his nose bled for three days. He, too, was going to give up readings. He will need the money from the readings. It is a way of getting by. But I ask all you poets what in hell are we doing to ourselves—why are we making ourselves into freaks when we are really some sort of priest or prophet or hermit. I ask you audiences to look deeply into yourselves before you go to the poetry reading and say, "What is it I want of this person, this human being, who is going to reveal his deepest thoughts?" If any of you have any answers, I would be glad to listen.

That was supposed to be the end of this column, but yesterday, February 24, the answer came. It came to my mailbox at Boston University (a place I seldom investigate—thus the delay). Here is the letter from one Janet Beeler:

Thursday night, Jan. 4th

Dear Anne,

I feel like I need to close the experience of this day by writing a note to you with a kind of oblique blessing of some sort—Oh, I hope you're home safely by now, snug and warm and protected. I wish you well, my friend.

I really don't know what to think about that surrealistic lunch—the overheated room, the strange food, the awkwardness of even the chairs.

Those men treated you in such a strange way—as though you thought of yourself as a kind of expensive freak. No, that's not it—they wanted to please, but didn't know how, so were patronizing, brusque, adolescent. And you of all people seem so worth protecting, and were so unprotected. I was very moved by you today—by who you are, or seemed to be. You seemed defenseless, for such a tough cookie. And I felt for your anxiety, and the attempts you make to get some distance from it, and what is happening, and to handle the various frustrations and pains and challenges.

Listen, the reading was fine. Oh, I was prejudiced, but I mean that I took care to ask some of the trapped Business Law kids what they thought. It seems important to tell you that one boy said, "It was mysterious." I take that as an affirmative compliment—good for him, he felt the mystery. The people I know that read you anyway were very positive—felt satisfied, even fortified. Maybe you don't care about that kind of news, but I did—I was fascinated—what would they make of those words! The contrasts of the profound meanings and the simple vocabulary struck one girl—well, good for her, too.

The only thing I'm feeling now is hungry—I wanted some time to talk. Isn't it strange, to have lived with you all these years—the poems among the last at night (in the company of Pound, Neruda, Rilke, my favorites)—to have lived through those parts of you, for your thoughts to have been part of my life, an intimate part. If you wrote different poetry—if you wrote farther from your marrow, it wouldn't be so. But there it is: my friend, the one who knows. And there you are. And I want to talk to you. Selfishly. I want to know the news from the fatherland, the news from the front. And the kids, how are they now? And you, what are the good things now? As though you owed that in some way because you've shared the bad news. And of course you don't have to share anything at all. It's just that . . . well, we've lived together. I'm sorry, Anne. I feel I'm grabbing, but it's a powerful feeling in me. It's okay. Well, look, I want to do something. You don't have to do anything about it, for Christ's sake, but I want to share something of myself with you. I've been writing too, for several years—never had much audience, or exposed myself, but these three poems were accepted by *Antaeus*. Anyway, I want to share them with you. You don't have to do anything, don't even read them if you're working. I just want something mutual, because your work is a precious part of my life. And I liked you a lot today. A lot.

Part of the blessing is that you have a good new year—new life, sweet new beginnings. If you have to come to Cleveland again, let me see you?

Love,

Janet Beeler

Who knows? Some day I may go forth on some jet to some college and look for that one person again and read my goddamned heart out.

HAYDEN CARRUTH

A Few Thoughts Following Professor Clausen's Essay

I.

No point of dispute occurs to me in my reading of Professor Clausen's essay, "Poetry in a Discouraging Time." What he says about the split between scientific and imaginative modes of thought, considered historically and culturally, is sound, part of our whole view of ourselves, I guess, and of our ancestors. Specialization of learning is a fact. Like all facts it carries within it its own inevitability. And specialization means the fragmenting of consciousness. We all know this, we've known it all our lives, and although Professor Clausen's recapitulation is clear and helpful, it does not add anything new to my awareness.

The difference between us is in point of view. I am more practical and hardheaded than he, or at least I like to think I am, for I have been a professional editor, dealing mostly with poetry, all my adult life, and have been also a serious, more or less constant poet, working in my shed with the actual problems of making relevant and integrated poems. For me the causes of poetry's continual recession have been less a matter of cultural or intellectual evolution than of immediate and primarily sociological circumstances. When I think back, I cannot recall a single serious writer from the time of Francis Bacon to the present who has rejected science or scientific thought. Shakespeare, Milton, Pope, Wordsworth, etc.—all incorporate the general scientific knowledge of their time in their work; it's there on the page. Even Eliot, in spite of his statements in prose about the "dissociation of sensibility," relied heavily in his poetry on concepts derived from the psychoanalysis and anthropology of his own time. What the hell, science is *interesting*. Who can have any feeling but warm fellowship for Pythagoras, over the millennia? Myself, many of my most contented hours, from boyhood on, have been spent in reading Faber, Muir, Einstein, Russell, Papa Darwin himself, to say nothing of more recent popularizers, Annie Dillard,

Part of a symposium in *The Georgia Review,* Winter 1981. Contributors were asked to respond to an essay by Christopher Clausen, later included in his book, *The Place of Poetry.*

Lewis Thomas, John McPhee, and others. When I canvass my own knowledge, I find, even though my schooling was long ago and based on scientific concepts originating in the nineteenth century or earlier, I still know something about relativity, indeterminacy, the conversion of mass into energy, various theories of functional cosmology, recent developments in biology, etc., and I know quite a lot—because my interests lead me in this direction—about animal behavior and conceptual ecology. My weakest sector is mathematics, but I remember at least the ideas of algebra, geometry, calculus, theory of numbers, etc., and I have a real fondness for Euclid. Not much to go on, a scientist might say. But did Shakespeare know any more about celestial navigation, did Wordsworth know more about the work of Lamarck? Moreover, I am certain I am not exceptional in what I know today; quite the contrary. In the poems that come to me by the tens of thousands, as in my own poems, I find the fabric of contemporary scientific knowledge, more or less generalized, taken for granted as one of poetry's contextual fields of reference. I am not thinking of poets like A. R. Ammons who have been trained as scientists. I am thinking of the numbers of us who have simply existed in the world one way or another and have followed out our normal instinct of curiosity to the extent permitted by our busy, specialized lives.

I can't help mentioning, because I am, foolishly or not, proud of it, that one of my own ancestors was among the great scientists of the seventeenth century, Isaac Barrow, the tutor of Isaac Newton at Oxford and originator of many concepts developed in Newton's *Principia*. And this reminds me that another distant relative, William Herbert Carruth, a nineteenth-century prairie American who became a scholar and was, I believe, a member of the founding faculty of the University of Kansas at Lawrence, wrote a poem called "Each in His Own Tongue," which had this line for its refrain: "Some call it evolution, others call it God." Not a good poem, but not altogether bad either, and a distinct *poetic* effort not only to reconcile but to integrate imaginative and empirical modes of perception. It went through scores of editions in the years between 1880 and the first World War, and it lay, in limp leather or embossed calfskin over boards, on I have no idea how many thousands of parlor tables; a great many. Americans of that time were not only hungry for a relevant poetry of ideas, they were also broadly enough informed to accept it and understand it.

No, the antiscientific people were never our genuine writers, nor genuine intelligences of any kind; they were our zealots, nuts, victims of intellectual hysterogeny. Plenty of them, God knows—here, there, and everywhere. But they have not usually been determinative in our civilization; I say not usually, because right now

I think they may be determinative, or close to it; I am not enchanted by the future. But there are still plenty of the others too—you, me, our friends and colleagues. We *do*, I insist, share among us not only a larger body of scientific knowledge than many critics think but a willingness to account for that knowledge and for the intellectual procedures which produced it in our own work as artists. What we, the serious writers, have always despised—not from the time of Bacon, but, significantly, from a hundred and fifty years later—is technology and commerce; as the subjugation of all our civil life by technology and commerce has accelerated, until now we are completely enslaved, so has our hatred become deeper, broader, greater in every way, a controlling thematic element in much of our writing. This is the schism. We on one side of the abyss, our massively technological and commercial civilization on the other; but we, the writers and artists, do not stand alone. I believe true scientists are standing with us, and in fact a large part of the general populace. Isn't this the fact of our particular demoralization, not quite like anything known in the past? We have a civilization in which a great number of people, probably a majority, are hopelessly and helplessly alienated from the structures and values of the civilization itself precisely because they perceive the doom of that civilization in the flaws of specifically human nature. They themselves are responsible; yet they can do nothing. They are paralyzed by their own staring eyes in the mirror of the world.

II.

So much by way of supplementing Professor Clausen's view with mine, from a somewhat different line of vision. I emphasize, however, that I have no disagreement with what he says; I think it is right and useful, although the question seems to me larger than his essay suggests. The additional points I wish to make can now be made quickly.

A. Clausen says that poets themselves are largely responsible for their alienation from the main line of cultural evolution in this country, and I largely agree. But I think the matter can be explained more simply. Critics in general do not like to discuss the "difficulty" (they always put it in quotes) of twentieth-century poetry, if only because they don't want to seem callow or simpleminded, although there are other reasons too. If one assumes, as I do, that the so-called revolution in poetic tastes and methods which was associated with Pound, Williams, H.D., and others of their generation was necessary and inevitable and would have occurred anyway, no matter who the rebel poets of that time might have been, then there is no point in arguing about it. It happened; it is a fact. Another fact is that the poetry written by the revolutionary poets was, and is, difficult to read. For the first time in the exoteric tradition of Western poetry, readers were presented with poems that they could not read without study. I don't wish to quibble. Obviously at all times those who had literary training could read Milton, Dryden, and Wordsworth with more immediate appreciation than those without such training. But it is also true that many, many people possessing no more than the ordinary literacy could read and enjoy the most important poetry of their own times; that is, up until about 1910. Then came the poetry that required study, more and more of it as the decades passed. This seems so obvious to me that I wonder why people evade it so persistently. Nor do I think I need define what I mean by *study* and what I mean by *reading*. Then who, pray tell, wants to study, especially after one's school days are over? Well, some people do, I know. But many do not, and it isn't because they are crude or unintelligent. Most poets and professors of my acquaintance will choose a political magazine or thriller fiction to read when they are choosing freely, not difficult poetry. Consequently, beginning about 1910 the audience for important contemporary poetry drifted away. This is not, I say plainly, a question of cultural lag. Young people today, those from intelligent families and good secondary schools, cannot read *The Waste Land* or the Cantos any more readily than could their parents or grandparents, i.e., with even a merely sufficient understanding. They must study. In short, much of the poetry of the revolution remains *permanently* difficult—and I don't mean like John Donne's, I mean damn near impenetrable—and in spite of sundry attempts to return to simpler poetry, as with the proletarian poets of the thirties and the beat poets of the fifties, poetry written in America today is still pervasively influenced by the work of the revolutionary masters. I know for a fact that in many creative-writing workshops the idea of difficulty is disseminated to the students, explicitly or implicitly, as a prerequisite of successful, which usually means fashionable, writing. But how can you have a fashion when nobody cares? Basta! It is so ridiculous! The more serious question of whether or not the study of these difficult poems produces results that are worth the effort is one that neither I nor anyone else can answer. I hope it does. But no matter what I hope, the *fact*, very disheartening, is that the general audience for poetry in America has vanished during exactly the same period in which thousands upon thousands of young Americans have submitted to such study in our colleges and universities.

(Let me add, although I'm not sure what it means, that I think Robert Frost in his best poems is just as difficult as T. S. Eliot and in many of the same ways, namely, in poetic structures and in the use of symbolic or associative reference.)

B. The effects of technology must be mentioned. I mean not simply as changing the cultural substance and context of writing, but as a direct cause of the lost readership we are talking about. I am sure I don't need to explain what I mean when I say that a very large proportion of Americans today have had their literary responsiveness, which is not the same as artistic or esthetic responsiveness, trained out of them by radio, television, and motion pictures. How important this is I don't know. I personally don't like it, not at all; but the widespread habit of reading poetry was made possible by a technological event—the discovery of printing from movable type—which occurred rather late in the evolution of poetry as a distinct formal art, and perhaps there is no necessary reason to believe that poetry will not survive when functional literacy has become a vestigial skill. Perhaps we rely too much on mere literacy or "letteredness." However, although the problem needs to be mentioned, I think for the present we can leave it to the psycho-semanticists to argue about.

C. What seems to me far more important is a development related to electronic technology, but fundamentally not a part of it: the observable and growing distrust of language in general. It began long before the advent of electronic transmission, and I do not mean in the nominalist/realist arguments of philosophers; I mean in the iniquity of the first publican who hung out a sign saying that his beer was "better" when his clients, relying on their senses, could tell immediately that it was awful. The iniquity has been augmented to utterly horrifying dimensions in our time. Constantly we are told that this or that commercial product or service, or even this or that candidate for office, is "better," when we know it cannot be true. (How my father, an honest newspaperman, used to rail against the "objectless comparative!" But that was in another country.) Children today are taught, in lessons compounded every five minutes, that untruth may be uttered with impunity, even with approval. Lying has become a way of life, very nearly now *the* way of life, in our society. The average adult American of average intelligence and average education believes almost nothing communicated to him in language, and the disbelief has become so ingrained that he or she does not even notice it. In short, the advertising business. I hate it with every molecule of moral feeling, the prior condition of esthetic feeling, left in my somewhat failing sensibility. Advertising is the most corrupt and corrupting mental activity of the human race. It has invaded and destroyed every sector of language. When most people no longer bother to read the newspaper except as a consciously offered travesty or as a means of ascertaining through numerical tabulations the results of yesterday's stock transactions and baseball games, how can they be expected to read serious literature? Get rid of advertising! It has not only destroyed language, it has directly caused the increase of violence in our civil life, of death and misery, of war. Extirpate it! A dream, no doubt. Yet in my projected nonviolent anarchist community I can easily invent ways to do without advertising. And when corrupt apologists, with their bland faces and fatty voices, tell me that advertising serves a socially necessary informative purpose, I snarl at them and tell them just what evil, damnable liars they are.

(Doris Lessing wrote once of "the thinning of language against the density of our experience"; a constant theme among writers of the past thirty years, the same idea essentially as the noninterpretive fragmentary metafictions of the trans-modernists today. But experience isn't at fault. How could it be? Fact remains always at the "inactive" level of fact. There can be no such thing as the "new reality" that many people, with philosophical abandon, now insist on. We—the enemies we harbor, the advertising persons, the manipulators of "image," the liars—are responsible for the thinning of language. I am convinced that a real artist will be thrown up eventually by any condition of existence, and he or she will possess the means to express that condition fully. The question is whether or not anyone else will be sufficiently uncorrupted to recognize what the artist has done.)

D. This leads back to the poets again, to their responsibility, their evasions. For if, in considering the disappearance of the audience for poetry, I do not emphasize the cultural complexity of poetic themes and modes as much as Clausen does, I nevertheless do believe that poets are failing more and more in the substance of their work. I mean they do not write relevant poems. How can they be blamed? Everyone is scared to death, everyone is seeking evasions; poets the same. Recently I too have become a professor, late in life and unexpectedly, which means I cannot speak with much academic authority; and believe me, I do not use the word *academic* in a negative sense. On the contrary, for me it signifies the application of systematic thought, a skill I admire and often envy. But I've "taught" three poetry workshops now, two on the graduate level and one on the undergraduate. So far not one student has turned in a poem that deals either directly or indirectly with the impending end of the world—*world*, fr. OG *wer-ald*, "man-era"—in nuclear war, an event which sober, studious, and careful scholars now predict will occur as soon as two years and certainly no more than thirty or forty years from this moment; that is, within the natural lifetimes of many who are reading these words and of all the students in my workshops. When I ask them, my students, why they avoid so obvious a fact of their lives, they say, "What can we do about it?" Most of the time, when I am overcome by the endemic and natural despair of our age, I agree that we can do nothing. Occasionally I experience a spasm of hope that if we rally ourselves sufficiently we may do something. But *in either case* I know, as a writer and teacher of writers, that no poetry which does not in general represent the feeling of human existence in its own time, no matter how rotten that feeling is, will capture the attention of intelligent readers. Poets who write endless poems about their grandmothers, their sex fantasies, their storm windows, etc., etc., etc., are escapists, and in this they cannot hope to compete with the writers of television scripts. From Goldsmith to Lawrence (or from Chaucer to Cheever), writers wrote about the controlling social phenomena of their times, whatever their immediate materials may have been. But today most poets are failing to confront the dominant fact of our existence. I don't say all poets. But "most poets," in this time of overproduction and overpublication, are what the public encounters, and one cannot blame the public for being bored.

In short, it is a sociological rather than a cultural predicament, although of course it is both and the two cannot be separated anyway. The collapse of art—for I do not think it is confined to poetry—as a functional element of our civilization is a part of the greater collapse of morale everywhere, beginning with World War I and growing by geometrical increments down to this present instant. The dissociation of imagination from generally perceived experience has become wider and wider, until now the breach is total. Poets have no audience but themselves. This is folly. I can't prove this statistically, of course, but I know that as an editor I receive more responses now to the work I publish than I have ever received before, and the manuscripts coming in from untrained people, who instinctively resort to poetry when they are deeply moved, continue to increase. These poems are usually awful, but they are also, significantly, simple and true. Catastrophe is always simple and true, a matter of rudiments. I have written elsewhere about the problems of publishing poetry, and I intend to write eventually about the problems of teaching poetry, which are equally important. But now I am saying something more important still: the only way to revive the poetic imagination in our time and in relevant relationship to our time is by head-on confrontation with our dread. Let the poem be simple, let the poet be faithful, and then the reader will come.

But before all this is the question of how to stay the supreme irrelevance that will be the end of the world.

July 4th, 1981

THOM GUNN

Two Saturday Nights
Rewriting a Poem

This is the story of how I took fifteen years to write a poem.

In 1975 I was reading the *Divine Comedy* in the course of a three-year attempt to grasp it as people do who have little Italian, a bit of Latin, and much French. I think that must be the way the young Eliot read it—out of the Temple Classics edition of around 1900, taking it Canto by Canto, first reading the English literal prose translation and then piecing together the Italian on the opposite page, reading it aloud as best I could, and taking it slowly, but at worst getting closer to it than if I had read it in the verse translations of Carey and Binyon. However far I may have been from *really* reading Dante, I certainly arrived at a sense of that extraordinary compression which must be one of the sources of his power.

I loved besides the combination of the cerebral with the visionary in a man whose ability, whose necessity, was to speculate about his own ranging imagination. And I was, not for the first time, much attracted by the tune of terza rima, a form with great potential for speed and condensation and inconclusiveness: when I think of Dante's verse form I get the image of a big dog running fast, its body packed with meat and muscle and import.

It was at this time that I wrote a poem about the Barracks, one of the most famous, one of the most lurid indeed, of the bathhouses in San Francisco during the 1970s. (It was the only one I ever heard of that was raided, not by the vice, but by the narcotics squad.)

Saturday Night

I prowl the labyrinthine corridors
   And have a sense of being underground
As in a mine . . . dim light, the many floors,
   The bays, the heat, the tape's explosive sound.
People still entering, though it is 3 A.M.,
   Stripping at lockers and, with a towel tied round,
Stepping out hot for love or stratagem,
   Pausing at thresholds (newness never ends),
Peering at others, as others peer at them
   Like people in shelters searching for their friends

Among the group come newest from the street.
　　And in each room a different scene attends.
In one, three portly men, each bare in his seat,
　　Passing a joint between them, as polite
As if at home in civilized retreat.
　　Next door, packed twining limbs seem in half-light
Continuous flesh unjoined to head or foot.
　　Next, one lies patient on his belly all night,
His special interest reared and resolute.
　　And here one waiting as his trip comes on
Stares at the handcuffs which his friend has put
　　Open before him, but his friend is gone.

I'm still on top of it, but only just.
　　Not hell, not even a phenomenon.
And yet tonight I'm full of self-mistrust . . .
　　Then one whose very eyes brightly conspire
Moves from the mob and touches me. Clear lust—
　　I suddenly flare up—fire in the mine, all fire!
It burns down to the self, the baths, the night,
　　Which grant me thus a great and good desire.
I think, at least for now, it's all all right.

I never published this poem because something dissatisfied me
about it, as if I hadn't quite told the truth in it. For all the qualifica-
tions he makes, its author seems limited and complacent. "Look, I
scored!" he says with the defiance of an insecure stockbroker.
Harold Norse once wrote a poem about a housepainter on his
lunch break: virile and juicy, he sits relaxed in the sunshine with
white paint still flecking his eyelashes; and first of all the poem
asks us to admire him from a distance—it is a beautiful moment,
perhaps *because* of the distance. (D. H. Lawrence would have had
him rightly warning the greedy: NOLI ME TANGERE.) But then
the poet, apparently, comes up and propositions him, because
they have sex somewhere and the poem subsides into a mere
boastfulness. I hate that kind of poem, but it was what I had
written here.

In 1975 I had recently been granted a new subject matter, one
which would have been unpublishable probably ten years before
and certainly twenty years before. It was still the time of Gay Libera-
tion, a phrase which now has a quaint but worthy ring to it. There
was talk of a "gay community," something I doubted existed. But
community it was, as Ellen Willis described it, in the course of a fine
article in the *Village Voice* (Jan. 24, 1989):

> The lesbian movement of the '70s was not primarily about liberating
> desire . . . but about extending female solidarity; for the gay male
> community solidarity was, at its core, about desire.

That's what we were a part of, a visionary carnal politics. No wonder Blake was often cited!

Something more. The 1970s were the time, as I heard someone say later, of a great hedonistic experiment. And the word experiment inevitably recalls to me the way people spoke for years about Soviet Russia. In the early 1940s, when I was at boarding school because of the Blitz, my mother wrote to me on the invasion of Russia: "Does this mean that the great experiment will fail?" (She was ignorant of Stalin's massacres.) And visionaries are much the same, whether they are political or religious or sexual. As hippies were the indirect heirs of the communists between World Wars, so we were the direct heirs of the hippies, drug-visionaries also. At the baths, or in less organized activity, there was a shared sense of adventure, thrilling, hilarious, *experimental.* In our deliberately distorted vision, we crossed gulfs as dramatic and enormous as those in John Martin's landscapes, on the huge pinions of our sexual momentum. We tried to make the ecstatic commonplace, each night of it a building block for an apocalyptic Holy City—a City of Eros.

> There are many different varieties of New Jerusalem,
> Political, pharmaceutical—I've visited most of them.
> But of all the embodiments ever built, I'd only return to one,
> For the sexual New Jerusalem was by far the greatest fun.

That was a spin-off of 1990. I wanted it to resemble the epigraphs to Kipling's stories. It was designed as an introduction to the poem I did eventually come to write at this time, which I don't think is much like Kipling in itself. I tried yet again because I thought some poet should do something about a great imaginative experience— the excitements and intensities of a bathhouse, with the druggy fantasy always bordering on the dangerous. I kept the first eleven lines from my old poem but after that I had to rethink the whole thing. This time, fifteen years after I had started it, it necessarily became a historical poem:

Saturday Night

> I prowl the labyrinthine corridors
>   And have a sense of being underground

As in a mine . . . dim light, the many floors,
  The bays, the heat, the tape's explosive sound.
People still entering, though it is 3 A.M.,
  Stripping at lockers and, with a towel tied round,
Stepping out hot for love or stratagem,
  Pausing at thresholds (wonder never ends),
Peering at others, as others peer at them
  Like people in shelters searching for their friends
Among the group come newest from the street.
  And in each room a different scene attends:
Friends by the bedful lounging on one sheet,
  Playing cards, smoking, while the drugs come on,
Or watching the foot-traffic on the beat,
  Ready for every fresh phenomenon.
This was the Barracks, this the divine rage
  In 1975, that time is gone.
All here, of any looks, of any age,
  Will get whatever they are looking for,
Or something close, the rapture they engage
  Renewable each night.
                    If, furthermore,
Our Dionysian experiment
  To build a city never dared before
Dies without reaching to its full extent,
  At least in the endeavor we translate
Our common ecstasy to a brief ascent
  Of the complete, grasped, paradisal state
Against the wisdom pointing us away.

  What hopeless hopefulness. I watch, I wait—
The embraces slip, and nothing seems to stay
  In our community of the carnal heart.
Some lose conviction in mid-arc of play,
  Their skin turns numb, they dress and will depart:
The perfect body, lingering on goodbyes,
  Cannot find strength now for another start.
Dealers move in, and murmuring advertise
  Drugs from each doorway with a business frown.
Mattresses lose their springs. Beds crack, capsize,
  And spill their occupants on the floor to drown.
Walls darken with the mold, or is it rash?
  At length the baths catch fire and then burn down,
And blackened beams dam up the bays of ash.

V. The End of a Golden String ✒️
                            Poets on Influence and Identity

WILLIAM STAFFORD

The End of a Golden String

My mother would say abrupt things, reckless things, liberating things. I remember her saying of some people in town, "They are so boring you get tired of them, even when they are not around." My children say very odd things. Their conversations, collected into a book I cherish called "Lost Words," can entertain. I came across a recent example, saved in notes from the old days. Two little ones pretending a telephone conversation:

"How are your children?"

"They're dead."

"Chicken pox?"

"No, the hear-ache."

These are just samples recollected. I could recall for hours. But the intent is to identify only, to snag one little point: what people say—the people around us—floods our attention and then passes; it alerts us, now and then jiggles our feelings or provides a sigh or a laugh, or a combination. "How are your children?" "They're dead." We can make these passing phrases recur, change their context, add a new, immediate feeling—and resonate with unexpected force. The everyday talk around us throbs waxing and waning interest and possibility.

I want to come back to this one little snagged point.

Sometimes a person says to a writer, "What great writer influenced you?" It is an engaging question. It almost always elicits a search for favorite authors, for passages to recall with satisfaction. Many of my friends can detect in themselves traces of pure gold—Hardy, Tennyson, Joyce, even veins of George Eliot or Shakespeare. Some find current swagger—in Mailer, or Carrie Jacobs Bond. The search for influence has appeal, as we can easily see. I would not want to spoil the fun.

Further, not just the living embodiments of former greatness take pleasure in this tracing of influences. Critics live by it. And teachers mix it with other ingredients to provide stretch and keeping qualities to the long, spinning spiel that serves them through class time and earns the daily bread. When I was in graduate school I was finely trained in this detection. For a spell of several weeks just before the ultimate pleasure of my orals, I could group selected writers into their segmented, linear schools—puritan strains of the

later seventeenth century, pre-Romantics sniffing toward Words-
worth. Less for boasting than for identifying, I would classify my-
self still as one able to slot pretty well through the whole College
Outline Series.

To identify neutrally this impulse almost universal amongst schol-
ars and teachers is to hint some questioning of it. But of course
writers are influenced by earlier writers. Of course there are
schools and trends in the arts. Of course in education we dwell on
the achievements of those who have gone before. Surely no one
could seriously question the system that has served so long and
been used, explicitly and implicitly, by our whole culture, in the
schools. Of course, and surely. But. I do want to give the relay-race
assumption in the arts a thump. It has served, and it still serves. It
lends itself to sustained scholarship. It is a life preserver for teach-
ers on the long float through the afternoon. But the relay-race
assumption distorts.

Admittedly, this issue is imposing. Writers have almost always
witnessed about their reliance on models. Writers read each other,
and imitate, and blend, and react to traditions in literature.
Teachers—and the most imposing and successful of teachers—
trace with their students the residues of earlier writers in the
achievements of later ones. The subtlety and reach and eloquence
in these weavings and recognitions must impress those of us who
learn in the tradition. We have all experienced the search and
discovery, the classifying and evaluating in terms of influences.

If you think about how flourishing and convenient the whole
pattern of sequential influence is, in practicing and assessing the
arts, you can see why I hesitate to make my turn and give the
thump implied by my careful approach. Further, I am in danger of
seeming to attack more or less than I intend. Here is the charge,
and the limit on the charge, that I want to bring: the accumulated
results, the convenience, and the wide acceptance of literary schol-
arship as a way of approaching individual works create a hazard for
all who would understand how art, the doing of it, comes about.
Literary scholarship, because of its convenience and success, calls
for special caution on the part of the teachers and students.

Let me try to untangle my charge, starting with the actual feel of
writing a new thing, something never before formulated. By an
easy gradient, I imagine a writer in the first degree of momentum
on a new work. All directions are out from the center, the condition
of stillness. A state of feeling, immediate surroundings, closest com-
panions, whatever begins to occur to the writer—all the influences,
stretching back through daily life, into early experiences, past fam-
ily talk, with a mother's encouragement or criticism—all of these

pieces hover for the next move. Out of all these pieces, some—for a writer—will be literary. To choose an extreme, maybe the writer puts down on paper what begins to be a sonnet. The most easily identified characteristics of the product will be literary, and the simplest, most mechanical elements will be the most easily identified. But the motivations, the pervasive influences, the distinctive elements that mark the writing will be available only to those who fall into the page as if into a strange land.

Elements easiest to identify and talk about are ones recurrent from other pieces of literature, but those recurrences are not the motivation or distinction or most significant parts of the work. The writer, even if induced by custom or laziness to do so, should not characterize his effort by predominant reference to other literary works. Each move grows out of resonance between an individual's situation and the emerging effects at the time of composition. Literature is not like a relay race, with a changing baton passed from person to person, but like something more horizontal and immediate, something that develops amid influences that for the most part are not literary.

It is easy to assume that any poem grew from another poem, but a regress into remote time, attributing each present to a literary past, ultimately runs out into some kind of present in which a person and a world encountered each other and sparked something not dependent on formulations but on involvement with material in an encounter from which original things grew. For a writer, that one-to-one encounter with materials is much more important than having a place in a sequence of writers.

Think of a person centered in a life and ready to follow leads into creating something. It might seem that such a person would need education, wide experience, and coaching in order to achieve anything impressive and intense in the arts. But any such person, no matter how remote, uneducated, and tranquil, is caught up in one, long cliff-hanger of a life which we might title "Inhale, Exhale": at any minute the experience of living can alternate from security to the most intense and dangerous of deprivations based on nothing more unusual than breathing. Viewed in this way, the artist is not so much a person endowed with the luck of vivid, eventful days, as a person for whom any immediate encounter leads by little degrees to the implications always present for anyone anywhere. A tradition may appear to an outsider as being crucially involved, but the "tradition" derives from sense encountering related elements, not from an intellect relating to a pattern.

I will descend all the way to a particular, to a poem, this one called "The Trip":

Our car was fierce enough;
no one could tell we were only ourselves;
so we drove, equals of the car,
and ate at a drive-in where Citizens were dining.
A waitress with eyes made up to be Eyes
brought food spiced by the neon light.

Watching, we saw the manager greet people—
hollow on the outside, some kind of solid veneer.
When we got back on the road we welcomed
it as a fierce thing welcomes the cold.
Some people you meet are so dull
that you always remember their names.*

The nearest to a tradition that I can discover for myself in this poem is in the last two lines, where I hear my mother's voice again, in a remark something like the one about people being so boring you get tired of them even when they are not around. But that literary influence I can claim is not all honorific. It does not come from emulation of a recognized model, but from helpless involvement in the mean feelings of a person so much like me that my style is my plight as a human being. And my poem is like a series of bumps into sensations I have under certain conditions in current life. If a scholar should tell me that my poem is a resultant from a tradition in satire, or a variation on so and so's reaction to the age of the automobile, I might plume myself on having a part in culture; but what the poem feels like is this—it feels like an extension of family gossip into trenchant statements to be made to people listening with a little more care than usual.

Now it may seem to you that in attacking the relay-race theory of literary production I am doing a minuet in an area not important to us. Maybe this concern of mine is trivial, but even a slight misplacing of emphasis might lead to big trouble, over the years, as we accept stances that give us little leverage with people who discover themselves prevalently involved in contemporary affairs and not coercively interested in establishing a theoretical relation to the past or to the accomplishments of persons whose lives apparently had little justification except as models for programmed citizens. Somewhere, each life has its validation, not in a sequence of ciphers influencing each other down through time, but in immediate encounters that have their own individual worths, no matter how

*From *Traveling Through the Dark,* Harper and Row. Copyright 1962 by William Stafford.

small. If this contention of mine lacks force, perhaps an example will help.

In traveling to lecture I have been asked often to train my remarks around some topic like "The Influence of T. S. Eliot on Current American Poetry." This topic I can recognize. I like to be able to relate my reading of T. S. Eliot to what I find happening now. It is even true that in my conduct on formal occasions I may find myself either being or refusing to be J. Alfred Prufrock; and I think that being—but especially refusing to be—J. Alfred Prufrock is an interesting maneuver amidst the values and lack of values around us. But in some strange way I feel that the influence of T. S. Eliot is more on other people than on current American poets. I see critics like markers in a channel, tugged by what they measure, but I see writers like minnows disporting themselves in flurries of action that avoid the current.

So it interests me that after a lecture on the influence of T. S. Eliot, many people, and especially young people, will often come up for a few remarks eddying around some such question as "What Is Really Happening?" "What Are American Poets Doing These Days?" And such questions as these bring me to the point of trying to reformulate the literary scene in such a way as to bring out a crucial difference between our way of feeling and earlier ways. Instead of tagging our time by means of adjustments in the usual ways of tracing literary influences from generation to generation, I would hazard something like this:

> Writers today in America are finding their way forward on the page by means of opportunities that occur to them as they use the language of the rest of life in conditions that invite sequential discoveries that validate themselves in terms of immediate feelings. No test of tradition is needed. No approximation to established form. No assessment as to congruence of the now experience with given or established experience.

A poem today is anything said in such a way or put on the page in such a way as to invite from the hearer or reader a certain kind of attention. Form or content will be validated by the writer's feelings and by the convergent feelings of readers, who will be caught up in the common language. Any suggestion that the language is depending on conventions established for purely "literary" experiences will be disquieting, not because such conventions were always disquieting, but because now we assume more than ever before that a convention is not a rule that makes legitimate a practice, but a temporary and changing statement of something we continue to discover: what appeals in practice establishes a basis for temporary formulations that can be called "rules," until a new discovery or feeling suggests a change, at which time not the feeling but the rule must give.

To assert a break with tradition, with certain conventions, with certain rules, is not to assert a break with order of some kind. What implications for writers, teachers, and students grow from the view asserted here? If the relay-race concept is downgraded, where do we turn? The turn toward a positive looms as troublesome, and no claim can be made for the adequacy of what follows, but here are suggestions for teachers ready to accept some opening moves. I will word the suggestions in terms of poetry, but I believe other forms of literature will yield to this approach.

My guide into open forms is suggested by my title, a quotation from William Blake's *Jerusalem*:

> I give you the end of a golden string,
> Only wind it into a ball,
> It will lead you in at Heaven's gate
> Built in Jerusalem's wall.

Writing or reading, a poem goes by sequential parts, accumulating its effect (or frittering it away) by its internal trends. Starting with anything, the pattern begins; the little thread leads onward. If the writer is masterful and ambitious, the string may very well break; and the result may be a document on a well-chosen topic, but it will not be a developed poem. If the reader is masterful and ambitious, the interpretation may be eloquent, but if it commands the materials on the page it may very well distort and impose rather than discover. If the writer knows the market and deliberately hits a trend, the result may be a negotiable piece of work—he may get it published—but it will lose that golden string of its internal consistency, and the result will not be an increment in art, but just a marketable product. If the reader knows literary history and traditions, and forces the poem into conformity, the interpretation may link the poem to some discoverable pattern, but only at the cost of neglecting some of what is individual in the poem.

The stance to take, reading or writing, is neutral, ready, susceptible to now; such a stance is contrary to anything tense or determined or "well-trained." Only the golden string knows where it is going, and the role for a writer or reader is one of following, not imposing.

Retreating into the snug little weaving shed of the writer, I would advance, timidly, an idea contrary to the scholarly, the masterful, the eloquent. Sometimes it seems to me that a writer habitually touches the earth, touches home, clings to all that passes. Even to start a poem is to unreel stingily from the starting place, and to make each successive move out of minimum psychic expenditure. Here is something that leads like a little thread. It is called "At the Playground":

> Away down deep and away up high
> a swing drops you into the sky.
> Forth it swings you in a sweep
> all the way to the stars and back—
> Goodby, Jill, goodby, Jack.
> Shuddering climb wild and steep,
> away up high, away down deep.

Let me say that a poem comes from a life, not a study. The influences pounce upon a writer, and any rules or traditions get buffeted. Entering the sequence—writing or reading—is entering what unfolds. It is easy to talk about a tradition. It is easy to adopt a concept of metaphor (my golden string is one). Sometimes it is enticing to speak about the danger of playing tennis with the net down, if you want to claim some rules. But for the writer each poem has its own net. The essential is some kind of lead, and then a willingness to allow the development. If I start telling a poem, and try to be alert about its connections, I find internal resonances rather than traditions of literature. Something of the tonality of my mother's voice, referred to at the beginning, recurs to me now; and I feel the bite of her disappointment in life, and a wry angle of her vision. My dashing brother getting out into the big world—he recurs to me—and my father taking me out for a ride in a racing car—right down by the big engine I crouched, while Martin Shamosko revved it out North Main. And the horizontal flood gets busy in something like "Fifteen":

> South of the bridge on Seventeenth
> I found back of the willows one summer
> day a motorcycle with engine running
> as it lay on its side, ticking over
> slowly in the high grass. I was fifteen.
>
> I admired all that pulsing gleam, the
> shiny flanks, the demure headlights
> fringed where it lay; I led it gently
> to the road and stood with that
> companion, ready and friendly. I was fifteen.

We could find the end of a road, meet
the sky on out Seventeenth. I thought about
hills, and patting the handle got back a
confident opinion. On the bridge we indulged
a forward feeling, a tremble. I was fifteen.

Thinking, back farther in the grass I found
the owner, just coming to, where he had flipped
over the rail. He had blood on his hand, was pale—
I helped him to his machine. He ran his hand
over it, called me good man, roared away.

I stood there, fifteen.

From this indulgence in young feelings, I want to step back, here
at the end of my witnessing about the primacy of feeling and imme-
diate reference. For my final bid I offer what claims to be a poem
and also a lecture, even a scholarly lecture. For this last piece I beg
your friendship and indulgence, as I attempt "A Lecture on the
Elegy":

An elegy is really about the wilting of a flower,
the passing of the year, the falling of a stone.
Those people who go out, they just accompany
many things that leave us. Death is only
bad because it is like sunset, or a long eclipse.
If it had a dawn for company, or came with
spring, we would need laws to keep eager people
from rushing into danger and thus depopulating the world.

So, I have turned the occasion for such sadness
around: those graceful images that
seem to decorate the poems, they are
a rediscovery of those elements
that first created the obvious feelings,
the feelings that some people cannot even sense
until they are built up from little losses
and surrounded with labels: "war," "catastrophe," "death."*

*From *The Southern Review,* Winter, 1973. Copyright 1973 by The Louisi-
ana State University.

The Luck of It

A poet approaches language in the spirit of a woodman who asks pardon of the dryad in a tree before he cuts it down. Words are inhabited by the accumulated experience of the tribe. The average poet adds about as much to the language as he adds to the nitrogen content of his native soil. But he can administer the force that resides in words.

It is the magic inhabiting the language that he administers, all the lived meaning that the noises have picked up in the days and nights since they were first uttered. He finds ways to revive that total meaning, or a part of it he wants to use, as he makes his verbal artifacts. His very attentive use of a word, associating it with other words used with equal attention (for no word is an island), astonishes us the way we would be astonished to hear a dryad speak pardon out of an oak tree. And as if this were not all elfin enough already, he does the job largely at a subconscious level. His intelligence stands around, half the time, like a big, friendly, stupid apprentice, handing him lopping-shears when he wants the chain saw.

In "Duns Scotus's Oxford," Hopkins demonstrates this magic of association in the tremendous energy of the opening and closing lines. "Towery city and branchy between towers;"—who would have imagined there was all that going on in those six words before they were joined in that sequence? And of Duns Scotus himself, the final line says, "Who fired France for Mary without spot." *Kinesis* is all, and the energy is in the words rather than in the thinky parts of man's mind.

Both superstition and modesty warn a poet against reducing his meager knowledge of these forces to theory. A poem I wrote a long time ago has come to seem to me an example of how much luck goes into the job. It was a breakthrough that I seemed at the time simply to stumble on as I went about my fairly methodical and fairly *safe* wording of experience. It was a poem that carried me into its own experience, demonstrating that simple mystery Frost has put: no surprise in the writer, no surprise in the reader. It's a poem called "A View of the Brooklyn Bridge," and I am still incapable of judging it as a poem, so strongly did it imprint itself as a revelation. Set down rationally, revelations sound like hallucination: this bush by the side of the road flared up and a voice spoke out of it—we very rational people feel foolish recounting it. But this is what happened: a series of associations, and the words they inhabited, came to me uninvited but because I was in a state of un-self-centered attention. This is apparently a rare state with me, because in the twenty-five years since then I have averaged about six poems a year. That is apparently as often as the muse can get my attention.

Before I introduce the document, I might say that it had per-haps one forerunner, a longer poem called "Love Letter from an Impossible Land"—a somewhat more willful performance but similar—that I'd written five years earlier, when I was twenty-three. Other than that, I think all the poems I had written before this were primarily rational attempts to word accurately something I thought I understood. This poem, and to a less conscious degree "Love Letter," were irrational acts of surrender to an experience I knew very little about but which I had a sudden sense was being offered to me.

A View of the Brooklyn Bridge

The growing need to be moving around it to see it,
To prevent its freezing, as with sculpture and metaphor,
Finds now skeins, now strokes of the sun in a dark
Crucifixion etching, until you end by caring
What the man's name was who made it,
The way old people care about names and are
Forever seeing resemblances to people now dead.

Of stone and two metals drawn out so
That at every time of day
They speak out of strong resemblances, as:
Wings whirring so that you see only where
Their strokes finish, or: spokes of dissynchronous wheels.

Its pictures and poems could accurately be signed
With the engineer's name, whatever he meant.
These might be called: *Tines inflicting a river, justly,*
Or (thinking how its cables owe each something
To the horizontal and something to the vertical):
A graph of the odds against
Any one man's producing a masterpiece.

Yet far from his, the engineer's, at sunrise
And again at sunset when,
Like the likenesses the old see,

Loveliness besets it as haphazard as genes:
Fortunate accidents take the form of cities
At either end; the cities give their poor edges
To the river, the buildings there
The fair color that things have to be.
Oh the paper reeds by a brook
Or the lakes that lie on bayous like a leopard
Are not at more seeming random, or more certain
In their sheen how to stand, than these towns are.

And of the rivering vessels so and so
Where the shadow of the bridge rakes them once,
The best you can think is that, come there,
A pilot will know what he's done
When his ship is fingered

Like that Greek boy whose name I now forget
Whose youth was one long study to cut stone;
One day his mallet slipped, some goddess willing
Who only meant to take his afternoon,
So that the marble opened on a girl
Seated at music and wonderfully fleshed
And sinewed under linen, riffling a harp;
At which he knew not that delight alone
The impatient muse intended, but, coupled with it, grief—
The harp-strings in particular were so light—
And put his chisel down for marvelling on that stone.

It *is* a poem of associations, isn't it? a gatherer as Robert Frost
used to call them. Let me gloss it a little.

I was living near the bridge that winter, and looked at it a lot. In
the house where I lived there were two artists who were good
talkers and my closest friend was an artist who was a good listener,
so I was probably seeing things with freshly peeled eyes. I can't
remember where the image of skeins came from—I had to look the
word up as I wrote this, but the crucifixion etching was a Rem-
brandt, I think one I'd seen at the Metropolitan where the wife of
one of the painters had a job. I had been more irritated than
wondering at my southern grandmother and a French woman I
knew who *cared about names and were forever seeing resemblances to
people now dead.* But in the openness of the poem I find no irritation
(although I suppose the word *forever* is gently irritable), rather an
affection for the old, for the associative-recollective process that is
characteristic of age and of this poem. It seems to have been a kind

of grace I was experiencing—an arrogant person in my late twenties—as I followed whither the poem led.

The image of *spokes of dissynchronous wheels* came into my head from aviation. I was still flying occasionally as a reserve pilot in the Navy, and when you fly propeller planes in formation you adjust the speed of your engine (by adjusting the pitch of your propeller) by looking through the blades of your own propeller at that of the lead plane until the blades appear to be standing still. I wonder what that image conveys, if anything, to a reader who hasn't observed the spokes of dissynchronous wheels or propellers.

When the poem first appeared in a book, I glossed the line about the engineer's name, as follows: "The Brooklyn Bridge was designed by J. A. Roebling who began the work in 1869 which his son W. A. Roebling completed in 1883"—an impulse of propitiation, perhaps? as if the engineer might be helping me with my job?

With one of the three painters in particular, the now well-known Canadian Jack Shadbolt, I used to have very rangy talk. *The odds against any one man's producing a masterpiece* had been the theme of last night's talk.

The paper reeds by a brook is borrowed I think from *Psalms,* but I know it came to me from a beautiful setting by Randall Thompson, a colleague at Princeton the year before. *The lakes that lie on bayous like a leopard*—am I boring you, reader, with all these fingernail clippings?—I had ferried a plane to the west coast that winter by way of Louisiana.

I made up the Greek sculptor and his anecdote, but *made up* is too willful a verb: the Greek boy and his muse came to me, and the story—his wanting to do something difficult with his mallet, and having it done instead without his effort or even consent—came to me as a story that I did not then understand, a story parallel to something that was happening to me in the fashioning, if I did fashion it, of the poem.

A final gloss, comprehensive of the whole forty-seven lines: the things I hadn't read! Whitman, Hart Crane, none of the poem's ancestors.

The opening up of form that occurred in the poem is something that had happened with me before, but more often from clumsiness or laziness than at the direction of the poem. To this day I feel surer that I'm communicating with the poem if a prosodic pattern declares itself. I have sacred texts about this.

Most of my poetry is metrical, though I have written some free verse, syllabics, etc. One reason I write metrically is very simple: I do this better than I do in the more open forms. But I think I have a more deliberate choice behind it: from first to last most of my poems have dealt with violent or extreme or *non-verbal* [italics mine] experience. Fitting such experience through a fairly fixed form helps me to more firmly re-create it, and so to come to terms with it, possibly even to partially understand it. The openness of the experience is brought into relation with the structures of the mind. (Thom Gunn, in a letter, 1970)

This is a fragment from a dialogue between Borges and a writing student at Columbia University (from *Borges on Writing*, edited by Norman Thomas di Giovanni, Daniel Halpern, and Frank MacShane):

> *Question: One can read the poets of the past and interpret what is learned into free verse.*
> Borges: What I fail to understand is why you should *begin* by attempting something that is so difficult, such as free verse.
> *Question: But I don't find it difficult.*
> Borges: Well, I don't know your writing, so I can't really say. It might be that it is easy to write and difficult to read.

Auden ("He thanks God daily / that he was born and bred / a British Pharisee," he says of himself elsewhere) talks about the problem as if the devices of prosody were our servants:

> The poet who writes "free" verse is like Robinson Crusoe on his desert island: he must do all his cooking, laundry and darning for himself. In a few exceptional cases, this manly independence produces something original and impressive, but more often the result is squalor—dirty sheets on the unmade bed and empty bottles on the unswept floor. (*The Dyer's Hand*)

But the fourth of these texts is the one I need most, and states the other half of what has to be a dialectic. Randall Jarrell, in his extraordinary appreciation called "Some Lines from Whitman," says:

> The enormous and apparent advantages of form, of omission and selection, of the highest degree of organization, are accompanied by important disadvantages. . . . If we compare Whitman with that very beautiful poet Alfred Tennyson, the most skillful of all Whitman's contemporaries, we are at once aware of how limiting Tennyson's forms have been, of how much Tennyson has had to leave out. . . . Whitman's poems *represent* his world and himself much more satisfactorily than Tennyson's do his. In the past a few poets have both formed and represented, each in the highest degree; but in modern

times what controlling, organizing, selecting poet has created a world
with as much in it as Whitman's, a world that so plainly *is* the world?
(*Poetry and the Age*)

And in the luck of the poem there is one other element: will the
poem work as well for the reader as it works for the muse and her
scribe? Can you step back from the poem and see what is *there*,
having been present when all its bright ambience burned and taken
down what the unearthly voice said?

In the magazine where some of my favorite poems have ap-
peared, for more than twenty years, a poem that I thought well
enough of to place at the front of my selected poems was read this way:

William Meredith's volume is prefaced by an elegantly thoughtful
foreword in which he tells us that although he may not have kept the
most promising poems, he has kept the ones "that try to say things I
am still trying to find ways to say, poems that engage mysteries I still
pluck at the hems of. . . ." As the patriotic sailor was heard to say,
staring out at the mid-Atlantic, it makes you feel kinda humble and
kinda proud. Meredith's poetry has all the virtues: decency, rever-
ence, gravity, quiet curiosity, and there is something very depressing
about it, as of poetry soft at the center.

The reviewer then quoted only the middle stanza of the opening
poem.

Winter Verse for His Sister

Moonlight washes the west side of the house
As clean as bone, it carpets like a lawn
The stubbled field tilting eastward
Where there is no sign yet of dawn.
The moon is an angel with a bright light sent
To surprise me once before I die
With the real aspect of things.
It holds the light steady and makes no comment.

Practicing for death I have lately gone
To that other house
Where our parents did most of their dying,
Embracing and not embracing their conditions.
Our father built bookcases and little by little stopped reading,
Our mother cooked proud meals for common mouths.
Kindly, they raised two children. We raked their leaves
And cut their grass, we ate and drank with them.
Reconciliation was our long work, not all of it joyful.

Now outside my own house at a cold hour
I watch the noncommittal angel lower
The steady lantern that's worn these clapboards thin
In a wash of moonlight, while men slept within,
Accepting and not accepting their conditions,
And the fingers of trees plied a deep carpet of decay
On the gravel web underneath the field,
And the field tilting always toward day.

His comment went on, and I have to confess that I think it's witty, though to this day I have been unable to find a revision of the poem—without betraying what I feel is its discovered language— that will make the metaphors of that second stanza less vulnerable to misfeeling:

> What kind of a meal are you cooking? Oh, I think a proud meal tonight. How do you raise your children? Kindly, thank you. It's all too beautiful and shaming to be true, establishing the poet as such a splendid understander, knower and forgiver that a slightly self-congratulatory atmosphere hangs over this poem and the whole volume.

In general, a poet tries to make misreading and mistaking of feeling impossible, by the same attention that he pays to exact rendering of the experience he is being initiated into. Clearly he is not always lucky in both phases of his intuitive work, and there is always somebody waiting at the third stage who can say with critical detachment, Meredith is no Whitman or Tennyson. But what an ordinary poet congratulates himself on is, I suppose, being a good scribe, taking the things down as the tongue declares them. And, of course, the luck of being chosen by the tongue in the first place.

DONALD JUSTICE

Bus Stop

Or, Fear and Loneliness on Potrero Hill

That fall and winter we were living in a rented house on Potrero
Hill. From the back porch on the second story, where the living
quarters were, you could look down into the neglected garden
below or off across hills to the bay and the lights of Oakland. It was
an exemplary view, but in a dark mood it could leave you feeling
remote and isolated. We seemed to be perched insecurely on the
top of an unfamiliar new world, teetering on the continent's very
edge. Every evening I would walk our dog, Hugo, up and down the
steep sidewalks, past the rows of narrow two-storied San Francisco
houses, as the sun faded across their pale pastel fronts. High
wooden fences surrounded some of them, and through the palings
you could see strange plants in tubs and the deep-hued blooms of
exotic flowers.

Our nearest corner, the intersection of Kansas and 20th Streets,
was a municipal bus stop. It seemed that often, just as we were
setting out on our walk, a bus would be stopped there, discharging
passengers. At that hour they would be city workers coming home
from their day in shop or office. There must have been an unusu-
ally long period of rain that year, two or three weeks of it, and I
remember the passengers one after the other opening their great
black umbrellas as they stepped down from the bus, which waited
purring and quivering in the mist and drizzle of early evening. I
sensed something symbolic in this, as if centuries hence it might be
recalled as part of an ancient urban ritual whose meaning had been
forgotten. And vividly there rose up before me a picture of the
raised umbrellas which had represented the dead in the last scene
of *Our Town*, called back now from the pages, years before, of *Life*
magazine.

Sometimes, as we walked, the streetlights would wink on all at
once, perfectly timed. Gradually more and more lights would be
visible in the upper windows of the houses. From the playground
you could see headlights moving along the Bayshore Highway just
at the foot of the hill; or, from another bluff, the distant shunting in
the Southern Pacific yards; all around, masked at times by fog,
hung the various glows of the fanned-out districts of the city. It was

beautiful. But the Potrero Hill of those days was like a lost village high in the Caucasus, with old Russian women peering doubtfully out from windows and doorways at passing strangers. All that fall and winter I felt like an exile, no part of the life around me. I knew none of the bus passengers alighting, no one in the lighted rooms above, certainly none of the wrinkled old women in their babushkas, who would yell and gesticulate sometimes at the quiet and well-mannered Hugo.

Such was the background from which "Bus Stop" gradually emerged. Other poems from that time share the same moods: "Poem to Be Read at 3 A.M." (with its own image of a burning light), "Memory of a Porch," "In the Greenroom," and "At a Rehearsal of *Uncle Vanya*." (I was with a theater company that year, The Actor's Workshop.) The somewhat visionary "To the Hawks" came just after.

Connections between the life a writer lives and the work that comes out of that life seem much more important now than I once thought them, and in fact I would insist on their importance. Even so, in my work I have preferred to deal with connections of this kind indirectly, which is, as I believe, the way of art. Thus it is not the mere undergoing of a terrible or a beautiful experience, neither suffering nor exaltation, which leads to poetry, at least not for me. Only when the experience itself, or more likely no more than some singular aspect or broken small tangent of it, comes somehow to be deflected or translated into something else, into some mysteriously larger other thing—which in another day might have been called the universal or archetypal—does any poem of mine begin to come into focus. I think of it as a merging of the personal with the impersonal; the singular commences to disappear into the plural.

But the exact relations between art and life are not legislated. We know that Dorothy had seen the ten thousand daffodils, too, but in the poem only William is left wandering "lonely as a cloud." So also did poor Hugo vanish from the Potrero Hill evenings of "Bus Stop," though he had been my faithful companion through many glooms. If he does survive now, it is only as a generalized ghost, one of

> The quiet lives
> That follow us—
> These lives we lead
> But do not own.

I did sometimes picture him, as the poem goes on to suggest, standing there, if I should die, puzzled but infinitely patient. That whole time in San Francisco, as a matter of fact, I went about, for reasons that scarcely enter the poem, in the grip of a fear of death. No doubt I did "own" Hugo, if it came to that, but I did not feel at all in possession of my own life. There were times when my life felt ghostly to me, and, as in some special effect contrived for film, I could picture the husk of my body left behind on a street corner waiting faithfully for the real self to return. But in writing the poem I was not tempted to spell out or to make very much out of so slight and evanescent a feeling, scarcely strong enough to register on the most sensitive emotional scale. As I concentrate now in an effort to bring back the time and the place, I see all at once and for the first time that the buses stopped at the corner were like a modern equivalent of Charon's ferry, and rain-wet 20th Street a paved-over Styx. The gathering gloom—mist, drizzle, twilight, fog—would have filled out the infernal impression. It seems obvious, now that I think of it, but even if so literal a transcription of what the scene suggested had then occurred to me—and it did not, not consciously—I would have kept it out of the poem. It would have been false, too explicit, too histrionic.

The first actual lines—I am sure of it, though I have lost or mislaid the worksheets—began with mention of the lights burning upstairs in unknown rooms. An image with overtones of Weldon Kees, no doubt, and of the very city from which, not quite a decade before, Kees had disappeared; only a block or two along Kansas Street his best friend still lived. I worked at lines meant to evoke the lives of the strangers in those rooms, a motif perhaps retrieved from "Anthony St. Blues," a much earlier poem of mine:

> Withindoors many now enact,
> Behind drawn shades, their shadow lives.

But I was too much absorbed in my own broodings to want to brood long on others; besides, they were very much like us, surely, which was a good part of the poignancy. I had my sense of exile and loneliness, my neurotic fear, my divided self all to find words and figures for, and there, in the very circumstances of daily life, in that extraordinary neighborhood, were facts and details vivid with symbolic presence, only waiting to be mentioned in right relation with one another in order to glow with meaning.

Finding the structure was no problem, as I recall. I had been trying to teach myself to write short free-verse lines; also short syllabic lines. I theorized that there was more control in the short line. A curious problem in syllabics had always interested me and nobody else, apparently, among all the poets—many more then—

attracted to that metric. It was the possibility of keeping the number of accents and the number of syllables the same from line to line, but without letting them fall together into the regular foot-patterns, iambs and the like, too often and too familiarly. It's a very technical matter, not awfully important, but it did interest me. Lines in syllabics had usually seemed to go better in odd numbers—sevens, nines, elevens—since the odd number was a help in avoiding iambics. But now I wanted to try *evens* and, to make it harder on myself, shorter lines than I had attempted or will probably attempt again in syllabics. My sense of syllabics is that as the count gets shorter the line gets harder to compose but, as though in compensation, more "musical," as people like to put it. In "Bus Stop" each line, it will be noticed, has only four syllables. (*Flowers* traditionally may be counted as either one or two syllables; in the line, "Black flowers, black flowers," it counts as one.) Some lines gave me trouble, however easy they may now look, but on the whole they did turn out to be more "musical" than average. The majority are autonomous, more or less end-stopped; they can be heard as lines, which is rare in syllabics. Readers who hear them as accentuals are not wrong to do so, for each line does have two accents. But if these were pure accentual lines no one could expect twenty-four lines in a row to fall by chance into the same syllable count. Because I was keeping this double count, the lines come very close, after all, to being iambic dimeter; yet to those who understand such intricacies, it must be clear that a few lines refuse to submit to the usual iambic conditions (lines 1, 20, and 24).

As for other sound-effect, mostly rhyme or something like it, the thought of calling the poem a song did enter my head, or even of subtitling it "An Urban Song," but a subtitle seemed pretentious. Even so, this was unmistakably a lyric poem, which by its nature could stand quite a lot of *sound,* and I was willing to seek out a fair amount of it, though not very vigorously. I wanted anything which had to do with the sound or "music" to come in very simply and in a completely natural way, almost as though by chance, and chance did, as always in such matters, throw up some coincidences of sound. My intentions in this, being largely impulse and instinct, I was able to carry out more successfully than with the meters. If rhymes showed up—and they did—they were to remain casual, not part of a deliberate scheme, not predictable. Repetition—a type of rhyme itself—turned out to play a larger role in the sound of the poem than the usual rhyming. The rule I set for myself in this was simple and indulgent. I would repeat whatever I wanted to, anything from a single word to a whole line, and at any time. The effect came to resemble what you get in a poem with multiple refrains, or, more fancifully, when several bells are set swinging at different timings. In the old ballads or in comic songs, not to mention in the master Yeats himself, the meaning of a refrain will seem to shift sometimes with its new context, and I made an effort to imitate that effect. The most obvious case involves repeating "And lives go on." First it is a complete sentence, signifying only that lives continue, persist, endure. But, chiming back in at once, it starts now a longer sentence which before it is done will turn the original meaning into something very different. The lives no longer plod along but are suddenly bright and giving light, beacons. A hopeful note, it seems now, looking back. Yet I was prouder of the more hidden repetition, for those who would notice it, between lines 4 and 23, *hours* echoing *ours*. One of the buried motifs of the poem— that of the displaced self—is here suggested, I would like to think, in the pun on *hours*, but quietly, secretly, perhaps escaping all notice. Read the lines again and see if it is there at all. Perhaps I have imagined it; or has everyone always seen it at once? It only remains to say that whatever the reader is willing to find in *burning* was probably intended, from the simplest turning on of lights to the ardent yearning of the self baffled in loneliness. But perhaps not. Only this instant has it occurred to me that at the end St. Augustine may have blundered into yet another Carthage, *burning, burning*.

Certainly the world seemed that year on the point of conflagration. Goldwater bullies had roamed Nob Hill, our navy was attacked by phantoms in the Tonkin Gulf, Khrushchev fell, China exploded a nuclear device, the first defiant Berkeley students were dragged roughly down marble staircases, and at Thanksgiving General Taylor took off on his futile fact-finding mission to Vietnam. By late February the official bombing of North Vietnam had begun. The theater company was breaking up, and I fled the city. It sounds dramatic now, but it did feel that way at the time. Not long afterwards, across the continent in Miami, I came upon most of the lines of "Bus Stop" jumbled together on a few pages of the old chemistry notebook I'd found in the Potrero Hill house and, unscrambling them now with ease, finished the poem in an hour or two.

(1983)

Bus Stop

Lights are burning
In quiet rooms
Where lives go on
Resembling ours.

The quiet lives
That follow us—
These lives we lead
But do not own—

Stand in the rain
So quietly
When we are gone,
So quietly . . .

And the last bus
Comes letting dark
Umbrellas out—
Black flowers, black flowers.

And lives go on.
And lives go on
Like sudden lights
At street corners

Or like the lights
In quiet rooms
Left on for hours,
Burning, burning.

ALICIA OSTRIKER

A Wild Surmise

Motherhood and Poetry

That women should have babies rather than books is the considered opinion of Western civilization. That women should have books rather than babies is a variation on that theme. Is it possible, or desirable, for a woman to have both? What follows here consists of some autobiographical remarks, offered on the assumption that my history as a writer has something in common with others of my generation; and a bit of exhortation addressed to younger writers.

My initiation as a woman poet occurred when I was in my first year of graduate school at the University of Wisconsin in 1960, writing poems as nearly resembling those of Keats, Hopkins, and W. H. Auden as I could. We were visited that year by a distinguished gentleman poet, to whom students were invited to submit work for scrutiny and commentary. I went for my conference hoping, of course, that he would tell me I was the most brilliant young thing he had seen in twenty years. Instead, he leafed through my slender sheaf and stopped at a tame little poem in which, however, my husband and I were lying in bed together, probably nude. "You women poets are very graphic, aren't you," he said, with a slight shiver of disgust.

Not having previously encountered this idea, I reacted in a complex way. Certainly I was hurt and disappointed. At the same time, something in me was drawing itself up, distending its nostrils, thinking: "You're goddamned right, we are graphic." I had not seen myself as a "we" until that moment. Like Huck Finn deciding, "All right, then, I'll *go* to hell," I had just decided "All right, then, I'll *be* a woman poet," which meant I would write about the body.

A year out of graduate school, in 1965, I found myself in Cambridge, England, composing a poem about pregnancy and birth called "Once More Out of Darkness," later informally dubbed by my colleague Elaine Showalter, "A Poem in Nine Parts and a Post-Partum." The work was drawing from the experiences of two pregnancies, during which I had written numerous bits and scraps without intending anything so ambitious as a "long" poem, and it was thickening like soup. One morning when it was about two-thirds done, I realized that I had never in my life read a poem about pregnancy and birth. Why not? I had read hundreds of poems about love, hundreds of poems about death. These were, of course, universal themes. But wasn't birth universal? Wasn't pregnancy profound? During pregnancy, for example, I believed from time to time that I understood the continuity of life and death, that my body was a city and a landscape, and that I had personally discovered the moral equivalent of war. During the final stage of labor I felt like a hero, an Olympic athlete, a figure out of Pindar, at whom a stadium should be heaving garlands. At times, again, I was overwhelmed with loathing for the ugliness of my flesh, the obscenity of life itself, all this ooze, these fluids, the grossness of it. Trying to discover a poetic form which could express such opposite revelations simultaneously, and convey the extraordinary sensation of transformation from being a private individual self to being a portion of something else, I had the sense of being below the surface, where the islands are attached to each other. Other women knew what I knew. Of course they did, they always had. In that case, where were the poems?

At this time I had not read Sylvia Plath's "Three Women," a radio play consisting of three intertwined monologues in a maternity ward. Nor in fact had I heard of Plath. I had neither read nor heard of Rich's *Snapshots of a Daughter-in-Law* (1963), Sexton's *To Bedlam and Part Way Back* (1960) and *All My Pretty Ones* (1962), Diane Wakoski's *Inside the Blood Factory* (1962) or Carolyn Kizer's "Pro Femina" (1963), in which the poet wisecracks that women writers are "the custodians of the world's best-kept secret, / Merely the private lives of one-half of humanity." Though I had read *The Feminine Mystique*, I had not read Simone de Beauvoir. My field was nineteenth century, my dissertation on William Blake. Consequently I did not know that I had the good fortune to exist in a historical moment when certain women writers—mostly in utter isolation, unaware of each other's existence, twisted with shame, pain, fear of madness or the fact of it, and one of them already dead by her own hand—were for the first time writing directly and at large from female experience. The early grassblade slips through some crack in the dirt. It enters the cold alone, as Williams tells us in "Spring and All." It cannot guess how the ground will soon be covered with green fire. What I concluded, ignorant that this "we" existed, was that no poems had been written on the subject of pregnancy and childbirth, first because men could not write them. Love and death *sí*, pregnancy *no*. Second, women had not written the poems because we all reproduce the themes of previous poetry. One doesn't need a conspiracy theory here, just inertia. But third, pregnancy and birth were, I suddenly realized, subjects far more severely taboo than, for example, sex. One did not discuss pregnancy or birth in mixed groups. It was embarrassing. Threatening. Taboo because men were jealous of us, did not know they were, and we had to protect them from the knowledge. Threatening because we have a society which in many ways adores death and considers life disgusting. (In the same year that I wrote this poem, Lyndon B. Johnson was sworn in as President of the United States, having campaigned as the peace candidate committed to ending our involvement in Vietnam, against Barry Goldwater, who wanted to bomb North Vietnam back into the Stone Age.)

"Once More Out of Darkness" was published in 1970, and has since generated other poems. On one occasion when I read it to a graduate class in Women and Literature at Rutgers, arguing that writing and motherhood were not necessarily mutually exclusive enterprises, someone remarked that it was one thing to write about pregnancy, where you could be symbolic and spiritual, but quite impossible to use the squalling brats as poetic material after you had them, messing around underfoot, killing your schedule. This seemed a gauntlet flung down, which I had to seize in order to defend my opinion that you can write poetry about anything; that night I wrote "Babyshit Serenade," a poem in which I complain among other things that men don't do diapers, one happy result of which was that a man I know wrote a fine and funny poem called "Finding the Masculine Principle in Babyshit."

On another occasion, a group of students who had absorbed a certain line of militant feminist doctrine popular at the time greeted "Once More Out of Darkness" with an overt hostility I had not met before (male audiences and readers when hostile to women's writing either feign indifference or ladle condescension onto you—my dear, what a wonderful natural poem you've written, they say, meaning they think it required no intelligence or craftsmanship). My suggestion to this group that motherhood for me was like sex, a peck of trouble but I wouldn't want to go through life without it, was intended to produce laughter and illumination. Instead it produced outrage—motherhood to them was a burden imposed on women by patriarchy—which I took personally and defensively. The poem I wrote in what must be called rebuttal is titled "Propaganda." All these poems, I might mention, are formally experimental: a result of emotional involvement combined with intellectual tension, and a feeling of stumbling from shadow into hot sunlight. Often my poems on mothering and children come from more normal, less intense states, and are more conventional poetically; for example, "The Wolves," in my first book, which I think is a nice thing but not a discovery.

I began my most recent work on motherhood, *The Mother/Child Papers,* in 1970, when my third child and only son was born just after we invaded Cambodia and shot the four students at Kent State University. It was impossible at that time to avoid meditating on the meaning of having a boy child in time of war, or to avoid knowing that "time of war" means all of human history. Adrienne Rich in *Of Woman Born* quotes a Frenchwoman declaring to her, when her son was born, "Madame, vous travaillez pour l'armée." Lady, you're working for the army. I had the despairing sense that this baby was born to be among the killed, or among the killers. What was I going to do about that, I who had been a pacifist since childhood, was then, and is now, a question. *The Mother/Child Papers* is, again, an experimental work for me, in the sense of posing formal problems correlative to moral ones. I begins with a section of prose about the Cambodian invasion paralleled with the delivery of my son in a situation of normal, that is to say exploitative, American medicine. A second section is a sequence of poems alternating between the consciousness of a mother and that of an infant, as the single fabric they are made of wears away and divides in two. Here a good deal of the excitement and difficulty lay in the attempt to imagine the changes in a newborn mind and invent a music for them. A third section consists of individual poems and prose-poems composed over the last ten years: a few scraps salvaged from the gullet of devouring Time, an enemy familiar to all mothers.

This brings me to the question raised by the activist and writer Alta, when she calls her book *Momma* "a start on all the untold stories." For women as artists, the most obvious truth is that the decision to have children is irrevocable. Having made it you are stuck with it forever; existence is never the same afterward, when you have put yourself, as de Beauvoir correctly says, in the service of the species. You no longer belong to yourself. Your time, energy, body, spirit and freedom are drained. You do not, however, lack what W. B. Yeats prayed for: an interesting life. In practical terms, you may ask yourself, "How can I ever write when I am involved with this *child*?" This is a real and desperate question. But can you imagine Petrarch, Dante, Keats, bemoaning their lot—"God, I'm so involved with this *woman*, how can I write?"

The advantage of motherhood for a woman artist is that it puts her in immediate and inescapable contact with the sources of life, death, beauty, growth, corruption. If she is a theoretician it teaches her things she could not learn otherwise; if she is a moralist it engages her in serious and useful work; if she is a romantic it constitutes an adventure which cannot be duplicated by any other, and which is guaranteed to supply her with experiences of utter joy and utter misery; if she is a classicist it will nicely illustrate the vanity of human wishes. If the woman artist has been trained to believe that the activities of motherhood are trivial, tangential to main issues of life, irrelevant to the great themes of literature, she should untrain herself. The training is misogynist, it protects and perpetuates systems of thought and feeling which prefer violence and death to love and birth, and it is a lie.

As writers like Rich, Dorothy Dinnerstein, Tillie Olsen, Phyllis Chesler, and Nancy Chodorow already demonstrate, it would be difficult to locate a subject at once more unexplored and more rich in social and political implication. Among the poets who have begun the exploration I would cite Plath, Sexton, Alta, Susan Griffin, Maxine Kumin, Lucille Clifton, Gwendolyn Brooks, Robin Morgan, Lisel Mueller, Sharon Olds, Patricia Dienstfrey, Alice Mattison, Marilyn Krysl—a beginning, a scratching of our surface.

The writer who is a mother should, I think, record everything she can: make notes, keep journals, take photographs, use a tape recorder, and remind herself that there is a subject of incalculably vast significance to humanity, about which virtually nothing is known because writers have not been mothers. "We think back through our mothers, if we are women," declares Woolf, but through whom can those who are themselves mothers, when they want to know what this endeavor in their lives means, do their thinking? We should all be looking at each other with a wild surmise, it seems to me, because we all need data, we need information, not only of the sort provided by doctors, psychologists, sociologists examining a phenomenon from the outside, but the sort provided by poets, novelists, artists, from within. As our knowledge begins to accumulate, we can imagine what it would signify to all women, and men, to live in the culture where childbirth and mothering occupied the kind of position that sex and romantic love have occupied in literature and art for the last five hundred years, or the kind of position that warfare has occupied since literature began.

GALWAY KINNELL

An Interview with Margaret Edwards

Sheffield, Vermont, August 27, 1976

Edwards: Do you have trouble writing about other people, espe-cially people you love, who might feel hurt by what you say?

Kinnell: I've felt some qualms, but not in the way fiction writers might. Since in a novel one has to present a whole, believ-able person, one tends to lift a lot of actual detail from the lives of people one knows best. This is OK—except when a recently di-vorced author tries to get revenge. But since verse isn't well suited to depicting people in any detailed way, this isn't a problem in most poetry. Shakespeare's sonnets tell us almost nothing about the per-son addressed, not even if it's a man or woman. In my own poetry there probably is less autobiography than there seems to be. It's often imagined that writers take actual persons and protect them with fictional names, but I seem to do the reverse—give actual names to more or less fictionalized characters. I think those I'm closest to know this and are not too upset.

Edwards: Do you think a person has to be crazy or unbalanced in some way to be a writer?

Kinnell: I guess there has to be something wrong with you. If everything were satisfactory, you might sing, as do the dolphins, but you certainly wouldn't sweat out long novels or involved poems. But crazy? No, not really. The people who are called crazy because they see through existence, those for whom there are no verities in this world, are surely the most gifted of us all, as far as poetry goes, but they are usually unable to write and perfect a poem. Rilke's very elevated sensibility was grounded in the capacity for unin-spired, plodding, hard work. Hard work concedes the reality of this world. Discipline, determination, and ambition—illusions for the people I'm calling crazy—are probably requirements for someone who wants to be a writer.

Then there's what you might call "real" craziness. As readers, we can't surrender to a work we feel has been written by someone controlled by paranoid suspicions and sick fantasies. The poems we love are those in which we believe we find the truest and most encompassing understandings. The poets we admire are the ones whose responses to experience we feel are reliable. In this sense the best poets are the sanest.

Edwards: What about the poems which manage to foist their dementia onto the reader?

Kinnell: Well, yes, many obsessed poems draw us in by their single-minded intensity. But even the maddest of these, the medieval romances and love poems, try to reach a whole understanding, even if like *Tristan and Iseult* they exhibit only the destructive side of their subject, the passion that leads to death. Among the handful of poets I like most are Christopher Smart and John Clare. Both wrote their finest poems while supposedly mad. But in these poems you find an incredibly intense clarity and selflessness, divine madness and divine sanity both at once. Here's a passage from "Jubilate Agno" that might give an idea:

> For the flowers are great blessings.
> For the Lord made a Nosegay in the meadow with his disciples and
>   preached upon the lily.
> For the angels of God took it out of his hand and carried it to the
>   Height.
> For a man cannot have publick spirit, who is void of private
>   benevolence.
> For there is no Height in which there are not flowers.
> For flowers have great virtues for all the senses.
> For the flower glorifies God and the root parries the adversary.
> For the flowers have their angels even the words of God's Creation.
> For the warp and woof of flowers are worked by perpetual moving
>   spirits.
> For flowers are good both for the living and the dead.
> For there is a language of flowers.
> For there is a sound reasoning upon all flowers.
> For elegant phrases are nothing but flowers.
> For flowers are peculiarly the poetry of Christ.
> For flowers are medicinal.
> For flowers are musical in ocular harmony.
> For the right names of flowers are yet in heaven.
> God make gardeners better nomenclators.

Everyone knows that human existence is incomplete. Among those who are especially troubled by this are those who turn to writing. Writing is a way of trying to understand the incompleteness and, if not to heal it, at least to get beyond whatever is merely baffling and oppressive about it.

Edwards: I take it you don't think writing makes a person more unbalanced, yet how do you account for the fate of Crane, Berryman, Kees, Jarrell, Plath, Sexton, and others?

Kinnell: A. Alvarez puts forward the theory that writing intensely about one's own pain increases the pain. I don't think it does. I can't demonstrate this. It's an article of faith. I think poetry brings us more, not less, life. When it happens that a poet commits suicide I find myself looking in the poetry for the flaws.

Edwards: Is this also true of Sylvia Plath, whose poetry seems to get better the closer she comes to death?

Kinnell: It's complicated. I'm not really sure. Often an element in the suicide of writers seems to be loss of creative power, a loss of interest—frequently brought on through too much drink, or giving up drink, or relapsing back into drink, I don't know which is the most deadly! In Plath's case there's none of this. In her last years she is more energetic, interested, and clear-sighted than ever. A terrible intensity comes over her, kindled on the emptiness, that makes it appear her art required her to destroy herself. Yet I think it's mistaken to see her as a doomed goddess. Her husband had left her. She was alone with her children. It was cold. Things were going badly. One of her reactions was to sulk, if one can judge by the poems. Suicide, or attempted suicide, is the ultimate form of sulking. She thinks her own woes are the only ones and ceases to understand that other people suffer, often more grievously than she. Other people don't exist in these later poems except to the degree they cause or reflect her pain. I am not taken by her use of Nazi concentration camps as a source of metaphors for her own situation. Also, it often seems she doesn't want to understand her misery so much as to intensify and perfect it. Each poem becomes a quest for the image that will lacerate her most. So her poetry is marked by self-absorption, self-pity, and melodrama. I know this is a harsh judgment. But you see, I respond very much to her poems, and it is these elements in myself, as much as in Plath, that I'm trying to be clear about. All criticism is self-criticism. What anyone says about anyone else is only provisionally true. In fact, when it comes down to it, we know very little about the real forces, the actual emotions, that drive a person to commit suicide. And I'm ready to concede that I could be wrong about the connection between a life and an art. There remains the rather romantic possibility that a destructive, despairing life can produce a poetry that gives us only health.

Edwards: Which poets of your generation do you think are writing well these days?

Kinnell: A number of poets who've been writing beautifully for years I'm glad to say still are. I'd give you a list, but they'd be poets you've known a long time. I'm struck by a few poets of my generation who've blossomed more recently. Doubtless they themselves feel it wasn't so recent. I've felt Philip Levine used to hold something back, as if for fear poetry would betray him into tenderness. In his recent poems, it has done exactly that. Donald Hall has stopped writing those poems crafted according to the best critical principles and has started writing what you might call simply *poetry*—saying in its own music what matters most to him. Their new poems are marvelous. Hayden Carruth's *Paragraphs* are among the most exciting new poems I've seen. Carruth has been unfashionable and unread for far too long. Another splendid "late-bloomer" is Gerald Stern.

Edwards: That's an interesting—and rather simple—description of poetry: "Saying in its own music what matters most." Do you, as a poet, think critical theory about poetry in general is excessively complicated?

Kinnell: I suppose some equally simple statement about poetry has been made many times, by those who react against a convention-ridden poetry, by Wordsworth and Coleridge, for example, or by Pound and Eliot. But perhaps it's too often taken for granted that the problem lies with a faulty poetic theory, and so can be solved by a correct theory. I suspect it isn't a matter of theory but a personal, psychological, question: whether one can get past the censors in one's mind and say what really matters without shame or exhibitionism. It seems to me the four poets I mentioned were quite lucid with regard to the evasions that the poetic conventions of the day encouraged their predecessors to practice, yet they in turn fell into evasions of their own—Coleridge less than the others.

Edwards: Sometimes I suspect you of thinking that form is itself an evasion.

Kinnell: I'd like to agree—but I'm really not quite that bad. Anyway it's a long story—one that someday I may write. All I'd say now is that I don't think the term "form" should be applied only to such things as stanzas of uniform size, rhyme schemes, metrical patterns, and so on—elements which may be regarded as external trappings. I think form properly speaking also has to do with the inner shape of the poem. Some of the most "formal" poems are rather formless in this sense: they change subject, lose the thread of their arguments, and lack the suspense and sense of culmination that come from the pursuit of one goal.

Edwards: This is one of those peculiar, but human, questions: Do you indulge any old habits, quirks, or rituals in the process of writing?

Kinnell: Not really. I prefer to write with a pen. And I must have a Smith-Corona portable circa 1935 to copy the poems with. I own three of these machines. They look a bit the way my poems feel to me. Also, they creak along at about the speed of thought—my thought, I mean.

Edwards: Do you feel unhappy when you haven't written for a long time?

Kinnell: Yes, a little, sometimes. In the last few years especially, when I've written less than earlier. It's irrational. It should be no great worry if it should happen that one stops writing. In fact it should be rather bracing to go on to something new. But it's not that way. Writing is the one trade you can't give up. The history of literature is filled with poets who've gone on all their lives desperately, doggedly, turning out verse to maintain the dream they are poets. Wouldn't it have been better if Wordsworth had taken up innkeeping or journalism? Rimbaud was the only one able to give it up, and that was probably because he hadn't been at it long. The difficulty is that by comparison other occupations are less interesting. To give up writing would be to close the door on one's deepest experiences. It is no consolation to think back on work already done. On the contrary, the *Moby Dick* in one's past is only a brutal reminder of how inattentive, shallow, and faithless one has become. The fear that comes from not writing is the fear of inner deterioration. They say that by tying a dead hen around its neck you can train a dog not to chase hens. There's nothing you can do about an aging poet—even if you tie around him a copy of the late poems of Wordsworth.

Edwards: Your speaking of hens reminds me of something I'd like to discuss. I teach The Book of Nightmares *and there are certain questions students often bring up. I'd like to ask you a few of them. First, "The Hen Flower." What is your fascination with hens? Why devote a whole section of the poem to this one creature?*

Kinnell: My family had a henhouse out behind our house until the Pawtucket city fathers zoned it away. I was very young then, perhaps six or seven, and I remember the chickens mostly through a few images. One is of my sisters plucking them. I don't suppose they ever stuffed a pillow with these feathers, or that we ever laid our heads on the feathers of a hen we were at that moment digesting—but it seemed a possibility. And I can see my father hatcheting the hens' heads off on the old grey log he'd set on end for the purpose, and then letting the headless creatures run about. I don't think any of the times I've killed hens myself are more vivid than these memories. Though not very personable, hens have an unusual psychic dimension, due, I like to think, to the suppression of their capacity to fly. When you hold their heads under their wings they slump into a strange coma. You might think they think it is the night, except that they do the same thing if you turn them on their backs and stroke their throats. They'll lie there for several minutes, apparently in a trance. Maybe the throat is their Achilles' heel, emotionally speaking, and they've fainted from too much. But they also fall out if you face them toward infinity—if you draw a straight line in the earth and hold them down with their beaks touching it. There are doubtless other mysteries in the hen.

Edwards: What about that "tiny crucifix" at the center of the earth? It has made some students assume you are Catholic.

Kinnell: I wanted to retain the Christian terminology, but to alter its reference. I wasn't trying to say that the cross of Jesus lives at the very center of existence. I was supposing that a body that presses down on the earth creates under itself a "shaft of darkness" that gets smaller and smaller as it approaches the center of the earth, until at the bottom it makes a formalized shape—which here happens, due to the form of the outstretched body, to be a cross.

Edwards: Could you say something about the "Dear Stranger" section? I find it hard to figure out. Explain the Juniata. Who lives there? And who is Virginia?

Kinnell: The Juniata is a river that flows through southern Pennsylvania. It's Virginia who lives near it. I guess that isn't clear. Virginia is an actual person I've had a long correspondence with. She is a mystic, a seer. She is one of those born without the protective filtering device that allows the rest of us to see this humanized, familiar world as if it were all there is. She sees past the world and lives in the cosmos. In an old issue of *Poetry*—or perhaps it was *Time*—there's a review of Malcolm Cowley's book of poems, *The Blue Juniata*. The review says the region Cowley writes about belongs to the past, no longer exists. So I allude to the fact that Virginia found it amusing to have her own sense of non-existence thus confirmed. ("You see," I told Mama, "we just *think* we're here.") In this case, the "I" is Virginia—that *is* confusing.

Edwards: Have you ever met her?

Kinnell: Only once. We had coffee together somewhere in Pennsylvania, I think in 1969. It wasn't a successful meeting. Mostly we warily circled those strange containers, each other's bodies. I think it's the opposite of what Plato thought. I think that if people know each other only mind to mind they hardly know each other at all. Later, it was again possible for us to write trusting letters and even to reestablish an intimacy, though we now knew it was in part illusory, being purely platonic.

Edwards: Students occasionally get confused as to who's speaking the various quoted lines in "The Dead Shall Be Raised Incorruptible." I'd like to have it spelled out, if you don't mind.

Kinnell: The person who says "Lieutenant! This corpse will not stop burning!" is just some soldier on some battlefield somewhere—presumably Vietnam, since death by burning characterized that war. The man with the broken neck is also a soldier, though in fact the lines came when I was thinking of victims of lynching in the American South. And it is the membranes, effigies, etc., the memories of itself left on the earth by the human race, which is imagined to have destroyed itself, who pray for earthly experience to continue no matter how painful or empty it has become. ("Do not let this last hour pass/Do not remove this last poison cup from our lips.") The line, "We shall not all sleep, but we shall be changed," is quoted from the Burial of the Dead.

Edwards: What about the man who addresses the Captain?

Kinnell: That's supposed to be a conversation during a hospital visit. The Captain comes to see his tailgunner who has been put in the mental ward. I copied down that speech nearly verbatim from what a man told me who'd been in the Korean war.

Edwards: Someone you knew?

Kinnell: No, it was a stranger. I was with James Wright and Robert Bly on a barnstorming tour of New York State colleges in the spring of 1966, giving poetry readings against the war, sometimes two or three in a day. After the final reading, at Cornell, the three of us went to an all-night diner in downtown Ithaca. We had spent a whole week talking about love and peace. The moment we walked into the diner a man with the peculiar clairvoyance of drunkards came weaving over to our table and said, "Want to fight?" James Wright, who has great presence and also a prodigious memory which can pluck the right phrase from any of a thousand movies, said, "We're not fighters, we're lovers." So the man sat down and told us his story. He had been the tailgunner in a plane assigned to fly over Seoul to protect the city from enemy aircraft. From time to time when he saw civilians in the streets he would fire a few bursts at them, sometimes wounding or killing them. After a number of such incidents, he was given a medical discharge. For the next fifteen years, evidently, he had remained unable to understand his behavior. As he talked, one moment he was boasting of the feeling of power the machine guns gave him as he fired at the scattering figures, and the next he was weeping with shame. So he had become the town drunk—or one of them. I wanted to get this schizophrenic quality into the poem.

Edwards: That section is followed immediately by "Little Sleep's Head Sprouting Hair in the Moonlight," a very sharp contrast.

Kinnell: Yes, well, it's a special time—those minutes— hours sometimes—we spend with little children in the middle of the night. I've always liked getting up and going to my children. I'm partly asleep myself—most of what we call personality, or individuality, we leave back there in our bed. The child, too, is half asleep. So we hold each other, creature and creature, clasping one another in the darkness. We probably have to know each other well by daylight for these cosmic hugs, almost devoid of personality, to be possible It is good for the child that the hugs take place, for during them something "sets" inside that will make it possible to experience a similarly primal embrace later on, in adult life, with a lover. It's like happiness. Everyone uses the word, but it's obvious that many don't really experience it and never will, probably because they were not disposed that way as little children.

Edwards: Could I ask about "The Porcupine"? In what way is it an "ultra-Rilkean angel"?

Kinnell: I was thinking—as I seem to do often—of the Ninth Elegy, where Rilke tells how the angels are attracted by ordinary, earthly things. The porcupine eats anything with salt in it—generally things we've handled a lot, that the salt of our sweat has soaked into. So, like Rilke's angels, the porcupine loves axe handles, doors, chair arms, and so on. A porcupine once ate the insulation off all the wires in my pickup truck, for the road salt. But it's mostly wooden things they like. Once they actually ate their way through the cellar door of this house. If they had climbed the stairs into the house itself, they would have reduced the place to rubble, since it is splashed—floor, walls, and ceiling—with my sweat. As it happened they didn't get in, because they ate down the cellar stairs on the way up. Farmers regard them as pests, and kill them on sight.

Edwards: I would like to go back to what you said earlier: "It's the opposite of what Plato thought. I think that if people know each other only mind to mind they hardly know each other at all." Once you said something that struck me in its simplicity of truth—we were talking about friendship and you said, "The body makes love possible." Just that. It was only a sentence in a conversation, but I've never forgotten it.

Kinnell: I remember that conversation. It was last fall, when you were driving me to the train in Montpelier. We had been talking about something Jean-Paul Sartre had been quoted as saying, something obviously spoken out of his own experience—which surprised me, since for some reason I had always thought of him as "mental," a theoretician, one of those who are just brains carried around by a body. He was talking about how deeply one communicates in a relationship that combines friendship with sexual love. He spoke about how language itself comes from the deepest place, from sex, particularly when love in involved. Our conversation had gone on I think to my days of teaching a correspondence-school course. But after all this talk in which I explain and explain and often feel I get nowhere, I think I'll keep still and leave at least that one phrase, which in its simplicity *does* seem to have the ring of truth, unexplained and possibly still true.

MAXINE KUMIN

Estivating—1973

The reason I am keeping a journal this season of the hearings and the horses is to put down those "bits of the mind's string too short to use," as Joan Didion once said. Things tie themselves together with little quote marks and perhaps the string crosshatches itself into a statement in time, who knows? My son, scanning the *New York Times* one weekday morning when it was heavy with financial articles of the technical sort, complained, "not even anybody good died today" and I hang onto that phrase as it reflects the kind of stasis I am in, estivating here.

I came away from the city the first day of June, no longer in the grip of one routine, promptly though voluntarily snared in another one, for my friend and neighbor across the valley has leased me two mares for the riding and gifted me with two foals for the caring. Some impulse toward order propels me into the nonpermissiveness of animals to care for, a schedule to adhere to. I think I am afraid of too much latitude—how else could I handle such large blocks of time? As it is, I sleep less and more lightly than I have in years. One night the bay mare, for reasons of her own, took out a railroad tie and twenty feet of fence board. A week later, the colt and the filly, having spent several hours worrying the top slide board out of its double fixture, exploded out of the barn at 2 A.M. and we went barefoot flapping after them. They wanted only to be in the paddock with the mares, it seems. We want them stabled at night, as they are too young and venturesome to roam. It is a return to the era of earaches and chicken pox and the nightmares of young children. Presumably, it serves some purposes, vague ones: the animal pleasure of touch, an aesthetic gratification, and it uses up some of my maternal obsessions. And is perhaps a way of hanging loose in between some more sustained efforts. Always the small terror of a prolonged block hovering just off stage, waiting to set in like an ice age. In any case, it makes me remember Orwell saying ". . . there has literally been not one day in which I did not feel that I was idling . . . as soon as a book is finished, I begin, actually from the next day, worrying because the next one is not begun and am haunted by the fear that there will never be a next one."

Noondays, I try to think up here in this boxy, pale blue room. I think of Virginia Woolf's aunt who did her the kindness of falling from her horse while riding out to take the air in Bombay and leaving her a legacy for life, enough for that room of one's own. The desk that I sit at in this room is an old oak piece left over from a schoolhouse when the century turned. It has a shallow pencil drawer and two sturdier deep ones and it stands on four unturned legs. Through the window it overlooks an equally unremarkable barn, once a dairy barn for fifty head of Holsteins. In the utilitarian manner of barns it is built into a slope so that one could in all seasons shovel the cow flops downhill and downwind. Years before our tenancy, an artist lived here and favoring the north light for his gloomy canvases—at least the ones he left behind are unremittingly dour in theme and muddy of color—he built an absurd sort of overhang from the haymow. It juts out like a Hapsburg jaw, looming halfway across the one-car-width dirt road that divides house and barn. I can sit here and watch swallows come and go through the gap tooth of an upper board where they coexist with the red squirrels. Yesterday, an owl, late awake in the mizzly weather, flapped his way in, presumably in search of mice. I hope he is snugly tenanted for a while, since he has a habit of hooting his way uphill tree by tree in the small hours announcing something. A very prepossessing paddock connects into the expired dairy farmer's dung heap, now leveled out and used as a shelter for the mares. Except they often prefer to stand out in a downpour, looking woebegone but cool.

From my window I can seen the strawberry roan mare tearing up grass by its roots, munching dirt and all, swashbuckling the flies and mosquitoes with her bug repellent-larded tail. Her coloring is rather like that of a redheaded woman, the freckled variety. This, I realize, stands for my four aunts, now deceased, who were always diminishing their spots with cocoa butter.

Privately, I call this mare Amanda and I am writing a cycle of poems for her. She is a sensible and almost never petulant creature, on the enormous side (Aunt Harriet?) with feet as big as dinner plates and the girth of a California wine keg. A broad white blaze down her face lends her a look of continuous startle (Aunt Alma's plucked eyebrows?). And of course that voluptuous golden tail and mane, brillo consistency. She knots these by rubbing on the fence. We spend hours together. I do the combing and she, placidly, enjoys the small sensual tugs of the bristles. Until I was twelve I suffered two heavy plaits of hair, continually coming unbraided. "Stand still!" my mother would say. "Your part is as crooked as Ridge Avenue." Now my mother's hair is as thin and white as spun sugar, coaxed from a baby-pink scalp. This is the kind of reflecting that comes of combing.

Meanwhile, the Watergate unfurls its tattered length daily and we catch bits of it between barn and pond. It is a wondrous decadence, this daytime *opéra bouffe*, beaming in over the hills to this isolated spot. We worm the babies in the middle of John Dean's testimony and at last I see a connection. Although it makes me want to be sick, I count the nematodes in the little ones' shit—forty the first day, fifty-six the next. I am making sure.

Carless, two miles from town, we ride the horses down the back way, through the covered bridge, along the old railroad bed, and come out at the laundromat which was once a station stop on the B & M line. We tie them to the VFW flagpole, fifty yards from the general store. It seems a fitting use. When we remount, milk, flour, butter, and beer in knapsacks, I see that Amanda has left a little pyramid on the lawn.

Mornings, early, we go for long trips over corduroy and dirt roads that have lost their destinations, although the county area map still notes the burying grounds and sugar houses of a hundred years ago. It is chanterelle time, their dry yellow vases nicely visible in the woods at this height. It is like looking for butter. I remember Laurie telling me that in Provence if you want to go mushrooming you must start at daybreak or the other foragers will have picked the woods clean. Here, we can go all day loading our burlap saddle bags with fresh edibles, and not meet another person. It is a delicious depravity, feasting on our find—how far we are from the real world! What does the mushroom know? Only to open the hinges of its gills and shower down its blind spores—white, pink, rusty brown, or the good black of the inky caps. It corrects itself, this fruiting body, it is phototropic. Thanks to gravity, something will fall on fertile ground, though most stay stuck on the gills like words on a page. I suppose I mean that love is like this; as evanescent, as easily lost, as mindless, blind, instinctual. Or it is all a metaphor for the poem, the genesis of the poem as unexpected as the patient mushroom you come upon.

Today I order 200 pounds of horse chow from the Feed and Grain Exchange in the next town. I do this by phone, apologetically, because I have no car and must ask for a delivery. The woman taking my twelve dollar order chats with me, a long and cordial conversation between strangers who will likely never meet. Afterwards, I think about the natural courtesy of it and all the city-surly bank clerks, taxi drivers, and cops who throw this moment into high relief.

Today, two startling finds: an enormous stand of ripe raspberries that fell off their stems into our pails, and yielded twelve jars of jam, and several fresh boletes of a kind I had never seen before. They matched in every way *boletus mirabilis,* which is native to the Pacific Northwest. We ate them gratefully for supper, enfolded into omelets and praised the name and serendipity of their arrival. The mushroom passion freshens with me year by year. Too bad it is such an esoteric subject for Americans—each genus is as distinct as broccoli from cauliflower. A broccoli poem would speak its own universal, but a boletus poem? They are, of course, the toadstools in *Alice* and all those dreadful fairy books of my childhood, each with an elf underneath. Little children are taught to trample them on sight as something nasty to be eradicated. A pity. Once you have eaten wild mushrooms, the dull store-bought agaricus is a poor substitute. I think of Thoreau's "a huckleberry never reaches Boston." I pickle some mushrooms, string others with needle and thread and hang them to dry. Extras I sauté and freeze, but they are a pale imitation of the fresh-picked-and-into-the-pot ones.

This morning I hoed between the corn rows and thought up ways to foil the raccoons who will unerringly arrive with the first ripe ears. A transistor radio tuned to an all-night rock and roll station? Camphor balls and creosoted rope around the perimeter? One of my farmer neighbors claims that balls of newspaper between the rows will keep them off; they dislike the crackle. What to make of the foraging and gathering in? One part thrift, one part madness; three parts inexplicable.

In Yeats's journal, the work sheets for "the fascination of what's difficult" contain these notes: "Repeat the line ending 'difficult' three times, and rhyme on bolt, exult, colt, jolt. One could use the thought of the wild-winged and unbroken colt must drag a cart of stones out of pride because it's difficult." ("I swear before the dawn comes round again / I'll find the stable and pull out the bolt.") But the domestication has got the better of me; lose half a garden and begin again. "Oh masters of life, give me confidence in something." Yeats again. So it seems I put my trust in the natural cycle, and bend to it. It is so far removed from self-improvement as to be an escape hatch. Nature pays me no attention, but announces the autonomy of everything. Here nothing is good or bad, but *is,* in spite of.

FRED CHAPPELL

The Function of the Poet

To ask the question is to answer it—on one level, at least. After that, the subject becomes complicated.

What is the function of the poet?

—Why, to write poems, of course.

And how does he go about performing this act?

First he determines that he has something to say. Then he decides upon the best way to say it, and after that it is only a matter of intensive clerical labor, interrupted by desperate momentary surges of inspiration. It is rather like working next to a lamp with a faulty switch; the light keeps flickering from dim to bright, but never quite goes out. . . . Except when it does.

But that first step is likely to be the steepest. How does he find something to say? And when he thinks that he has found a promising subject, how does he decide that it is genuine and that he has anything to add to what centuries of poets have already said? For he knows very well indeed that there is no original subject for poetry any more than there is a new and original human emotion that he can feel and which no one else has felt before.

This guaranteed lack of originality is at once the poet's burden and his comfort. He recognizes that he must find new approaches to old subjects, that he must find new combinations of words and new arrangements of such poetic materials as rhyme, meter, caesura, and metaphor; but he can take heart from the fact that other people have felt the same emotions that he proposes to arouse or to recall with his poem. They may not have been able to articulate these feelings or even to know exactly what it is that they have felt, but he counts terribly on the brotherhood of man, on the consonance of human sympathy, in order to arouse these feelings again in his audience, to define and to refine them, and if possible to ennoble them. And he cannot cheat: he cannot casually trigger the same well-trained neural responses that advertisers, demagogues, and sloganeers have so often used and abused.

The poet discovers something to say by putting himself in position to discover it. "Chance favors the prepared mind," said Louis Pasteur; and this proposition determines the poet's regimen: to learn to observe, to become friendly with the tools of his craft, to attempt to understand his own mind and his behavior, to feel continually the contours of experience. Then something is bound to happen that has a poem in it or about it. In fact, such events are taking place all the time, even in the poet's purview, but he is not always receptive. The kind of attention that the inception of a poem requires is not always accessible. Randall Jarrell's comparison, that a poet searching for a poem is like a man standing in a field during a storm, hoping to be struck by lightning—not once but many times—is an apt one. But it is easy to see how such as effort is bound to take its toll.

The emotions the poet feels are the same ones we all feel and often upon the same occasions. He is elated at the onset of spring, during parades, while falling in love, upon getting a raise in salary, at the opening of baseball season, at weddings. He is sad at funerals, during the breaking up of love affairs, upon the disappearance of a species of animal or plant from the earth, at the prospect of continued suffering and injustice among the nations, at the continued exploration of the bottomless abyss by his favored baseball team. The difference between the poet and the rest of us is that he must say something more eloquent than "Hot dog!" when he feels good and "Oh phooey!" when he feels bad.

And there is where the difficulty lies.

He is going to delineate, dramatize, and heighten a simple emotion by the use of complex means. He is going to attack this feeling, or surround it, or seduce it, with his words. He must choose a form and a manner in which to ply his blandishments upon his subject matter, and how shall he meet this new girl of his dreams? Will she be attracted to him by the patched and faded blue jeans, the torn T-shirt, the rebellious punk haircut of free verse? Or will she more readily disclose her beauties to the man in white tie, top hat, and regular meter? Or to the soft spoken humorous gentleman in the tweed jacket which disgorges from its breast pocket a blue-iris-colored silk handkerchief bearing a scent of gardenia?

There is no way for the poet to know the answer to this question. Yet he has to make a beginning. If the poem he wishes to write is a love poem, he is acutely aware that there is a long and bulky tradition of love poetry peeking—or glaring—over his shoulder, and he must decide how he wishes to position himself in relation to this tradition. If he finds in his feelings for the beloved a certain complexity which prevents the full-throated celebration of joy—so that he cannot simply sing like the birdies sing—and that there is a firmness in the texture of his thought, then he may well choose the sonnet as the form which is most fitting to his thought and to the urgent impulse behind it. Having chosen to write a sonnet, he knows where he stands in relation to the long tradition of love poetry. It may not be the most comfortable position because he has put himself in competition with Elizabeth Barrett Browning and George Meredith and Robert Lowell and Longfellow—and now that we think about it—with Shakespeare and with Dante. If it were a foot race, he would feel the encumbrance of a ball and chain.

He may decide to eschew the sonnet and to begin instead with a line of poetry that stretches in capital letters all across the page a string of obscene epithets testifying in one fashion or another to his passion, or at least to his virility. This is to say, he has chosen the radical rather than the traditional mode of verse. Perhaps he believes that he has chosen the modern over the ancient. But of course the modern is in a sense already ancient; it too is a tradition and he finds that he is in competition with Allen Ginsberg, Blaise Cendrars, Clayton Eshleman, and Robert Creeley. These poets too offer some mighty tough competition. And, to make the situation worse, he still has not escaped competition with Dante and Wordsworth and Shakespeare. They are still there and their presences now seem more than insurmountable; they look positively glowering.

Nevertheless, he is going to write his poem. It is in him to write, and he fails himself and the poem if he does not attempt to set it down. He picks up his pencil with a mixture of feelings difficult to describe and impossible to analyze, but he does feel—when the work is going as it ought—one thing quite clearly. "This is what I was born to do," he thinks.

He knows that poetry is what he was born to do because, like all the rest of us, he has to do a lot of things he was not born to do. It is incumbent upon each of us if we strive for contentment in our lives to be happy in our work. My Uncle Fudd used to tell me to try to be the best there ever was. "I saw you installing linoleum the other day," he said. "If that is what you're going to do you should try to be the best linoleum installer in the world."

All right, Uncle, I'm willing to try. But nothing is going to make me say that I was born to install linoleum. Linoleum installers, unlike poets, are made, not born.

That is the poet's first and last rationale for what he does. He writes poetry because he cannot help it. The discipline of poetry is lodged as securely in his body as an athlete's talent is lodged in his rather more comely body. And he justifies his existence in part by remembering that there are societies upon the earth without the use or even the concept of money, without the concept of athletic competition, even without a clear concept—according to the anthropologist Bronislaw Malinowski—of fatherhood. But there is no society of human beings, in past record or in present view, that lacks the concept and practice of poetry. Poetry is an activity, or way of thought, or habit of language, that is built into the human physiology.

And this fact makes it a little easier to get past the first and highest hurdle: the necessity of having inescapably to be a poet.

Now, having faced up to his destiny and produced his poem, what does our little man do next?

Why, he looks all about for someone to admire his work.

This situation is the more intricate one. The poet may have been born to produce poetry, but no one in the course of human time ever felt that he was put upon the globe in order to read poetry. It is a catch-as-catch-can proposition, this search by a poet for his audience.

He is not going to find much of an audience. He knows that already because it is historically—perhaps prehistorically—a part of the poet's predicament. The ancient Greek poet Callimachus and the Roman Horace after him both proclaimed their contempt for the vulgar crowd that simply did not appreciate their fine and clever words. *Odi vulgus,* they wrote: "I hate the mob." Milton wrote for fit audience though few. Whitman found a nifty way out by declaring that every man is his own poet and that he, Walt, had no more claim to be listened to than anyone else we might meet in the street. But this attitude is only the obverse of that of Horace and Milton, and the only people who know what Whitman's sentiments are in this regard already read the poems in which he outlines them.

Another solution to the problem of audience was broached by William Butler Yeats. Disgusted by and contemptuous of the middle class he found to be lacking in proper interest in poetic genius and nationalist literature, he decided to invent his audience, to write for an ideal reader. Yeats's ideal reader was of course an Irishman; he was also a fly fisherman, a man who gave up his whole attention to the art of casting flies, who went out at dawn each morning to practice his art. He describes him as "a wise and simple man," and vows to write for him "one / Poem maybe as cold / And passionate as the dawn." But he admits, is forced to admit, that his fisherman in gray Connemara cloth is "A man who does not exist, / A man who is but a dream."

Yeats's solution, ambiguous as it is, probably represents the way most contemporary poets resolve the problem of audience. The poet writes for a single ideal reader or for a small group of sympathetic readers. These latter may or may not exist in reality. He hopes for a larger number of readers and he knows that they do not exist—or that they exist only as scholars, for whom his poems are not regarded as poems so much as raw material for the profession of literary scholarship. The poet himself is perforce a scholar—of literature, of science, of politics, of any number of specialties—and he thinks with dismay of the kind of operation contemporary scholarship may perform upon his verses.

It was Yeats who also wrote the line, "Tread softly because you tread on my dreams." That is the kind of attitude that gets no sympathy from reviewers and critics, much less from scholars. Literary scholarship has become the kind of business it never was before in the western world, and as the personal motives of scholars become more selfish, so do their analytic methods become clumsier. Trying to tread softly with deconstructionist criticism is like trying to perform an entrechat while wearing snowshoes. The poet knows this disheartening fact, that his most careful readers will be critics afflicted with the virus of some strain of exotic theory. So how does he deal with that knowledge?

If he is wise he ignores it or forgets it. But we are not always wise. Sometimes he may try to outfox the professional critic. If a critic is learned, why then a poet too can be learned: he can seek out abstruser theories written in more obscure languages than ever a critic has dreamed of. He can build his poem on matrices of fractal geometry, borrow rhyme schemes from Provençal dance forms, and decorate them with allusions to Cambodian architecture. He can publish the poems with a flourish of his hand that seems to say, "There you go, buddy. Try to figure that one out!"

But this is a lost cause. The poet is a single person, writing one poem, no matter how lengthy or complex he makes it. The critics hunt in packs and time is on their side, as well as the traditional academic resources. Someone in the future is likely to pay them money for flushing the poet's errors and trivialities and even some of his achievements out of hiding.

So if the poet knows that scholars are likely to make up the largest number of his immediate audience, he tries to hope that this will not always be the case, that readers with less specialized interests will come to his work at last and evince a different kind of appreciation, an interest more personal and perhaps more aesthetic in nature, and less colored by merely professional concern.

But he can find this audience only if he is willing to satisfy its expectations. The poet thinks he knows what his readers want from him: his duties, as they have been defined over the millennia, are stable. The first responsibilities of the poet are to teach and to delight. Or, putting it in proper formulation: to teach by delighting. People come to his poems in order to learn things that they did not know, or to be reminded of things that needed to be remembered in fresh fashion. They gain this knowledge or rejuvenate these memories because the poet delights them with his use of language. He makes everything sound like fun. If ever a reader wrote to a poet, upon reading his volume and closing it up, a letter that said: "I'm glad I read your book. I had a good time and I learned a lot," then the poet might well feel that his life had been justified and that he could retire from the vocation. He could not, of course; one can retire from a profession but never from a vocation. Yet he might feel that he had accomplished most of what he had set out to do in his art.

But he never gets a letter like that. Usually he gets a letter saying, "Dear Jim-Bob, I enclose a copy of that gruesome review of your new book that I told you about on the phone. As I said, I don't agree with a word of it, but I thought you ought to see it." Or a letter that says, "Dear Mr. Hotpoet, I am a junior at Ragweed High here in Raw Neck, Utah, and I have been assigned to write a paper on your work. Will you please write me a letter telling me what your books are all about and how you came to write each one, and could you please reply by return express mail as I have kind of let this paper slip and it is due real soon, like I mean real SOON." Or he receives a letter that says, 'Dear Mr. Birdbard, I don't read poetry, but I saw your name on a book in the store and want to know if you are any kin to the Birdbard family in Goosejuice, Oregon. My aunt Flimsy Thimble was once married to a Birdbard and she said they were a rum bunch. I was curious if you might be one of the Oregon Birdbards." Many letters like these and then a few others that deserve their own butterfly nets, but never ever a letter that mentions teaching and delighting.

The poet himself might have a difficult time justifying the old justification. Haven't those terms changed over the centuries? Have they not broadened? Or have they narrowed?

What is it that the poet can teach? Will not a prudent person go to his minister for moral instruction or to a philosopher for ethical enlightenment and ontological speculation? Will he not apply to the scientists to know about atoms, hummingbirds, and the motions of tides? For understanding of human character will he not open the books of Freud, Jung, and William James? For history he will go to historians. When he reads about these matters in the poet's works, is he not merely getting the words of the true experts in secondhand prettified manner?

This question puts itself in simple terms: Is there any subject besides himself and the art of poetry that the poet is qualified in this day and age to teach?

And as for delight—well, what kind of fun can the poet offer that has half the attraction of Nintendo? Or, come to that, a fourth? Make it a tenth. We shall not even mention the other activities that the poet must compete with: movies, recordings, concerts, sports, television, and driving about amiably in convertibles.

Maybe we can help the poet out by making some elementary distinctions. Let us propose that *to teach* is not the same thing as *to instruct*. There are some things we learn in order to know them and some things we learn in order to live with them. If you wish to learn how to drive a car safely or how to manufacture hydrochloric acid, then it will be better not to turn to books of poetry for instruction. But if you wish to know or to remember how it feels still to be in love with a person who has done you most dreadful wrong and to search desperately for a way to forgive that person so that you can go on loving, then Facts on File is no help, nor the IBM PC Computer Operator's Manual. We need to learn, probably, the basic skills of driving automobiles only once; the other lesson, how to feel and behave in a difficult love affair, we must learn again and again. Then we turn to poetry.

As we normally do in other situations.

I do not know how to report this next observation from my personal experience without seeming to gloat—which I most certainly abhor to do. I shall only say that it has happened more times than a few that people who have aggressively attacked the whole idea of poetry in my hearing or who have belittled me for practicing it have sent me their own poems to read and comment upon when they have been faced with personal catastrophes and sorrows and poetry has been unwillingly wrung out of them. The usual occasions are the deaths of family members or of close friends and the hymn-meter verses produced are genuine in feeling. Then, when the hurt hearts ease a bit and time performs its secret assuaging ministry these nonce-poets take up their old attitudes again and relish teasing me about my uselessness in society.

It is difficult for people to understand that the poet might have a function. I fly about our busy nation in airplanes fairly frequently. Sooner or later my seat-mate on the plane will ask me what I do for a living. For years and years I replied that I was a schoolteacher. A meaningful pause. Then: "What do you teach?" And trying to be truthful for a moment I would answer: "I teach English." Another pregnant pause—and then either one of these two replies: "I guess I'd better watch my grammar," or "That was my very worst subject in school."

This conversation deteriorates immediately, in my opinion.

These days I'm elderly and gray and paunchy and don't care much any more. When the shiny young executive looks up from his printouts for a moment to ask me what I do for a living, I say, "I'm a poet." Then comes the longest pause you could ever imagine; the Byzantine civilization comes and goes while this nice young man ponders. Finally comes his sentence, the phrase that enables him to turn back to his figures and bottom lines with equanimity, dismissing me and my concerns to Etruscan obscurity. "I suppose," he says, "there's not much money in that."

I might reply in turn, "Oh, yes and no. Some years better than others. Only pulled in half a mill last year, but this year looks pretty good." I never say that sentence, but I might with perfect ease. Everyone lies on airplanes. And anyhow, Willie Nelson could say it, after adjusting the numbers upward quite a bit. Mr. Nelson is a poet, after all. So are all the pop singers. They only write a different kind of poetry than book poets do and have slightly different goals in view.

It is easy to forget that we live—or drown—in a sea of poetry. Not only popular songs but advertising jingles, political slogans, mnemonic rhymes, street jive, and a hundred other activities are informed by the energies and formal usages of poetry. Television advertising has taken over from the surrealist movement of the 1920s and 1930s its wild imagery, its disclocated logic, its irreverence, and its shock value. Television has not managed to capture the innocent heart of that movement, but it has stolen its fruitful mannerisms right and left.

And we could trace with greater or less effort the various influences of poetry upon the popular arts and commerce and industry, and it would not be too difficult to make out a good case for the tyranny of literary aesthetics over American business practices. Even so, such influences are but by-products of the poet's purposes and in large degree probably irrelevant to them.

For he is still most of all concerned with what his work can do within itself. He is still concerned with teaching and delighting. But he knows, and maybe he has had to learn again lately, that delighting and entertaining are not the same thing. It is true that weak poetry can delight us when it is put to music—we have already mentioned Willie Nelson. But the delight of serious poetry (even when it is humorous in nature) is of a different kind.

There is an intensity of purpose about it that more casual productions do not approach. And there is in it an enormous respect for its subject matter, so much respect that the techniques of more popular art forms are rejected as lacking in respect. And there is a corresponding respect for the intended audience of poetry that the popular arts do not try to match. The best serious poetry expects that its readers shall be warm and empathic personalities, with intelligence and taste and deep concern for the truth. Sometimes, in responding to these expectations, certain readers may take on some of these qualities, though I would not strongly suggest that fine literature has the power to transform for the better the character of its audience—not many of them, anyhow, and not for very long. The popular arts do not usually hold such respectful expectations about their audiences: they cannot afford to because such expectations must be met with great care and painstaking time must be spent in composition and construction.

It is this kind of respect that makes poetry suspect in the minds of many people. Its very seriousness makes poetry seem unserious. Mr. Ted Turner likes to advertise his Cable News Network as being the most important of television networks because it broadcasts news and nothing but news. Still we remain unconvinced, you and I. The news may be *urgent* now and then, or quite often, but it is rarely *serious*. If we really regarded the news as serious we would bind our newspapers in leather or cloth and preserve them in our shelves, publish our novels and poems on newsprint and throw them away weekly. But it is the other way round, of course, because we know what is serious. It is the very old news that Sophocles brings and the Gospel of St. Luke and *The Bridge* of Hart Crane. But, as Ezra Pound observed, these poets still bring news, whereas the latest dispatches from eastern Europe will be out of date by the time they arrive upon our shores.

One way that the poet attempts to teach by delighting is by leading his readers to appreciate the excellent qualities of one subject or another. It may well be that his girlfriend comes first to mind—or a rainbow, a daffodil, a bottle of wine, a painting. In fact, when we come to the objects of nature even the homeliest and most insignificant may serve as cause for meditative appreciation by the poet. Examples are myriad, but here is a little poem by Edward Thomas, called "Tall Nettles."

> Tall nettles cover up, as they have done
> These many springs, the rusty harrow, the plough
> Long worn out, and the roller made of stone:
> Only the elm butt tops the nettles now.
>
> This corner of the farmyard I like most:
> As well as any bloom upon a flower
> I like the dust on nettles, never lost
> Except to prove the sweetness of a shower.

There it is, as simple as ever we could wish, a celebration not only of the generally uncelebrated nettle, but also of the dust that settles upon it. We are not surprised by the poem, except by its modest excellence. It does, after all, what we expect poets to do, to find a new way to praise something of our lives, and a new object to praise. The delight an interested reader takes from the poem is out of all proportion to its length and the putative importance of its subject matter;

and the delight is, as I can aver after long acquaintance with these eight lines, perennial. I never come to them without a sense of anticipation or leave them without a feeling of satisfaction.

And the only trouble with my experience is that it is I who report it. A poet is expected to respond warmly, thoroughly, and accurately to the poetry he reads. Perhaps it is seen as a part of his job to support the fraternity of poets in the way that doctors so famously support the medical fraternity.

What is wanted then is a reader who is not poet nor critic nor scholar who will respond as warmly to Edward Thomas's lines as I do and who will react as carefully. Are there such readers? At one time or another in a poet's career, he doubts that there are, for he never hears reliable report of such a legendary creature. The tree surgeon does not repair after supper to his copy of *The Faerie Queene;* the disc jockey does not interlard his hectic patter with allusions to *Piers Plowman;* the weary farmer does not give up his Superbowl Sunday to a fresh perusal of Shakespeare's sonnets. In fact, as soon as we suggest these individual possibilities they sound farfetched, silly.

Yet such readers do exist, and it is over a period of time that they make themselves known. It may take generations, but word does at last get out that Herman Melville repays at least as much as Longfellow the time it takes to read him. William Blake ascends to the ranks of the greatest English poets; Thomas Traherne is discovered and enjoyed; William Faulkner is distinguished from Erskine Caldwell, Nathanael West from Horace McCoy. And at the same time the names of many of the proud are humbled and brought low.

A patient and secret cadre of readers is at work in this process, overcoming the vagaries of the popular press and the perversities of critical theory. Some of these readers are inevitably academics, steady scholars and teachers of benevolent and searching curiosity. There is a traditional intercourse among them wherein new ideas are tested and overlooked authors of worth are reclaimed. But there are other readers too, beautiful amateurs and skillful collectors of books, persons whose reading is wider than it is profound and more guided by love of adventure than by accepted critical opinion. These readers are almost completely immune to the fevers of contemporary fashions in reading, though they enjoy good new work equally with the older when they are certain they have found it.

These are the voluptuary taxonomists of literature. They read for pleasure, and the pleasure of reading has become so keen for them that they are eager but patient to discriminate, to enjoy as much as possible of every sort of literature, not merely the so-called respectable sort. They are able to immerse themselves in reading so earnestly, so longingly, that their experience of books is the best part of their experience of life, and finally these two experiences are joined as one, life and literature commenting upon one another at equal length and with equal authority.

I am so happily convinced that such readers do indeed exist that I have tried to draw the portrait of one of them. The poem is called "The Reader" and it is dedicated to my mother-in-law, Helene Nicholls:

The Reader

Beside the floor lamp that has companioned her
For decades, in her Boston rocking chair,
Her body asks a painful question of the books.
Her fingers are so smooth and white
They reflect the pages; a light
The color of cool linen bathes her hands.
The books read into her long through the night.

There is a book that opens her like a fan; and so
She sees herself, her life, in delicate painted scenes
Displayed between the ivory ribs that may close up
The way she claps the book shut when she's through
The story that has no end but cannot longer go.
It doesn't matter what the story means;
Better if it has no meaning—or just enough
For her to say the sentence that she likes to say:
Why do these strange folks do the way they do?

And yet they comfort her, being all
That she could never be or wish to be;
They bring the world—or some outlook of its soul—
Into her small apartment that is cozy
As the huddling place of an animal
No one is yet aware of, living in
A secret corner of a secret continent,
An animal that watches, wonders, while the moon
Rides eastward and the sun comes up again
Over a forest deep as an ocean and as green.

This poem is my picture of one kind of ideal reader and if I am asked whether I believe that such a reader actually does exist I shall not know how to answer. For the purposes of my writing, for the purposes of my teaching of literature, this attentive reader does indeed exist. After all, it is for these same purposes that I myself exist and when the time comes that I must inevitably give these purposes over I shall no longer exist in the same way that I do now. I shall be a different person and the world that I inhabit shall be much changed also. And not, I think, for the better.

Meanwhile—*allons, citoyens!* Let us keep scouting faithfully through the poetry books, the good old ones and the good old new ones. Because there are more things in heaven and earth than can be dreamed by the dullard, the barbarian, and the postmodern literary theorist. And not only more things, but better ones.

Acknowledgments

"Robert Frost and the Better Half of Poetry," from *Predecessors, et Cetera: Essays* by Amy Clampitt. Copyright © 1991 by the University of Michigan, all rights reserved. Adapted from a paper read at the Frost Place, Franconia, New Hampshire, and first published as "The Better Half of Poetry" in *Grand Street*, Summer 1985.

"Dull Subject," from *Curiosities* by William Matthews. Copyright © 1989 by the University of Michigan, all rights reserved. Originally published in the *New England Review & Breadloaf Quarterly*.

"Improvisations of Form and Measure," from *Halflife: Improvisations and Interviews* by Charles Wright. Copyright © 1988 by the University of Michigan, all rights reserved. Originally published in the *Ohio Review*, number 38, 1987.

"The Interrupted Scheme: Some Thoughts on Disorder and Order in the Lives of Poets and the Lives of Poems," from *Richer Entanglements: Essays and Notes on Poetry and Poems* by Gregory Orr. Copyright © 1993 by the University of Michigan, all rights reserved. Originally published in the *AWP Newsletter*, November 1988.

"What Does Art 'Imitate,' and How?" from *Old Snow Just Melting* by Marvin Bell, published by the University of Michigan Press, 1983. Copyright © 1993 by Marvin Bell. Reprinted by permission. Originally published in the *American Poetry Review*, May/June 1975.

"Notes on Poetic Form" from *The Line Forms Here* by David Lehman, published by the University of Michigan Press, 1992. Copyright © 1992 by David Lehman. Reprinted by permission.

"Sea Level" from *Working Time: Essays on Poetry, Culture, and Travel* by Jane Miller. Copyright © 1992 by the University of Michigan, all rights reserved. Originally presented as a lecture for the Ohio Literary Festival in Athens, Ohio, in May 1990, and subsequently published in the *Ohio Review*, number 45, 1990.

Interview "With Linda Wagner" from *Tales Out of School: Selected Interviews* by Robert Creeley. Copyright © 1993 by the University of Michigan, all rights reserved. Originally published in *Contexts of Poetry* by Robert Creeley (Donald M. Allen, Grey Fox Press) and revised for the "Art of Poetry" series, *Paris Review*, Fall 1968.

"The Pure Clear Word: An Interview with Dave Smith" from *Collected Prose* by James Wright, edited by Anne Wright. Copyright © 1983 by the University of Michigan, all rights reserved. Originally published in the *American Poetry Review*, May/June 1980, and later reprinted in *The Pure Clear Word* by Dave Smith, University of Illinois Press.

"The Hole in the Bucket" from *Living Off the Country* by John

UNDER DISCUSSION
David Lehman, General Editor
Donald Hall, Founding Editor

Volumes in the Under Discussion series collect reviews and essays about individual poets. The series is concerned with contemporary American and English poets about whom the consensus has not yet been formed and the final vote has not been taken. Titles in the series include: